Picking Up

Picking Up

ON THE STREETS AND BEHIND THE TRUCKS WITH THE SANITATION WORKERS OF NEW YORK CITY

ROBIN NAGLE

Farrar, Straus and Giroux | **New York**

Farrar, Straus and Giroux
18 West 18th Street, New York 10011

The Library of Congress has cataloged the hardcover edition as follows:
Nagle, Robin.
    Picking up : on the streets and behind the trucks with the sanitation workers
of New York City / Robin Nagle. — 1st ed.
       p.   cm.
    Includes bibliographical references and index.
    ISBN 978-0-374-29929-3 (alk. paper)
    1. Sanitation workers—New York (State)—New York.   I. Title.

HD8039.S2572U66 2013
331.7´61628442097471—dc23

                                                        2012028941

Paperback ISBN: 978-0-374-53427-1

Designed by Abby Kagan

www.fsgbooks.com
www.twitter.com/fsgbooks • www.facebook.com/fsgbooks

For ZXDN, who is my heart

The LORD shall watch over your going out and your coming in,
from this time forth for evermore.

—Psalm 121:8

Contents

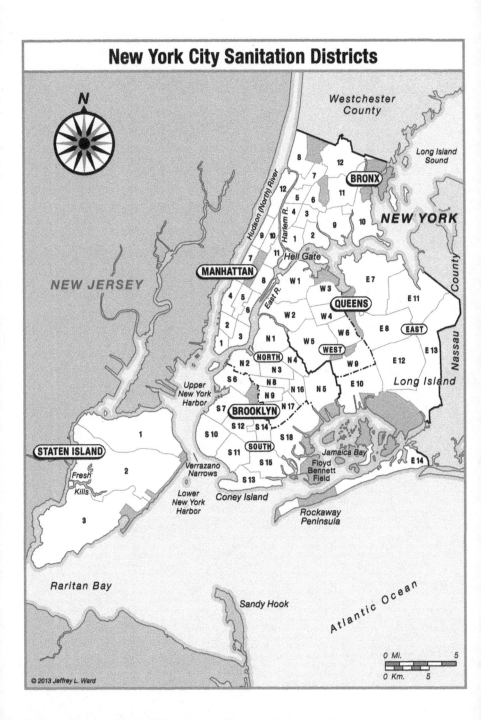

New York City Sanitation Districts

N

Westchester County

Long Island Sound

BRONX

NEW YORK

Hudson (North) River

Harlem R.

Hell Gate

East R.

MANHATTAN

NEW JERSEY

QUEENS

NORTH

WEST

EAST

Long Island

Nassau County

Upper New York Harbor

BROOKLYN

SOUTH

Jamaica Bay

Floyd Bennett Field

STATEN ISLAND

Fresh Kills

Verrazano Narrows

Lower New York Harbor

Coney Island

Rockaway Peninsula

Raritan Bay

Sandy Hook

Atlantic Ocean

0 Mi.   5
0 Km.   5

© 2013 Jeffrey L. Ward

Author's Note

This book is based on my work and research with New York City's Department of Sanitation. Certain individuals portrayed in these pages preferred to remain anonymous, so I gave them pseudonyms, as indicated in footnotes. The chapter "You Are a San Man" combines some of my own experiences on the job with stories told to me by other Sanitation personnel. Portions of "Garbage Faeries" and "On the Board" appeared in the April 2011 issue of *Anthropology Now*.

Picking Up

Prelude: Center of the Universe

I don't usually name my trucks, but this one I call Mona, after the sound she makes when I push her toward her top speed. She has other quirks typical of a collection vehicle with many miles on the odometer. Her shocks and seat springs stopped softening the jolts of the road long ago, and her side-view mirrors shimmy so hard that cars behind me look like jittery smears.

I am heading south during the evening rush hour on the Major Deegan Expressway in New York City, carrying a load of densely packed garbage to the dump (more properly called a transfer station). As I thread the truck's thirty-five-ton bulk through thick traffic, well aware that no one is glad to see me, the engine's steady keening aligns with my own sense of caution. Though I own the road—few motorists will play chicken with a garbage truck—fifty miles an hour is plenty fast enough for me.

Just before the Major Deegan becomes the Bruckner, I descend from the highway to the gloomy streets of the South Bronx. Only recently has the neighborhood started recovering from decades of decay and neglect. I bump over a rutted road, cross a set of train tracks, and drive carefully onto a scale, where an unsmiling young man takes my paperwork. Diesel fumes and river water scent the air. Once the truck is weighed, I move toward the dump itself, a vast barnlike structure a few hundred yards farther on. Other trucks are already waiting, so I pull up to the end of the queue (never a line), set my parking brake, and ponder Mona's noise again. Perhaps it isn't a keening. Maybe it's a truck-ish manifestation of our journey's ritual gravitas, a mechanical form of circular breathing that lets her intone a single note without pause. She is the ten-wheel equivalent of a chanting monk.

This is a story that unfolds along the curbs, edges, and purposely forgotten quarters of a great metropolis. Some of the narrative is common to cities around the world, but this tale is particular to New York. It centers on the people who confront the problem that contemporary bureaucratic language calls municipal solid waste. It's a story I've been discovering over the past several years, and from many perspectives.

The job of collecting Gotham's municipal waste and sweeping its streets falls mainly to the small army of men and women who make sure the city stays alive by wrestling with the challenge of garbage every day, fully aware that their efforts will receive scant notice and even less praise. This army makes up New York's Department of Sanitation, the largely unknown, often unloved, and absolutely essential organization charged with creating and maintaining a system of flows so fundamental to the city's well-being that its work is a form of breathing, albeit with an exchange of objects instead of air molecules. Or maybe its work is tidal: ceaseless ebbs and floods created by an almost gravitational pull between global economic forces that relentlessly shape both physical geographies and political landscapes. Just as a cessation of breath kills the being that breathes, or the stilling of tides would wreck life on earth, stopping the rhythms of Sanitation would be deadly to New York.

In many ways, the story is difficult to tell because it has no natural beginning or end—so let's start in the middle.

Garbage transfer stations are not on most tourist itineraries, nor are their neighbors charmed by their ambience. It's safe to say that dumps are largely despised, as is the continual parade of large, loud trucks that feeds them.[1] The public loathes the loads these carriers move, their comings and goings that never stop, the potholes they gouge into surrounding streets, the fouling exhaust, the trailing smell of trash that sometimes reaches farther than the laws of physics suggest is possible. We hate that transfer stations have to exist at all, no matter how remote their locations.

I'm thinking about how such structures came into being in the first place—surely we could figure out a better way to manage our discards—when a horn behind me breaks my reverie. Dump workers have been letting vehicles onto the tipping floor a few at a time, and there's a gap between me and the rest of the queue; I pull forward.

Then it's my turn. My gut gives a familiar flutter of excitement, and I take Mona across the threshold. Of course she chants. Though we understand this place to be odious, it is nothing less than the juicy, pulsing, stench-soaked center of the universe.

The smell hits first, grabbing the throat and punching the lungs. The cloying, sickly-sweet tang of household trash that wrinkles the nose when it wafts from the back of a collection truck is the merest suggestion of a whiff compared to the gale-force stink exuded by countless tons of garbage heaped across a transfer station floor.[2] The body's olfactory and peristaltic mechanisms spasm in protest. Breathing through the mouth is no help, and neither gulp nor gasp brings the salvation of fresh air; there's none to be had.

While the stench throttles nose and throat, deafening noise assaults the ears. Collection trucks are loud anyway, but their sound is considerably amplified when several gather inside a huge metal shed and they disgorge their loads all at once. Piercing backup beeps and roaring hydraulics are accompanied by shrieks of metal against metal, and the acoustic onslaught reverberates off the walls like a physical force, so intense that it takes on a kind of aural purity. Workers who spend their shifts inside the facility wear fat red headphones, but those of us only passing through must suffer the cacophony. The best way to communicate is with hand signals.

Then there's the remarkable interior landscape. The floor of the cavernous space—it feels as big as a few football fields—is three-quarters buried under garbage piled higher than our trucks. Mist meant to suppress dust falls from nozzles on the distant ceiling and blends with garbage steam rising from the heaps to create a sepia haze that obscures corners and far walls and makes the trash recede into yawning darkness. An oversized bulldozer lumbers across the mass as if sculpting it. The mounds quake beneath its weight like the shivering flanks of a living being, some golem given sentience by an unlikely spark that animated just the right combination of carbon, discards, and loss.

The reek, the howling, the gloom—a newcomer would be forgiven for thinking he's stumbled into a modern-day staging of the *Inferno*. In the Third Circle of Hell, where the gluttonous are doomed to spend eternity wallowing in filth, even a poet as gifted as Dante couldn't make it worse than this. The Fourth Circle, in which the avaricious must bear great weights that they use to assault one another in perpetuity for the sins of hoarding and of squandering, is also perfectly represented. Trucks and bulldozers stand in for human beings, but the task of moving enormous burdens is similarly endless.

Those burdens are terrifying not only because their existence requires a place like the dump but also because of their provenance. They are made of material objects once distinct but now mashed indiscriminately into that single abhorrent category called garbage. Things never meant to be together are smeared and swallowed and dripped into one another, their individual identities erased.[3] Such transmogrification—or is it transubstantiation?—suggests that, despite appearances to the contrary, the physical world is always ephemeral. If we ignore the dump, we can more easily ignore the simple and chilling fact that *nothing* lasts.

Though I've made many trips to this place, the moment of arrival always amazes me. I nearly bring Mona to a complete stop while I gape and listen and try to take shallow breaths. Then I notice a red-headphones man motioning me to an empty space at the edge of the pile. I wave an acknowledgment and swing the truck around, listening as her backup beep joins the surrounding tumult. I set my brakes once again, jump down, pull the pins, then raise the hopper and activate the mechanisms that will eject her freight into the gigantic heap behind her.[4]

A Buddhist prayer of thanks said at the start of a meal acknowledges that the food about to be consumed is "the work of many hands and the sharing of many forms of life." So is the accumulation at a garbage dump. The garbage here and in every other dump the world over reflects lives lived well, or in desperation, or too fast, or in pain, or in joy. Even without the status of worth or a claim of possession, each bag stuffed with trash, each wad of spent tissue, every shred of shrink-wrap, every moldy vegetable and maggot-covered turkey leg, hints of countless stories. Archaeologists of contemporary household waste have demonstrated this; indeed, insights that the field has given us about our own past often rest on analysis of nothing more than the garbage of civilizations long dead.[5] We understand such artifacts to be treasures.

Less tangible and more metaphysical is the sense that all of these unloved things hold traces of their former owners. Marcel Mauss, an early twentieth-century sociologist, proposed that even when an object "has been abandoned by the giver, it still possesses something of him."[6] The original notion referred to gift exchanges in small-scale or tribal societies, but the point can stand for any Thing that has passed through a life and been cast off. Imagine if we were capable of a form of empathy that lets us know one another by savoring the aura we leave on the things we have touched. We would go to a dump to get drunk on one another's souls.

But we haven't yet evolved such sensitivities. We generate our dregs, we create their hazards, and then we invent the dump as one of the places to which we banish them so that we can pretend they won't harm us. But who plays the role of Charon, ferrying our deceased belongings out of our daily lives and across what River Styx into the imagined safe zone of the dump?

Or, to put it more bluntly: Who keeps us safe from ourselves?

Part One

COLLECTION

1. Garbage Faeries

It was a radiant autumn morning. Tree leaves and car windows sparkled. The garbage bags that filled the back of our collection truck shimmered as Ray Kurtz pulled the handles that activated the bawling hydraulics of the hopper blade. Eager to be useful, I leaned against the load so no errant pieces would fall out, then stepped aside while the blade moved down and pushed the pile into the truck's body. The machinery howled a note higher as it finished its cycle.

Kurtz was a loose-limbed blond who looked younger than his forty-eight years. He had a mullet, an easy smile, a gently self-deprecating sense of humor, and about eighteen years as a New York City sanitation worker—or "garbageman," in common parlance. His partner, who threw bags toward us from farther up the curb, was Sal Federici, a dark-haired fifty-something with more than twenty years on the job. Federici, tall and lean, was enigmatically quiet and a liberal smoker. Kurtz had been a few-packs-a-day man himself until the emphysema diagnosis.*

---

*These two names are pseudonyms. The real Ray and Sal preferred to remain anonymous, as did many other people whose stories are told here.

I was working behind a garbage truck so that I might better understand some of the human costs and labor requirements of waste. All of us create trash in great quantities, but it's a troubling category of stuff that we mostly ignore. We particularly ignore how much care and attention it requires from a large, well-organized workforce. What would life be like if the people responsible for managing the waste of contemporary society were not on the streets every day? What do their jobs entail? Why don't they get the kudos they deserve? These are urgent questions, and since I live in New York, I decided to look for answers among the men and women of the city's Department of Sanitation. The best way to learn about their work was to do it with them, a notion that eventually inspired me to get hired as a san worker, but I started my research by accompanying Sanitation crews in various parts of the city—which is how I found myself behind the truck on that beautiful morning, marveling at the light and trying not to get in Kurtz's way.

Both Kurtz and Federici had spent their careers in a Sanitation district called Manhattan 7, and both had enough seniority to be regulars in section 1, the district's plum assignment. The 1 has a reputation for clean garbage. The bags don't often break and maggots are less common, even in summer's heat.

Every crew starts their shift with a long oaktag card, formally called the Daily Performance Record but more commonly known as the 350, on which their supervisor has written that day's route (pronounced like "grout," not "root").[1] A route is figured in lines called ITSAs—Individual Truck Shift Assignments—that indicate the specific block and side of the street to be collected, and in what order. The south side of Eighty-Fourth Street from Broadway to Central Park West, a distance of three blocks, is three lines. This particular example would be written "84, B'Way–CPW, s/s." If both sides were to be collected (abbreviated on a 350, logically enough, as b/s), it would constitute six lines.[2] Kurtz was explaining some of these details while we worked. Federici just smiled, taking drags on his cigarette between bag flings.

Kurtz was the driver and Federici the loader, but both men tossed bags. That particular day, on a block of fastidiously restored brownstones near Central Park West, we were doing house-to-house.* We picked up the garbage left in front of one small building— a town house or a modest apartment complex or a church, for example—and then moved the truck forward a stoop or two to get the pile that waited in front of the next small building, and the next, and the next. The quiet morning streets had been our domain when we started at 6:00, but by about 7:30 more and more people with pressed clothes and closed faces were emerging from doorways and descending stoops. It felt odd that our day was already well under way while these sluggards were only now heading to work, but my colleagues didn't pay them much attention. The passersby paid us even less.

The workforce of Sanitation is surprisingly small. New York's 8.2 million residents are served by fewer than 10,000 Sanitation employees (9,216, to be precise: 7,383 uniformed personnel and 1,833 civilians), all of whom make it possible for the DSNY to carry out its three-part mandate.[3] The first two parts involve picking up the garbage and figuring out where to put it. Sanitation makes sure that more than six thousand miles of streets are swept several times a week and that the city's eleven thousand tons of household trash and two thousand tons of household recycling are collected every day.[4] Both these tasks are organized by the Department's Bureau of Cleaning and Collection. Most of the people who work in uniformed titles are assigned to BCC. Once the trash is off the streets, the Bureau of Waste Disposal has to put it somewhere. The problem occupies many fewer people than are required for cleaning and collection, but BWD accounts for a quarter of Sanitation's $1.35 billion budget.[5]

*A glossary of DSNY lingo can be found on page 227.

Snow removal is the Department's third duty. Snow does not belong to any single bureau. The public might assume it's a concern only during the cold months, but everyone on the job, in every title and in every office and among all ranks, will tell you that the many tasks required in preparing for winter make snow a year-round focus.

Behind these organizational divisions stands an eclectic assortment of support personnel. Mechanics, lawyers, plumbers, architects, engineers, electricians, analysts, carpenters, and a host of others keep the physical and political machinery of the Department moving smoothly.

The Manhattan 7 garage serves the Upper West Side neighborhood, which is where I was working with Kurtz and Federici. It's one of the fifty-nine districts into which the Department divides itself across the city. Districts, or garages—the words are interchangeable—are managed through seven borough-based commands. (There are five boroughs in New York, but Sanitation splits Queens administratively into West and East, Brooklyn into North and South.) Manhattan has twelve districts, as does the Bronx; Brooklyn North and Brooklyn South have nine districts each; Queens East and Queens West have seven each, and Staten Island has three.

Every district is commanded by a superintendent who oversees a team of supervisors, also known informally by their older title of foremen. Supervisors directly manage the sanitation workers who drive the trucks, pick up the trash, and operate the mechanical brooms. Supervisors also serve as intermediaries between what happens on the street and what happens higher up the Department bureaucracy. Until 2011, their responsibilities were organized according to sections, the smaller units into which districts are divided.

Geography, staffing needs, and equipment allocations vary from one garage to the next. Manhattan 1, for example, is a small district of just three sections. M1 covers the Wall Street area, runs about 20 collection trucks and 15 recycling trucks a week, and hosts 55 workers, officers, and support staff across all shifts. A big district like

Brooklyn South 18, by contrast, has seven sections, runs 150 collection and 66 recycling trucks every week, and has 168 workers. Queens East 13, so big that it's called the Ponderosa, covers eight sections out of two garage facilities. Each week, about 185 collection trucks, 72 recycling trucks, and 200 workers serve the neighborhoods of Laurelton, Rosedale, Bellerose, and Queens Village.[6]

If truck allocations are the measure, Manhattan 7, which has five sections and runs about a hundred collection and fifty recycling trucks a week, is the borough's second busiest.[7] Four of M7's five sections boast trendy shops, lace-curtain restaurants, and a surfeit of luxury residential real estate, which varies from well-kept single-family homes and block-square prewar palaces to big-box newcomers like Donald Trump's mammoth structures on a former rail yard overlooking the Hudson River. In the 5 section, the district's northernmost, Spanish is heard as often as English, and corner bodegas are more common than high-end retailers. It's easier to find small diners not famous for their coffee than cloth-napkin establishments requiring reservations. Columbia University, edging the top of the 5, inflects the streets with a college-town accent. Garbage in the 5 is supposedly heavier and messier than in the rest of the district and is alleged to attract more rats.

Kurtz, Federici, and I were making our way down a street lined with tall sycamore trees and elegant town houses when all at once, as if she had materialized out of the remarkable morning light, a muse appeared. She was tall, slender, in her mid-twenties, with flawless olive skin, large eyes, full lips. Her hair, neat behind her shoulders, bounced lightly in sync with her brisk footsteps. Surely, I thought, this was the inspiration for Richard Wilbur's poem "Transit," which starts, "A woman I have never seen before / Steps from the darkness of her town-house door / At just that crux of time when she is made / So beautiful that she or time must fade."

As we turned to watch her, time did fade. So did our focus on our work.

"What use to claim that as she tugs her gloves / A phantom heraldry of all the loves / Blares from the lintel? That the staggered sun / Forgets, in his confusion, how to run?"[8]

Never mind the sun—Kurtz was the one who was staggered. He leaned against the truck, folded his arms, and gazed at her; when a trace of her perfume reached us, he closed his eyes and inhaled deeply. I imagined tendrils of fragrance curling cartoon-style around his chin, tickling his nose with a long feminine finger. He smiled hugely, his eyes still closed, and I smiled as well to see a man so frankly enjoy the sight, and scent, of a woman.

I didn't know it yet, but that morning on the street I was also observing a man who could stare so blatantly because any potentially disapproving members of the public wouldn't notice him doing it. In fact, as Kurtz knew well, passersby didn't even see him. Years on the job had taught him that when he put on his uniform every morning, like Federici and every other sanitation worker in the city, he became invisible.

In mechanical brooms or driving the truck, san workers are merely obstacles to be skirted. When I worked parade cleanups in warm weather, I quickly learned that it was useless to ask bystanders who lingered against the barricades to move back just a little. The coarse bristles of my hand broom were going to scrape their sandaled feet, but even when I stood directly in front of them saying "Excuse me" over and over, they didn't see or hear me. It's not that they were ignoring me: I was never part of their awareness in the first place.

Uniforms in general change the way any worker is perceived. The man or woman wearing a uniform becomes the Police Officer or the Firefighter, the Soldier, the Doctor, the Chef. Individuality is subsumed by the role that the clothing implies.[9] But the sanitation worker is more than just subsumed by a role. Because of the mundane, constant, and largely successful nature of his work, his uniform (its official color is spruce) acts as a cloaking device. It erases him. He doesn't carry guns or axes, no one begs for him in a 911 call, he is not expected to step into a crisis, to soothe an emergency, to rescue innocents.[10] Instead, his truck and his muscle punctuate the rhythms of a neighborhood at such regular intervals that he becomes a kind of informal timepiece.

Effective garbage collection and street cleaning are primary necessities if urban dwellers are to be safe from the pernicious effects of their own detritus. When garbage lingers too long on the streets, vermin thrive, disease spreads, and city life becomes dangerous in ways not common in the developed world for more than a century. It is thus an especially puzzling irony that the first line of defense in any city's ability to ensure the basic health and well-being of its citizenry is so persistently unseen, but the problem is hardly unique to New York.

John Coleman, president of Haverford College in the early 1970s, spent part of a sabbatical working for two weeks as a "garbageman" near Washington, D.C. His route took him to a tony suburban neighborhood late on a Saturday morning.[11] "I thought this might mean more talk back and forth as I made the rounds today," he mused. "While I wouldn't have time to talk at length, there was time to exchange the greetings that go with civilized ways. This was where I got my shock."

Both men and women gave me the silent or staring treatment. A woman in housecoat and curlers putting her last tidbit of slops into the pail was startled as I came around the corner of her house. At the sound of my greeting, she gathered her housecoat tightly about her and moved quickly indoors. I heard the lock click . . . Another woman had a strange, large animal, more like a vicuña than anything else, in her yard. I asked her what kind of dog it was. She gaped at me. I thought she was hard of hearing and asked my question louder. There was a touch of a shudder before she turned coldly away. A man playing ball with his two young sons looked over in response to my voice, stared without a change of face, and then calmly threw the next ball to one of the boys. And so it went in almost every yard.[12]

No wonder people gaped at him or turned away. By speaking to the householders he met on his route, Coleman had transgressed. Invisible laborers are not supposed to make themselves noticed. They are meant to do their work and move along, heads down and mouths shut. Though most householders would admit, if pressed, that the people who tote away their garbage are important in the larger scheme of things, it doesn't mean they must acknowledge the one who does the toting. Heaven forfend!

Here's an especially illuminating and depressingly common example of Invisibility Syndrome, one I've heard from junior Sanitation folk and seasoned vets alike. A san man reaching to pick up a bag of trash encounters a dog walker who lets Fido let loose at that exact instant on that exact bag. Imagine the san man in motion, his body bent so he can grasp the slick plastic of the bag, finding himself face-to-face with a dog's raised leg and liquid output. A variation on this theme is that the dog walker plops a sample of the pooch's poop precisely where the worker is reaching, in which case the worker in motion closes his fist not around the ear of the bag but around a bagged (or sometimes unbagged) pile of shit.

The situation presents a few choices. The worker can ignore it. Or he can politely but firmly point out to the dog walker that her behavior is offensive. Or he can become irate. A new hire still on probation is wise to stay quiet, though he in particular will often find that the most difficult choice. A san worker with a few years on the job who is familiar with this moment knows that nothing he does or says will change the dog walker's attitude or behavior—in fact, even a polite comment from him will most likely inspire invective—so he usually doesn't bother to respond.

But to another man with a few years on the job, or perhaps the same man on a different day, the rudeness can carry an unexpected prickle, maybe even a sting, that ruptures his calm. In the versions I've heard, the san man who decides to protest always starts by speaking respectfully, which may or may not be true, and the dog walker always responds with obscenities, which I believe. The curses are variations on the command that the san man mind his own goddamn business, an illogic I especially like. That garbage Fido is soiling? It *is* the san man's business.

When the dog walker starts unloading expletives, the san man faces another choice. He can ignore her and continue his work. Those who take this path explain to me that they had to say *something*, even though—as predicted—the dog walker refused to hear it. But another worker, having opened his mouth in the first place, will sometimes further tease what now qualifies as a frayed interaction. The most popular strategy—a surprisingly spontaneous consensus, since there is no section of any codebook that recommends this reply—is to volunteer to deliver fresh dog shit to the dog owner at her job. Perhaps she would like it in the middle of her computer keyboard?

As one would expect, the suggestion provokes new outrage from Fido's owner, usually along the lines of "How dare you talk to me that way?" or "Who the fuck do you think you are?" or every civil servant's favorite, "Watch your mouth, you stupid asshole; I pay your salary." Once in a while the affronted citizen will formally complain, in writing or by phone, but the Sanitation officer hearing the offense likely experienced the same situation when he was on the street and will do little except make soothing noises to the complainant, along with assurances that the intolerably bad-mannered sanitation worker in question will suffer harsh consequences, which is nonsense.

There are exceptions to san workers' invisibility. Building supers and porters often help throw bags into the back of the truck. Small children sometimes stop to talk to the crew and watch them work, especially if the hopper blade is making an extra lot of grinding, crunching noise while it pulverizes something big, like a stove or a couch. Old people often watch closely, too; sometimes they offer thanks or querulous criticism. And motorists notice sanitation workers, but usually only after they turn onto a narrow street, come halfway up the block, and find themselves stuck behind the truck—the very same truck that was right there, easily visible from the intersection, before the motorist made the turn.

An alarming number of people seem to become cretins when they slip behind the wheel of a car. Or maybe a particular species of New York driver is prone to a form of magical thinking. When this person sees a street blocked by a working collection truck and makes the turn anyway, he must believe that he can cause the obstacle to vanish if he just concentrates hard enough. When that strategy fails, it seems that the driver attempts an alternative ensorcellment: if he says the right spells—that is, if he's rude enough—*then* the truck will disappear.

Woe unto that motorist. Excessive honking, yelling, and cursing are excellent ways to invert the standard relationship between seen and unseen: the san man does not seem to hear the horn or the curses, nor does he see the car. Astute observers will notice that—is it possible?—the more grief they get, the slower a crew moves. Indeed, some workers add an extra cycle of the hopper for every honk of a horn. The men have nowhere to go except the end of the block and then the block beyond that, and they are not interested in working faster every time someone in a car is inconvenienced. Moreover, this particular motorist is the umpteenth idiot to throw profanities at them, and they are thoroughly unimpressed. (Who's invisible now, suckah?)

I witnessed a near fight one morning when a man in an SUV worked himself into a froth while the delivery van in front of him was slow to squeeze past our collection truck. When the SUV pulled up next to the Sanitation crew, its driver asked, in accented English and with spittle flecking his lips, why they didn't move the *fucking* truck over a few *fucking* inches to allow the goddamn cars to pass. The two san men turned as one to look at their truck. If it were any closer to the cars parked at the curb, it would have taken off those cars' side-view mirrors. The men turned back to the motorist.

"Move it over where?" asked the driver, a stocky African American man in his fifties. "I'm supposed to climb out over the cars? Or over the loader's seat?" The motorist, a vein pulsing in his forehead, insisted that the truck had room to spare, that the san men were fucking *idiots* if they couldn't see that.

The loader, a young man, stepped forward. Earlier in the morning, he had been talking with pride about his parents, who had immigrated to New York just before he was born. He leaned down until his face was inches from the motorist's.

"Why don't you go the fuck back where you came from, you little shit," he said quietly. "No one wants you in this country. You can't even speak fucking English."

Had the motorist not been pinned by a seat belt and a car door, he likely would've taken a swing at the loader. Perhaps he considered disentangling himself and leaping from his car, but when he paused to converse with the crew, he had created a fresh traffic jam, and car horns were blaring anew. He glowered, spilled a few more curses, and stepped on his accelerator, his tires squealing as he zoomed toward the intersection.

The loader explained to me that even if it gets you in trouble, some insults you must answer, because are you a man or aren't you a man? If his supervisor had overheard this exchange, however, or if the motorist had taken note of the truck number, the street, the time of day, or the loader's name embroidered on his sweatshirt, the worker would almost certainly have been banged (that is, he would have received a formal written complaint). If it had come down to a he said/he said account, the motorist could have been faulted for starting the feud, but he would have suffered no repercussions.

Despite public perceptions to the contrary, guys will, in fact, take the truck around the block now and then to relieve the traffic backed up behind them. A dewy-eyed woman with a hitch in her voice can sometimes get a crew to move the truck out of the way in a heartbeat—but not always. Work is work, and often there are two dewy-eyed women for every three cars stuck. A short-lived policy from the Department required workers on some routes to move the truck every time it impeded traffic, a scheme that provoked great skepticism among the rank and file. Such thorough accommodation to motorists ensured that collection routes were never completed. Crews spent their shifts driving in circles.

The sociologist Wayne Brekhus might point to sanitation work as an example of an "unmarked" element of daily life.[13] The world around us is more completely comprehended if we look for phenomena that are usually unnoticed—unextraordinary, he calls them—and therefore unanalyzed. They stand in contrast to things, relationships, identities, or behaviors that are marked, claims Brekhus; these garner a lot of attention and are often used as examples that purport to illustrate larger realities, but recognizing only marked phenomena distorts our understanding of the world.[14] Brekhus makes the case that important truths are lodged within the unmarked and the unseen.

Municipal recycling programs are a good example. They are central to waste management strategies in towns and cities all over the world and are usually accompanied by rhetoric about how recycling helps save the planet. It's an unfortunate claim. While such programs have many benefits, they don't do squat for global environmental health.[15] Yet curbside recycling, a marked component of what's considered responsible ecological stewardship, receives real resources and support while other, less obvious, more complicated choices that have the potential to make a real difference, like a more politically engaged citizenry and government incentives against various forms of large-scale pollution, are largely unmarked and so are ignored.

San workers recognize that they are engaged in unmarked labor and are themselves unmarked laborers. One afternoon a san man listened passively as his supervisor yelled at him for something or other. When the rant subsided, the worker said wearily, "C'mon, Eddie, what are you getting so upset about? It's only garbage." The phrase is common. Following a difficult time "chasing garbage" after Department resources had been diverted for a large snowstorm, a district superintendent received low marks from his superiors for the efforts of his garage. Like everyone else, he was bone tired from consecutive weeks of twelve- and thirteen-hour days. He took his responsibilities seriously, and the criticisms stung. But then he shook his head dismissively. "It's only garbage," he said, sighing.

Labors of waste certainly qualify as unmarked, but a sanitation worker is not physically invisible. Haverford's John Coleman wasn't wearing a magic cloaking device when he was collecting garbage, nor do New York's Sanitation crews become see-through when they're on the street; rather, their consistent state of not-there-ness is a status given to them by the larger culture. When going about their everyday chores, sanitation workers are *willfully* unseen by the public.[16]

Garbage itself is the great unmarked and purposely unseen result of a lushly consumptive economy and culture. The work is further unmarked and unseen because it exists along both physical and cognitive edges. A sanitation worker's career is focused on objects and debris that others have decided merit no further attention and that are in transition out of the home to a "final" resting place. He occupies in-between physical spaces—the street, yes, but specifically the curb, the alley, the end of the driveway. He moves garbage, the ultimate unloved Stuff, to areas zoned mostly for industrial uses. He starts and finishes his workday in a garage that is usually on the outskirts of a neighborhood. He is the intercessor between the uncomfortable here and now of an individual's own refuse and a safely mythical "away."

But there's more. His work is preventive, not reactive, and thus it becomes marked only when it's *not* done. A steady joke and truism among san workers is that they get attention on only a few occasions; one of them is a missed pickup. Systematic garbage collection was instituted in New York less than 120 years ago, but since then the public has come to rely on the service as commonplace and unexceptional.[17] No matter the circumstances—a blizzard, a terrorist attack, a blackout, a hurricane, a fire that razes a garage—the garbage gets picked up. The sanitation worker is as unremarkable and as certain to arrive as the morning sun.[18]

A reader of a certain ilk who has stayed with me this far may be growing impatient. "Yeah," I imagine him saying, "so garbagemen—er, 'sanitation workers'—don't get much attention. So what? A lot of different kinds of workers don't get much attention. Why should I care about sanitation people?"

An excellent question. The quick answer, which consternates even some people on the job: because Sanitation is the most important uniformed force on the street. No city can thrive without a workable solid waste management plan. If sanitation workers aren't out there, the city becomes unlivable, fast. Before problems of rubbish and street cleaning were solved, much of New York was infamously filthy. Thousands upon thousands of people who had no choice but to endure streets shin-deep in all manner of debris, whose homes were airless rooms and lightless cellars, died in extravagant numbers of diseases that even back then were largely preventable. Responses to this constellation of horrors came from many quarters, but effective garbage collection was one of the bedrock foundations upon which reform was built. Certainly police and fire, corrections and transportation, child welfare and education, are all essential to a healthy city, but New York's history proves that neither cops nor firefighters nor teachers can function effectively for the city as a whole when the streets they travel and the neighborhoods where they work and live are buried in waste.

The claim extends beyond public health, and the second reason for Sanitation's importance has two factors. San workers are key players in maintaining the most basic rhythms of capitalism. Material consumption always includes, though seldom acknowledges, the necessity of disposal. If consumed goods can't be discarded, the space they occupy remains full, and new goods can't become part of a household.[19] Because sanitation workers take away household trash, the engines of our consumption-based economy don't sputter. Though this is a simplistic description of a dense and complex set of processes, the fundamental reality is straightforward: used-up stuff must be thrown out for new stuff to have a place.

Contemporary consumption and discard habits represent a use of time that has no historical precedent.[20] We depend on our ability to move fast, and so assume the briefest relationships with coffee cups, shopping bags, packaging of all kinds—encumbrances we must shed quickly so that we can maintain what I call our average necessary quotidian velocity. Such velocity is connected to our identities, which have never been more malleable; consumption is the mechanism we rely on in this moment of time to declare and recognize distinctions of class, education, political leaning, religious belief.

By this logic, sanitation workers are absolutely central to our physical well-being as residents of a metropolis and to our sense of proper citizenship within a hyper-paced world, even while the work of sanitation remains bluntly physical. Despite unprecedented technological sophistication, the labors of waste literally rest on the bodies of men and women whom we routinely stigmatize. The radio ad for a dating service asks, "Why settle for a garbageman when you can have a stockbroker?" A woman offers a sanitation worker that day's newspaper, and as he thanks her, she asks hesitantly, "You can read, right?" A cartoon of a couple at a nice restaurant shows the woman, looking distressed, explain to her date, "When I said I wanted someone in uniform, this wasn't what I had in mind." The man, surrounded by flies, wears a jacket from Joe's Garbage Service. A newspaper story about a college football scandal quotes an administrator justifying false grades for school jocks by explaining that he wanted his athletes to get jobs at the post office instead of having to become garbagemen.[21] Tourist shops all over New York City sell knockoff FDNY and NYPD gear, but little or nothing from the DSNY. Chain stores, other retail outlets, and even some colleges in the New York region give discounts to cops and firefighters but not to sanitation workers. And every sanitation worker of a certain age remembers the teacher yelling that if he didn't get good grades, he'd end up a garbageman.

The stigma smarts, but it is especially disturbing because, according to the federal Bureau of Labor Statistics, sanitation work is one of the most dangerous jobs in the nation, with significantly higher injury and fatality rates per labor hour than policing or firefighting.

Families whose loved ones become sanitation workers often cite the absence of guns and flames as a reason to be glad for the job. "I didn't want to get shot one day," a new hire told me, explaining why he turned down the chance to be a cop. It's true that as a san man he's not likely to have someone pull a gun on him (though it has happened), but he is quite likely to get beaned in the head, or punched in the gut, or scored on the legs with a random assortment of blunt or sharp or jagged objects. Various toxic substances inside the trash he's handling can cripple or even kill him. And while he's working in the street, his chances of getting clipped, crushed, or run down by traffic are alarmingly high.

New Yorkers know none of this. "They put their garbage out at night," quip old-time Sanitation personnel, "and think the Garbage Faeries make it all go away." The city's Garbage Faeries are workers who wear dark green uniforms, drive loud white trucks, and lift, in some districts, their share of twenty tons of trash every day; whose families must adjust to a schedule that allows two days off in a row only once every several weeks; who, when they are junior hires, find out only at the end of one shift when and where their next shift starts, which can bounce them all over the clock and sometimes all over the city for weeks, months, even years; who spend their working hours handling heavy machinery and stepping in and out of traffic; and who suffer an array of debilitating and sometimes deadly injuries, regardless of how careful they are. Roughly a quarter of them are African American, slightly fewer than a fifth are Latino, and a little more than half are white, though within that category are many who make a sharp distinction between Irish and Italian.[22] Regardless of their ethnicity, their time on the job, the families who depend on them, the specific assignments they take, the physical hurts they endure, or their crucial role in the city's well-being, when the Garbage Faeries put on that uniform, it's as if they cease to exist. This had bothered me for a long time.

2. In the Field

It started when I was ten years old. The forest where my father took me camping seemed so pristine that I could almost pretend we were its first human visitors—until we discovered, just behind our campsite, an open-air garbage dump about forty feet square. Fat flies buzzed moldy orange peels, empty soup cans rusted near a single sneaker, and balls of crumpled aluminum foil glinted next to spent Tang packets. There was even that signature stink.

I was astounded. How could my fellow campers be so thoughtless? Obviously, they had no problem letting their garbage become someone else's problem, but *whose*, exactly? Were they assuming the services of a special Forest Ranger Trash Brigade? Was a garbage truck scheduled to appear via some road I hadn't noticed?

The memory is vivid because it was one of those awful childhood moments when a certainty is exposed as a lie. I had assumed that adults cared about respecting wild forests, but the woodland trash heap was proof that some people, even those who presumably liked to go camping, didn't give a hoot. The realization left me angry, confused, and eventually fascinated.

The behavior of a few careless campers was merely a small example of what most of us do all the time, on a much grander scale, with objects we no longer need and no longer want. We toss trash in a litter basket or put it on the curb in bags or in garbage cans behind our homes or drop it down an apartment building chute or drive it to the local dump or even, yes, let it fall on the street or toss it from our car windows, and never think about it again.

Such casual unthinking is evident in the peculiar construction in English of "throwing" our garbage "away"—an act both emphatic and vague. We don't "put" it away, which would imply saving it, or "place" it somewhere, which suggests handling it with care. We "throw" it, thus putting it far from ourselves, to an "away" about which we know little. In today's developed nations, "away" means landfills or recycling facilities or waste-to-energy plants (the modern versions of incinerators, which used to be called destructors and before that were known as crematories).

In New York, "away" has been the city's shoreline, the bottoms of marshes and gullies and outhouses, the rocking ocean. These choices put trash out of sight but also kept it close: 20 percent of today's metropolitan region, and fully 33 percent of lower Manhattan, is built on fill, much of which was created from rubbish.[1] Like many cities around the world, contemporary New York rests on top of its own buried history.

In the first half of the twentieth century, "away" was scores of hastily constructed incinerators and dozens of sloppy landfills. They were put in place by Robert Moses, the city's so-called master builder, as part of his long-term solid waste management plan, but most lasted only a few decades.[2] When they were shut down one after another, ever greater quantities of municipal trash were shunted to a single landfill on the west shore of Staten Island. It was established in 1948 on a tidal wetland called Fresh Kills, and Moses promised it would be open for only three years, but its footprint kept expanding as its hills kept growing; by the early 1990s, it was the city's only waste-disposal option. The landfill was finally closed in 2001. Now Gotham's garbage travels as far as Ohio and South

Carolina before reaching its "away" (where it will confuse generations of archaeologists in the distant future).

I knew none of this when I left home and started to make my way in
the world. I knew that I had great curiosity about trash, but I thought
my questions were weird because I didn't hear anyone else asking
them. By the time I moved to New York City, I was used to keeping
quiet about my musings. They made people chuckle; they marked
me as odd.

There were kindred spirits in the world, and I'd have found
them if I'd known where to look. One was the artist Mierle Laderman Ukeles, a tall, slender woman with flowing hair and a deliberate cadence of speech. After her first child was born, Ukeles was
struggling to reconcile her responsibilities as a parent with the apparently incompatible calling of her work when she had an epiph-
any. Maintaining the well-being of her child was itself an art. In fact,
she realized, *all* maintenance work—unrecognized, monotonous,
repetitive, essential—could be art.

The discovery inspired Ukeles to propose an entirely new genre.[3]
One of its first expressions was a performance piece in 1976 called
I Make Maintenance Art One Hour Every Day. Based in an office
building in lower Manhattan that was also home to the downtown
branch of the Whitney Museum, it involved three hundred window
washers, security guards, janitors, cleaning women, and elevator mechanics. Ukeles spent weeks with them across all shifts and asked
them to do their chores as usual but to consider designating their labor as art for an hour a day. She took Polaroids of each of them while
they worked, and they told her whether the pictures showed them
doing maintenance work or maintenance art. She labeled the photographs accordingly and mounted them in the Whitney's exhibition
space; by the time she was done, 720 images covered an entire wall.

A glowing review ran in *The Village Voice*: "Housepersons of the
world, rejoice! If urinals and soup cans can be art, why not ordinary

activities like sweeping?" The reviewer said that the project had "real soul," and mused, "If the Department of Sanitation . . . could turn its regular work into a conceptual performance, the city might qualify for a grant from the National Endowment for the Arts."[4]

Of course. What more basic maintenance work was there in New York than that of the city's own municipal housekeepers, the Department of Sanitation?

As Ukeles tells the story, the *Voice* review prompted a phone call from the commissioner of sanitation, who asked her, "Want to make that kind of art with 10,000 people?" "I'll be right over," she replied. Soon after, she was appointed the DSNY's artist-in-residence, an unsalaried position she has held ever since.[5]

She spent a year and a half preparing for a performance artwork called *Touch Sanitation*, her debut piece with the Department. Over the course of eleven months between 1979 and 1980, she followed a carefully planned sequence that took her to DSNY garages, landfills, incinerators, repair shops, section stations, lunchrooms, broom depots, and offices. She accompanied sanitation workers in every section of every district, walking out the routes with them, staying for the entire shift and longer, coming back day after day. During her journey, she met and shook hands with every sanitation worker in the city—eighty-five hundred at the time—and said to each, "Thank you for keeping New York City alive."

When I learned about Ukeles's work, I was riveted. Here was a person—a *woman*—who not only thought about trash and about the people who pick it up but also made their concerns central to her own. And she didn't consider them from a distance; she got up close and personal with them, the better to bring attention to their efforts and to celebrate their labors. Many decades earlier, at the turn of the nineteenth into the twentieth century, New York had formally recognized and even cheered its street cleaners, but few remembered that history, which made Ukeles all the more extraordinary. When she was doing *Touch Sanitation*, no one else was grappling with similar themes (and few have since).[6]

Ukeles gave me much to ponder as I tried to figure out what to do with my life.

Cultural anthropology is a discipline with a complicated and trou-bled history, but its basic tenets point to the creative potential inherent in human existence.[7] An anthropologist wants to understand worldviews that are sometimes radically different from her own, then tries to discern which parts of those perspectives are unique and which are found in other societies. With its focus on cultural practices and social structures of large- and small-scale societies around the globe, anthropology reveals that across time we humans have created an astonishing variety of political structures, economic practices, timekeeping systems, marriage rules, religious teachings, kinship patterns. Tradition and habit can give the weight of Truth to assumptions about how the world works and how relationships within it are supposed to be structured; to me, anthropology's biggest revelation is that most of these Truths, and the social contexts in which they fit, are inventions. We make them up. Maybe not consciously, and certainly never all by ourselves in a vacuum, but our customs and habits and cultural predilections are not immutable.

Anthropology took me through graduate school, but I wasn't studying garbage, and I missed it. After I finished my degree, it was time to make rubbish central again, so I put together a seminar called Garbage in Gotham: The Anthropology of Trash. My students and I considered things like the fickleness of value or worth.[8] We pondered how understandings of time have changed over the last century or two, what that has to do with our connections to "goods," and what happens when goods go bad.[9] We weighed the economic and social factors that encourage wasting versus those that inspire conservation.[10] We looked at categories of thought that are set apart from casual discourse—categories that almost require bracketing, like death, for instance, and garbage—and explored the implications of such segregation.[11] We learned that mechanisms of disgust and structures of morality might be closely connected.[12] We studied how other peoples understand and confront waste, and read about the connection between definitions of order and definitions of sacredness.[13] The history of infrastructural developments connected to waste management, especially in cities, revealed aspects of urban history that were new to most of my students.[14] And the conundrum of personal versus corporate versus government responsibility for waste in various manifestations inevitably provoked lively discussions.

But the most memorable part of the semester was always our visit to the Fresh Kills landfill on Staten Island.[15] A Sanitation supervisor took us to the unloading pads where crane operators dug out barges filled to the brim with hundreds of tons of trash. He showed us Payhaulers, mammoth dump trucks with wheels that seemed nearly twice our height, and front-end loaders with buckets the size of cars. For the tour's finale, we went to the landfill's open face, where we watched compacting bulldozers that looked big enough to push over entire buildings as they moved across broad fields of freshly dumped trash. Or rather, we tried to watch them; the machinery was hard to see through the hordes of vulture-sized seagulls that swooped and dipped and bombed the inexhaustible food source.[16]

My students knew before they saw it that the landfill was huge—according to folk wisdom, it was so big that it could be seen from space—but nothing prepared them for its sheer audacity. The bulging hills seemed to go on forever and hinted at forces once human-made but now, perhaps, autonomously geological.[17] Fresh Kills was a concentrated manifestation of immense material might—the discards of a great city molded into peaks and valleys—and also of extraordinary logistical daring: How were the people who worked there not overwhelmed by the perpetual flood of trash? Garbage moves in what the industry calls a waste stream, but this colossal expanse could only have been built for a waste deluge. It seemed large enough to accommodate the refuse of an entire nation, not just of a single city.[18]

Maybe New York was unwittingly imitating indigenous peoples from the northwest coast of North America who were famous for extravagant feasts in which vast quantities of goods, amassed over years—blankets, hunting tools, food, cooking pots, huge copper ingots—were brazenly destroyed. This was one element of a ceremony called potlach. The goal was to prove one's power by obliterating more property than rivals could ever match. But if Fresh Kills stood for our potlatch, who and where were our rivals?

Throughout our studies, the questions that most caught my imagination were also those that held my students' interest and that were especially vivid at the landfill. Just as objects are given value, so are labors. What is the status of a sanitation worker? Who takes the job? What is the work like, on the street or at the dump?[19]

An anthropologist learns about the lives of a group not her own by doing fieldwork. As it was structured from the discipline's earliest days, fieldwork requires a practice called participant observation.[20] The idea is to immerse oneself in the ways of a particular group or society, learn as much as possible about their worldview, and share those insights with the larger world. The more my students and I explored labors of waste, the more I knew it was time to start working with the people whose lives were centered on exactly those concerns. It was time to get into the field.

I wrote a proposal for an ethnographic research project that asked, in essence, what it's like to be a sanitation worker in New York today and why that's important to know, then sent it to the DSNY. I was pretty sure that mine was a unique request, and I knew I'd have to prove that I wasn't out to dis the Department. I followed up the letter with a phone call asking if I could come down to Sanitation headquarters to introduce myself and explain my plan. The reaction was less than enthusiastic.

That conversation was the start of a back-and-forth that turned into a kind of fieldwork unto itself. No one in Sanitation ever told me to get lost, but no one let me move my idea forward, either. After months of persistently knocking on the door of the DSNY through letters, e-mails, and phone calls, I was getting exactly nowhere, except to earn a thorough education in bureaucratic stonewalling. "We'll call you back." "Can you send that proposal once more? I seem to have misplaced it." "We'll have to check with so-and-so, he's on vacation for a few weeks." "I'm sorry, I didn't get that message, what did you want again?" "No one can meet with you this month. Maybe next month."

Meanwhile, my class visits to Fresh Kills caught the attention of the public relations staff at my university. They alerted *The New York Times*, and a reporter and photographer accompanied us on a trip to the landfill in the spring of 2000. I asked the reporter if the DSNY had given them permission to tag along; she shrugged and said she was pretty sure. The resulting story ran above the fold on the front page of the paper's Metro section a few weeks later, complete with full-color pictures and a long text.[21] It was wonderful—not fluffy, but not negative. It was syndicated nationally. Bill Griffith did a *Zippy* comic strip about it. The BBC phoned for an interview. My bosses were delighted.

I hoped that the *Times* piece would convince someone at the DSNY to sit down with me, but it made no difference. The wall remained impenetrable until finally, after many more months of letters and phone calls, I was given an appointment late in the summer of 2001. The person who had been in charge of the Office of Public Information was gone, and no one had yet been appointed to take his place. Perhaps staffers reasoned that they could meet with me, turn me down once and for all, and I'd disappear, thus ensuring one less headache for their next boss. I anticipated their thinking, however, so I marshaled my most compelling arguments. This was it—the chance I'd been waiting for, begging for, for almost two years, and I didn't want to blow it. On an unusually pleasant afternoon at the end of August, I found my way to the seventh floor of 125 Worth Street.

Kathy Dawkins, acting deputy commissioner of public information, sat behind an imposing wooden desk in a high-ceilinged office. I'd spoken to Dawkins a few times on the phone. She was a no-nonsense woman accustomed to dealing with reporters who often got the story wrong. Sitting in a chair next to me was Al Ferguson, now a three-star chief but at the time a superintendent.

I made my case, taking care to sound friendly but professional. Sanitation workers are the most important people on the streets of New York, I said. They are essential to the city's well-being, but the public doesn't really know what they do. Except sometimes briefly after a snowstorm, they don't get the respect or attention they deserve. I wanted to get to know them and their labors, I explained, so that I could write a book showing the world how critical and how difficult their work is, a book that would reveal how much sanitation workers and the Department that stands behind them merit praise and respect. Please, I begged inwardly, I come in peace. I bow to your gods. I will smoke the pipe with you. We will trade daughters and join our tribes in harmony. Please. Please. Please.

Dawkins and Ferguson listened politely. When I was through, they said that they would give my request more thought and get back to me. While it wasn't a firm refusal, it wasn't what I'd hoped to hear, but I couldn't think of anything else to say to help my cause. I thanked them for their time and was about to gather my things when, as an afterthought, I asked if they had any other questions, if there was anything we hadn't discussed that they wanted to touch on.

"Yes," said Dawkins. Her voice was hard. "How did you get a *New York Times* photographer and reporter onto Fresh Kills without our knowledge or permission?"

She was talking about my class tour nearly sixteen months earlier.

"They didn't have permission." It was a question, though I said it as a fact.

"No."

"I asked them; I thought they had permission."

"You were the one who requested the tour; you should've made sure."

"Of course . . ." I nodded slowly. I had the sensation of a kind of scrim lifting and once-familiar scenery becoming newly stark. Or maybe it was like, all along, I'd needed eyeglasses with a strong prescription but never knew it until a pair was plunked onto my nose.

"So . . . I made a mistake." I looked at Dawkins.

"Oh, yes."

Not just a mistake—a *big* mistake. Throughout its history, the Department of Sanitation has been put-upon and belittled by news organizations, freelance writers, and journalists of many stripes. It has been mocked in public venues, neglected at city functions, found wanting in every imaginable way. At the same time, it has grown from its disorganized start in the 1880s into a highly stratified, rigidly bureaucratized, often retributive institution that, despite colossal obstacles, gets up the trash of New York every day. One doesn't do anything that earns the Department publicity unless the Department has as firm a hold as possible on the message and on its delivery, a goal that it can't always achieve but that it strives for nonetheless.

The story that ran in the *Times* was positive—Sanitation came out looking quite good, I thought—but the crucial missing piece wasn't anything in the text or pictures. It was the fact that no one at the DSNY had seen it coming. All of a sudden one weekday morning, prominently positioned in one of the world's most influential newspapers, there were color photographs and a lengthy article about a college class hiking around one of the Department's most important but controversial facilities. To have a negative story in a major media outlet was bad, but to have a significant story that no one knew was going to run, regardless of its tone, was worse.

I shivered when I imagined the recriminations that must've sounded from the commissioner to the deputy commissioner to the public information staff, probably to Dawkins herself. It looked as if I'd done an end run around the very people whose permission I should've secured, and they were most displeased.

I sagged in my chair. "This means you can't trust me, doesn't it."

"It makes it much harder," conceded Dawkins.

"And if you can't trust me, you can't let me do this project."

She didn't reply.

I left Worth Street deeply discouraged. I couldn't think how to redeem myself with Dawkins and her colleagues, or what my next steps should be.

In 2002, a new mayor came to town. The people whom Michael Bloomberg appointed as agency heads reflected a more openhanded management style than had been the norm for many years. His commissioner of sanitation was not skittish about an outsider proposal that involved his agency, in part because his connection to the job had already transcended the fleeting brevity of mayoral administrations.

John Doherty, a slender man with a piercing look, is one of the few people in the Department's history to start on the street and end at the top. In 1960, after he learned that an old neck injury disqualified him for the Fire Department, he came on as a sanitationman (the official job title—yes, as a single word—from the 1950s until the 1980s) and rose through the ranks to become commissioner in 1994. He retired to California in 1998, but when Bloomberg invited him to take up his old post, he put his beloved motorcycle in mothballs and moved back to New York to resume command of the agency he knew perhaps better than anyone alive.[22] When Doherty returned, Vito Turso joined him.

Turso is occasionally mistaken for the TV personality Geraldo Rivera or the singer Tony Orlando. He has a fondness for puns, a passion for golf, and an abiding love for the job, even though it's not always easy to get out the good word about the DSNY. He headed

Sanitation's Office of Public Information from 1978 until 1990 and was working in the private sector when city hall reached out to him.

Two friends with hooks in the Department spoke to Turso on my behalf, and he agreed to meet. After several conversations, he let me start exploring the Department's archives; at the time, the collection consisted of a few boxes on a shelf in his office. For such a small trove, it was full of treasure. I spent hours immersed in more than a century's worth of annual reports, snowstorm summaries, descriptions of stables and garages and landfills. It was a scholar's delight, though his staff probably wished their cubicles had doors when I found it hard to resist reading various gems aloud.

Sweep magazine, a small quarterly that the Department published between the late 1950s and the early 1970s, was one rewarding discovery. Every issue included guest editorials from celebrities (such as Eleanor Roosevelt), book recommendations from the DSNY's director of engineering (*Municipal Refuse Disposal*, by the American Public Works Association, was a favorite), profiles of Sanitation personnel with unusual hobbies (a nationally ranked bodybuilder; a speedboat racer; a knitwear designer). I learned from *Sweep* that there were eleven incinerators in New York in 1962, that incinerator workers had their own union, and that the DSNY once had its own fleet of tugboats. I read an account of Leopold Stokowski's stint as guest conductor of the famous Sanitation Department Marching Band. There were profiles of the new Central Repair Shop built in Queens in 1964 and details of early collaborations between the city and a novel new civic organization called Keep America Beautiful.[23]

The archival research was fascinating, but I needed to be in the field, which meant I had to earn Turso's trust. I spent as much time as possible in his sights by lingering over those written records, copying dozens of pages from older documents by hand. After much of the summer and part of the fall, after many talks with Turso, and after a thorough case of writer's cramp, I started to press gently for access to a garage, and at long last the way was cleared for me to visit Manhattan 7.

At the time, M7 was crammed atop a pier on the Hudson River at Fifty-Seventh Street and the West Side Highway.[24] On a dusky autumn morning about half an hour before roll call, I walked past a canopied salt mound, a fleet of quiet trucks, a wall of plow blades stacked like majestic parentheses, and a corrugated shed that housed a small body shop, then climbed the battered wooden steps to the trailer that held offices for the district's superintendent, supervisors, and clerks. The linoleum inside was worn, and the air carried the sharp smell of the disinfectant used to excess in every New York Sanitation garage, police precinct, subway station, jail, public school. (It is so pervasive in city-controlled spaces that it could be Gotham's signature perfume, maybe with a name like L'Essence de la Municipalité de New York.)

When I arrived at M7, I felt well prepared, but the depths of my ignorance were about to be revealed. I knew nothing of the real forces that shape the job.

3. On the Board

"How much time you got?"

The question surprised me when first I heard it—how drastically our lives would change if we knew the answer!—but no one was referring to our ineluctable mortality. In the context of the job, it asks how long you've been wearing a Sanitation uniform, which is a way of ascertaining status. One worker will often ask it of another when they meet for the first time because it immediately establishes their places in the Department's hierarchy. It makes clear who has what kinds of rights over work assignments and chances at over-time, who gets dibs on choice transfer opportunities, who is closer to retirement.

"Five years" might be one response.

"Got you beat" is the reply if the questioner has been on the job longer. The happiest day in a new hire's short career is when an even newer hire arrives, because then the original new hire is no longer the juniorest man (or woman) on the roster.[1]

The issue of status is only one of the many ways in which time rules the job. Within the DSNY, time is a chart of progress, a point of argument, a cause for punishment. It is carved up, meted out, negotiated, swapped. It translates wages and tonnages into success or failure. It shapes the day, the month, the accumulation of years that becomes a career, and the most fundamental sense of self.[2]

Time's touchstone is the operations board. Every Sanitation facility has one, and all boards give a detailed snapshot of what's going on. A glance shows who is working where, with whom, on which specific truck or spreader or mechanical broom. It changes every day, and whoever rules it has considerable power.

A typical board is about five or six feet high by twelve or fifteen feet long, though sizes vary. Horizontal slots running all the way across are met by vertical lines that run top to bottom. Tucked into the slots are white and colored cardboard tags, about three inches by ten. Everyone has a card, including officers. Different colors correspond to different sections of the district. On each card is printed a last name and first initial, a number, and a date. The number is the list number for that uniformed employee, a calculation based on how well she did on the civil service test that is the first step toward employment, and the date is her first day on the job. These two details determine her seniority, which is another way of saying they determine most of her work life for most of her career.

If someone is on vacation, that's on the board. So is anyone out sick, on jury duty, on bereavement leave, sent to a different district, excused with pay, away without leave—all is revealed by the location of the cards in the slots. Charts are there, too.

A chart is the single day in the week besides Sunday that a sanitation worker or officer is scheduled to have off. Unless a uniformed person works in the Safety and Training Division or at Sanitation headquarters on Worth Street or in only a few other places, he has Saturdays off only once every few weeks. His other days off vary according to a schedule so complex that it occupies both sides of a densely lined, number-riddled . . . chart. Hence the lingo.

The chart system results from the job's manpower requirements, which are determined by continual and meticulous accounting. Every element involved in the task of collecting garbage is measured to the smallest possible increment, translated into fractions of cents, and then forecast into dollar requirements. A sanitation worker's eight-hour shift is strictly prescribed. How long it takes to get to the start of a collection route, the length of the route itself, how long to finish a specific street or section of blocks, to travel to and from break or lunch, how long break lasts, how long lunch lasts, what route to take to and from a dumping point—these are only some of the many variables measured, anticipated, recorded in space (miles) and time (minutes).

Miles driven in what kind of truck, the length of time any trip takes on any day in any set of conditions by any possible route (GPS helps with this), the tons of trash collected per day, per shift, per route, per line, per crew, how many gallons of motor oil and hoist oil and antifreeze glugged into how many vehicles, the numbers of lug nuts securing how many tires on how many vehicles in how many garages, tire abrasian rates per annum—it's all calculated, quantified, budgeted. The Department can anticipate overall rates of wear for collection trucks driven across all three shifts (it's pretty fast) versus those used only for two out of three shifts (much slower). Predictions of costs for near-term and long-range planning are calculated using such data, which are collected and interpreted by number crunchers in Sanitation's Office of Management and Budget.

Based on the wealth of detail gleaned from these many quantifications and on decades of experience, the Department looks at how many sanitation workers it needs across a six-day workweek and calculates an outage factor of 1.5. It means that for every person at work, plan on another half a person to fill in any gaps. When four trucks are scheduled for collection with eight people to work them, twelve people are on payroll for that assignment. If the original eight workers go out with the four trucks, the four extra people are given work elsewhere, usually in a garage where there's a shortage. Every day by late morning, the Department looks at the next day's labor needs across the entire city, sees where it has too many workers and where there are not enough, and issues orders to correct the imbalance. The orders go from headquarters to the borough commands to individual districts, where they become the responsibility of the person charged with setting the board.

A knot of people gathers in front of the board at the end of every shift in garages and broom depots around the city, checking to see where they'll be and what they'll be doing the next day. If there's been any trouble with a particular worker, it's sometimes first noticed when unusual arrangements show up on the board, an event that can set off hours of speculation and debate. When senior workers with a regular schedule check the board, they're mostly just confirming what they already know. Junior workers can rarely predict their next shift, so the board is their source of vital information. Regardless of what it tells them, juniors can count on getting the scut assignments—like baskets.

A crew on baskets rides a street or an avenue from corner to corner and empties public litter baskets. It is the most Sisyphean of chores because, unlike a collection route, a basket route never ends. When the crew finishes one pass, they go back to the top and start over. It used to be that one worker drove while the other hefted, riding the running board between stops, and every so often they'd trade. Then the union demanded that the running boards be removed from the trucks, arguing that they weren't safe.[3] Now one worker drives and the other walks, making basket routes much slower and more tiresome.

The tedium can inspire mischief. Like one time when Sal Federici, my buddy from M7, was on baskets. Sal hated baskets.

Somewhere in the middle of his first pass, Federici came upon a particularly dilapidated can. It was the old kind, made of orange metal webbing, and looked barely solid enough to stand, much less hold garbage. He was supposed to empty it and return it to the street, but instead, on a lark, he tossed the entire thing into the back of the truck, pulled the handles, and sent it up. He liked the way it screeched and bent into sculptural shapes under the blade. He was ready to go his merry way when he felt a tap on the shoulder and turned to see an elderly woman glaring at him.

"You just threw out a perfectly good public garbage can," she scolded. "You destroyed city property, and I saw you do it." So much for his invisibility.

"Oh, no, ma'am." Federici didn't hesitate. "It went into the truck to be serviced. In a few minutes it'll come out the front, polished up and good as new. We do this every now and then to cans that need a little maintenance."

The woman's eyebrows rose nearly to her starched blue hairline as Federici jumped on the back step, waved goodbye, and motioned his partner to drive on, quick.

Baskets go to juniors, but sometimes there are exceptions. One Sunday afternoon a week after a heavy snowstorm, the M7 garage was loud with workers' banter as they searched for dry gloves and hunkered into their jackets. Lunch felt shorter than usual as they geared up to head back out. Every able body was on mandatory overtime for the eighth day in a row, but today they were chasing garbage for the first time since the storm had diverted all energies to clearing the streets. Sidewalks all over New York were clotted with black garbage bags. Some of the piles near big residential buildings were shoulder-high and nearly a block long.

We had been out for a long time already, working steadily in freezing sleet, but with a twelve-hour shift there was still a ways to go. Many of the trucks from the morning were loaded out, so some men had to run relays, which meant they would take a full truck to the dump in New Jersey, empty it, and bring it back.[4] Relays only require the driver, so the loaders counted on downtime.

Not that day.

The super was calm but adamant. Whoever didn't take a relay would do baskets. I watched as guys with more than two decades on the job looked at him as if he were suddenly speaking Urdu. They knew that he knew that no worker with their seniority had done baskets in years. One man, the number three in the garage, got up in the super's face. What the fuck are you talking about? he asked loudly. Fucking baskets, the super replied evenly. I got seniority, said the first. The super smiled just a little. On mandatory overtime, he reminded the san man, there is no seniority.

It sparked much complaining, but the super got what he was after. He hadn't intended anyone to do a basket route. Instead, just as he'd anticipated, every man not running a relay took out a second truck and kept chasing garbage.

I once heard a pretty female sanitation worker with about three years on the job ask a popular superintendent about transferring into his garage. "But you won't put me on baskets, right?" she pleaded. She might have batted her eyelashes a little. It was a ridiculous request. Seniority is seniority. The super would be pilloried by the union and by management if he messed with the list. Had the woman been a man, it would have been an almost comical request, but because she was female, the implications could have cost the super his job if he had agreed to do it. She didn't transfer in.

It took me a while to understand the intimate role that time plays across all aspects of the work. In the beginning, I was too distracted trying to decode what seemed to be indications of unwelcome.

I had initially planned to be at the M7 garage several times a week at the start of the day shift, hang with the guys during roll call, then join different crews on their routes. While we worked together (because naturally I'd help load out the truck), I would ask them questions, they would tell me wise and funny stories, and I'd take careful notes. We would become friends. Maybe they would even come to see me like a cousin or a sister. After enough time and enough research, I would combine their stories with relevant anthropological analysis and show an enraptured world the indispensable and mesmerizing insights of sanitation workers.

I believed I had an entirely straightforward and eminently feasible research design. Besides that, my intentions were noble and my passion was real. I looked forward to an enthusiastic welcome from any Sanitation garage in the city.

As it turned out, my presence delighted no one. Neither the sanitation workers nor the officers were even slightly interested in my research. For reasons that are obvious in hindsight, no one wanted to talk to me. At all.

DSNY personnel have had far too much experience with journalists and other reportorial types who arrive with a smile, a notebook, and a few questions, stay for a day or a week, then go off and concoct stories full of innuendo and inaccuracy that are splashed across headlines and newscasts. When I, too, showed up with a smile, a notebook, and a few questions—never mind my spiel about championing their cause—I unwittingly fit the same model. The men decided that my unusual cover (anthro . . . what?) was a not-very-clever attempt to hide my real motives, whatever those might be. One faction was sure I had been sent by the commissioner, or maybe by the city's Department of Investigation, to be a mole within the garage. This argument found supporting evidence in my appearance: obviously, such geekiness could only be meant as a disguise. Another faction argued that I wasn't a spy but instead had come to trawl for men. Why else would a middle-aged woman want to spend time in such a male-dominated place?

The district super, following orders from downtown, assigned me to a crew already proven safe to put in front of media, having been filmed not long before for a documentary about garbage. Willie Bryant, an African American man in his early thirties, was so slender and tall that I immediately nicknamed him Stretch. A military veteran, he took pride in keeping his uniform crisply ironed and sometimes looked askance at his colleagues' less attentive attitudes toward their appearance. His partner, Andrew "Mac" MacBurney,* was a short white guy in his forties who had come to Sanitation

*Not his real name.

from Transit, where he had been a bus driver. When I asked why he switched, he said darkly, "Because this trash doesn't talk back."

Morning roll call was loud as many men gathered in the small space. One clutch was in front of the board, gesturing to it and arguing. I didn't know what they were talking about, but it was clear that Willie and Mac, both juniors, were the subject of more than a few comments. Much later I learned that they would normally have been running relays on the afternoon shift, but because of me they'd been given a collection route on the day line. The crew usually assigned to that route had been bounced to something else, and they were not happy.

Oblivious to these machinations, I connected with Willie and Mac on the street and did my best to help them load out the truck by dragging and lifting and tossing bags and cans. They were amused by my efforts, but they didn't tell me to stop, and during that first day in the field I learned several lessons.

1. Clothes matter. Not wearing gloves or boots while picking up garbage is dumb (Mac, seeing my predicament, lent me gloves). Not wearing a uniform while picking up garbage side by side with sanitation workers attracts attention. I made a mental note to get basic uniform pieces so that I'd keep my hands and feet safe, and so that I might blend in at least a little.

2. Language matters. According to the DSNY, garbage goes in a "collection" truck, and sanitation workers who put the garbage in that truck are "on collection." It alters the sense of the work ever so slightly. ("Do you have any hobbies?" "I collect garbage." "Ah. Do you put it in scrapbooks? Shadow boxes? Is your collection valuable? Did you inherit it from a grandparent, perhaps?")

3. Garbage is extremely heavy, and I had no idea how to move it without doing myself harm.

4. The truck is loud and dangerous. Even on the first day, I heard stories about injuries and accidents that had maimed men for life. Working next to the truck, I couldn't hear Mac or Willie unless

they half shouted. Watching the blade in the back scoop trash into the truck's compactor body, I was impressed by its force and by how often debris meant to go up was hurled back out instead.

5. When garbage is the organizing frame of reference, familiar geographies are radically changed. I was no longer just someone who thought a lot about trash; now I was one of the people picking it up, and instead of upscale residential blocks lined with lovely homes and trees, I saw clots of dark bags, metal cans, plastic bins that went on and on and on. Our route that day did not include large bag stops, but even the modest lines of our house-to-house assignment mocked me; the garbage was part of an infinite, orgiastic display of humanness at its most mundane, disquieting, and mesmerizing.

6. Garbage has a stubborn ontological persistence that I had never fully appreciated until the first day I worked with a crew. Garbage Is, always. We will die, civilization will crumble, life as we know it will cease to exist, but trash will endure, and there it was on the street, our ceaselessly erected, ceaselessly broken cenotaphs to ephemera and disconnection and unquenchable want.

I asked Willie and Mac if they ever turned a corner and groaned at the work ahead of them. "Sometimes," said Willie. "Never," said Mac.

7. A visitor to a Sanitation garage cannot, as a general rule, hang out in a space exclusive to the workers, especially if no one knows her yet. I figured this out the hard way when I wandered into the lunchroom and sat down. Affronted by my presence, unwilling to talk with me, and even less willing to let me listen to him and his buddies, some anonymous san man asked the district superintendent to ask me to leave, which the super did, though the task made him awkward and apologetic.

I was confused and a little hurt, but over time I came to understand why it happened, and when I sat down in the same lunchroom again many months later, after having become a regular presence in the garage, I was welcomed. I never learned who didn't want me there back in the beginning, but the story of my earlier eviction evoked much laughter. Though the warmth that my compatriots extended to me came more slowly than I'd anticipated, as I sat at the table and listened to their stories and jokes and gripes and teasing, I was grateful for it—and felt very much at home.

Part Two
IN TITLE

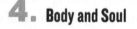 Body and Soul

It's always been about the body. Biceps and forearms bulge when hands clench the ears of tied bags or the rims of cans while lumbar vertebrae part, then meet, and femoral heads turn deep in hip sockets as the body bends; rotator cuffs round over ribs as the worker's shoulder joints hinge and release to fling a bag or lift a bundle.[1] In the summer especially, flesh shines as sweat trickles down necks, squeezes from inside elbows, drips from brows, chins, and earlobes, darkens T-shirts, soaks bandannas and hat crowns. Whether the laborer is scrawny or broad, tall or short, graying or baby-faced, a woman or a man, the body in motion is a thing of beauty—though such sensual, slow-motion consideration of these labors is rarely given.

As with any grueling physical effort, the trick is in the pacing. Crews can load out with twelve or fourteen tons before lunch, but that speed is costly. Injuries are more common, and even without a tear or sprain, aches are scored more deeply and fade more slowly.

In New York City, sanitation workers are taught how to bend and lift in the safest, most efficient way possible, but the lessons are difficult to impart; new workers are sure they know it already. During training, lift curriculum sometimes turns into a quiet Q&A as new-bies grill their instructors about what the job is *really* like, how to secure an assignment close to home, which garages should be avoided no matter what, how long it might take to make the truck. These questions are real and important, but so is the physics of picking up. Few sanitation workers forget their first days hoisting trash. The soreness of the early months seems to find muscles that most of us never knew we had. It comes to pass that as each of us develops our own version of the proper technique for moving heavy weight, we unwittingly follow tradition. "Some administrators contend that if a [sanitation worker] is worth keeping," noted the authors of a 1941 tome about garbage collection, "he will soon learn by himself the best and easiest ways to manipulate the containers."

The book, called *Refuse Collection Practice*, was written by the American Public Works Association, founded in 1937. New strate-gies for problems of urban infrastructure included time-motion studies and prim ideas about bureaucratic efficiency. It is telling that APWA's attention fell so quickly on solid waste; its debut pub-lication, *Street Cleaning Practice*, was released in 1938. *Refuse Col-lection* was its third (after *Sewer Rentals*). The book's scope was impressive, offering suggestions drawn from a study of 190 cities across the United States and Canada.

The physical demands of the work inspired examples of what were considered best practices. "Some [garbage] collectors prefer to lift the containers to their shoulders or heads for carrying them to collection vehicles," said the authors. "The easiest way to lift a can . . . is to raise it quickly and evenly to about knee height, and then, without loss of momentum, to boost it with the knee high enough to get a hand under the bottom of the container at about shoulder height. From this position the containers can easily be placed on the shoulders or head or the lift can be continued by pushing the receptacles into collecting vehicles."[2]

An illustrating photograph shows an African American man in a cap, gloves, boots, and knee-length bib apron balancing a tall tin tub full of junk on his left shoulder. The adjacent picture shows a white man in hat, gloves, and boots (no apron) with a wide wash-tub, also heavy with debris, balanced on his head. The text does not say whether he's wearing padding under the hat, though it explains that some men prefer this method because "wide receptacles are somewhat easier to balance in this position."

The tubs in the pictures are in good shape, with no discernible bent edges or rusted-out holes. For the purposes of illustration, they're probably not maggoty, nor are they dripping local brews of leachate, the "garbage juice" created by rotting putrescibles. They look scrubbed enough to hold something harmless—children's toys? laundry?—after their loads of junk and rubbish are dumped.

Such is not, however, the state of most contemporary garbage cans (one doubts they were so pristine back in 1941, either). The pictures brought to mind the strident demand of a politician one afternoon at a city council hearing. She represented the Lower East Side, a vibrant and overcrowded neighborhood that hosts dozens of high-rise public housing projects. In her district and elsewhere in the city, rats were the front-page problem du jour.[3] The council member claimed that rodents came to dine on the contents of hundreds of housing project garbage bags. The rats made the council member unhappy, but the bags made her unhappier. In the hearing, she peppered Commissioner Doherty with questions about alternatives to the bags and finally insisted, almost in a shout, that he make a vow, then and there, on the record, in front of the world, to replace all of those bags with metal, lidded garbage cans.

She glared at him in the moment of silence that followed. Then Doherty's Staten Island twang reverberated through the room. In his many decades on the job, he told her, he'd had a lot of experience with metal garbage cans. Cans were worse than bags. They got dented almost immediately, and then their lids didn't fit, or the lids were lost, or the lids were never used. The handles broke off. The bottoms, the sides, the rims, rusted out, and the rust spots became jagged edges that were dangerous to anyone handling them. Before the bottoms rusted through, water and garbage juice collected and stewed, exacerbating the odor while letting maggots thrive. Cans, he said firmly, did not do anything to solve the rat problem, and they had to be replaced so often that maintaining the supply required a full-time effort. He concluded his disquisition by assuring the council member that, no, he would not make a vow to replace plastic garbage bags in Lower East Side housing projects, or anywhere else, with metal cans. The woman stomped out of the room.

Metal cans are still used here and there, though plastic varieties—containers, san workers call them—are more popular. But the most common way to put out trash for pickup is in plastic bags. They rise in mounds on garbage day and range in size from a few plump gallons to a long 120-gallon style. These bigger ones are called sausage bags or body bags and usually require two people to lift (though a few extremely strong workers enjoy showing off by lifting them solo).

Plastic bags make the primary labor of waste—getting garbage up off the street—a simpler effort than it used to be, but they impose their own methods of hoisting. While lifting and toting remain basic to the job, resting a load anywhere on the body, let alone on top of the head, is anathema. No sanitation worker with any self-respect or common sense would ever carry a bag, a tub, a box, a sack, or any other garbage receptacle by placing it on his body the way the APWA book recommended. The first time I tried to use my knee to get better heft with a particularly heavy bag, my partner stopped me immediately.

"Don't do that," he said sternly. "You'll get cut. Do what you have to do to get that bag into the truck, but *never* let it touch you."

When Michael Bloomberg launched his first campaign for mayor in 2001, his would-be constituents weren't sure what to make of him. He wasn't as smooth as conventional politicians, and he spoke his mind rather freely, a refreshing contrast to the communications lockdown typical of his predecessor's administration. But once in a while, he managed to shoot off his mouth and sound foolish, like the blunder he made that June during a stump speech to the West Side Chamber of Commerce in Manhattan. He was discussing negotiations with the city's municipal labor unions. "I bet I could find statistics," he mused, "that say being a sanitation worker in this day and age is more dangerous than being a policeman or a fireman." [4]

It sounded like one of the candidate's biggest gaffes yet. A spokesman for the Uniformed Firefighters Association called Bloomberg "way off base." "I think he should go back and check his statistics," agreed a representative of the Patrolmen's Benevolent Association. The story was picked up by the Associated Press, and soon Bloomberg was pissing off police and fire personnel all over the country. Delighted New York Democrats added the remark to their "Bloomberg's Bloopers" Web page.

Perhaps Bloomberg's comment seemed insensitive because of its timing; he spoke just ten days after a blaze in Queens killed three firemen. In separate letters to the police and fire unions, he kind of apologized (though he blamed the reporter who quoted him "in such an unfortunate context") and reassured both union presidents that he never intended to downplay the risks faced by their members. [5]

But here's the thing. Bloomberg made no gaffe. Bloomberg was correct. Being a sanitation worker *is* more dangerous than being a police officer or a firefighter. It makes sense that members of the city's other uniformed forces would disagree, because most are no more knowledgeable than the general public about the hazards of sanitation work. But for them to be offended, to feel that the assertion somehow insulted them, underscores my point about the depth of ignorance that surrounds the mission of the DSNY. Bloomberg's campaign spokesman said his boss never meant to imply that taking out the trash is as dangerous as facing a gun or fighting a fire. The comparison, though common, is invalid. Sanitation workers don't take out the trash. You and I take out the trash. Sanitation workers take care of what happens next, and that's when the danger gets real.

"Collecting refuse has long been known to be dirty, strenuous work," notes the economist Dino Drudi in a study for the Bureau of Labor Statistics. "Less well known is that it is among the most deadly occupations." He calculates that compared to all job categories measured, refuse work has "10 times the overall on-the-job fatality rate," which puts it in a category that the BLS calls "high-hazard."

> Refuse collecting invariably involves jumping off and on trucks, carrying trash containers, and walking on streets, alleys, and parking lots. Refuse collectors often have to collect from both sides of a street; they work in close proximity to large collection vehicles that stop and start frequently. Sometimes these vehicles obscure them, which both inhibits their ability to spot approaching traffic, and blocks them from the view of approaching drivers. Not surprisingly, vehicles inflict most fatal injuries involving refuse collectors, for example, being run over by the refuse truck or struck by a passing vehicle, sometimes after falling from the truck.[6]

The BLS calculates that as of 2011 (the most recent year for which figures are available), "refuse and recyclable materials collectors" hold down the nation's fourth-most-dangerous job, after fishermen, loggers, and aircraft pilots.[7] The figures are equally startling when compared to other uniformed occupations. Sanitation workers are many times more likely than their counterparts in Police or Fire to be killed on the job.[8]

Few sanitation workers know any of this when they're hired, and most who stay long enough to qualify for full retirement benefits will not be killed on the job. But they all learn from their earliest days on the street that they will get hurt. The first risk is not to the back, as I'd assumed, but to the legs. Many routes require workers to move between parked cars, where the edges of oddly bent license plates can slice shins and calves. It's an injury that happens more frequently when the worker is moving fast, but even if he moves at a careful pace, he'll eventually get scraped, stuck, sliced, and/or bruised. Garbage-can rims catch knuckles, rip cloth and skin. Cuts from broken glass sever tendons, tear ligaments and muscle, leave scars. Straightened coat hangers, cutoff can tops, exposed nails, jagged piping, will puncture, scrape, and cut. Hypodermic needle sticks have always been especially unnerving, and plenty of workers endured the agonizing wait between potential disease exposure and test results.[9]

The parts of the body that allow for rotation and flexibility are also vulnerable. Knees stiffen, rotator cuffs and hip joints wear, spinal disks herniate, lower backs seize up. It takes only a few wrong twists to convince a worker that he must respect the right way to squat, grab, lift, and throw bags, to lift and empty baskets and garbage cans. Gloves and boots are essential protective wear, but on wet days, when workers usually wear rubber gloves, the rubber can slip. Ask anyone with time on the street how often he has reached for a wet bag, grabbed hold firmly, and pulled—only to smash himself in the face when his grip slipped.

Then there are those moments when the compactor blade hits solid objects and catapults them back out of the hopper. Bolts, nails and screws, plastic bottles, cans, shoes, food debris, mattress springs, wood fragments, glass shards, become lethal projectiles. Workers tell routine stories of getting hit in the chest, head, back, arms, and legs. One man I worked with on Staten Island reminisced about the time someone had thrown away a bowling ball. When he tossed it in the truck and pulled the handles, it came back at him as if shot from a cannon, caught him in the belly, and knocked him out. The driver, who thought his partner was on the back step, didn't notice that the fellow was missing until he'd turned the corner. When the driver went back to look for him, it took a while to find his unconscious body because he'd fallen into the tall grass by the side of the road.

More pernicious hazards aren't as obvious as airborne bowling balls. These affect the pulmonary, cardiac, and circulatory systems. A state-mandated worker-safety sign posted in all DSNY facilities sets a serious tone but cannot possibly be enforced: "You have the right to know! Your employer must inform you of the health effects and hazards of toxic substances at your worksite. Learn all you can about toxic substances on your job." It would be difficult, if not impossible, to catalog all the toxins to which sanitation workers are exposed.

The most unpredictable poisons come from the trash itself. Pressure from the hopper blade often pops the bags and hurls their contents. Pulverized Christmas tree ornaments and Christmas tree needles, lightbulb fragments, construction dust, house paint, barely coagulated cooking oil, urine-soaked kitty litter—to draw from a long list of examples—become ammunition. Powdered substances are especially unsettling. One morning we dropped an innocuous-looking bag in the hopper, and when it ruptured under the blade's pressure, a cloud of dark green powder billowed forth. It was disturbed again by every load we sent up. We didn't know what it might be, but its smell was slightly chemical, and we were certain it was something we didn't want to inhale. It brought to mind a story I'd heard from a foreman with a decade and a half on the job who was nearly asphyxiated by a lungful of soot he inhaled from a burst bag. When he turned to run, frantic for air, his partner caught him in the gut with a well-placed punch, a kind of Heimlich-maneuver-on-the-fly, that knocked him down—and that gave him back his wind.

San workers generally don't stand directly behind the truck when the blade is cycling, but staying to the side isn't always safe, either. One afternoon Ray Kurtz showed me the back of his and Sal's uniforms. They were covered by large blotches of some mysterious substance—oil, he speculated—that had showered them when a bag in the nearly full truck popped and its contents were forced out the sides of the hopper in unexpected geysers.

Those stains were only a nuisance, but they're not always so benign. A worker on Staten Island was behind the truck one day when an illegally dumped bag of sewage sludge exploded, splashing him in the face and mouth. He nearly died, and it was three weeks before he could be sent home from the hospital. When another Staten Island san man was running up his route and turned from the truck toward the curb too quickly, he punctured his eyeball on a tall metal skewer protruding from a recycling can. Yet another worker lost four toes on his left foot when he slipped under the front wheel of the truck as it moved along the curb; another lost two fingers to the hopper blade when his hand became tangled in the cord that tied a bundle of paper.

Similar anecdotes about injuries are easy to find; everyone has them. And the entire DSNY workforce can tell the story of what happened in 1996, when Michael Hanly and his partner were working their regular route in the Brooklyn neighborhood of Bensonhurst.

Hanly, who had twenty-three years on the job, didn't think anything of the garbage bags and trash containers set out for collection on New Utrecht Avenue near Eighty-Fourth Street. It was the usual pile that awaited him at this stop, one of the last on the route. He tossed a load in the hopper and was just turning away from the truck when the blade bit through a bag and broke open a jug of liquid concealed within it. The resulting geyser that hit Hanly full on was a 70 percent solution of hydrofluoric acid.[10]

His funeral, which drew nearly two thousand Sanitation people from across the city and around the region, made the television news. No one was charged for his murder.

Hanly's death was a shocking tragedy in part because it was such a horrific way to die, but more mundane circumstances can be equally heartbreaking.

Frank Justich, a sanitation worker out of Queens West 1, was a handsome, dark-haired man with the beefy build of a weight lifter who looked much younger than his forty-one years. That was partly because of his ponytail, but even more because his liveliness and warmth made him seem downright youthful.

Small children on his routes in Astoria looked for him; Justich nicknamed one toddler Hucklebee, which became the boy's excited cry every time he saw a collection truck. But it wasn't just the children. When he came to know a man on his route who shared his fondness for motorcycles, Justich dubbed him Marlon Brando. The guy was delighted.

Justich's chivalry was famous. Old ladies all over the district had stories about how he carried their groceries or helped them cross the street, while old men talked about the time he helped open a stubborn gate, or assisted one of them up steep steps, or moved heavy trash from their backyards to the truck. Justich noticed even those elderly who could only watch the world from their windows. He waved and smiled at them, and these frail seniors, like some of the children, watched for him with happy anticipation.

Commuters who crossed paths with him were glad to say hello, to talk. "I could not tell you the name of any Sanitation crew that serviced my area over forty years," said a man who lived on Justich's route. "I knew Frankie's name."

When he worked baskets, Justich didn't just toss their contents into the truck and drive off but took the time to go after things like the bent pizza boxes that always seemed to pop to the sidewalk and the crippled umbrellas that decorate curbs like tormented art after a rainy day.

And he was never without his sketchbook. One morning on break with his buddies at their favorite coffee shop, he sketched a portrait of the school crossing guard working at the intersection and then gave her the drawing as a gift. She framed it. He sketched the owners of the bakery where he bought treats to share at roll call. All his coworkers had pictures of themselves that Justich had drawn. ("He made us better looking," said one.) He reached out to them in other ways, too. "I remember when I first came to the garage in April 2004," recalled another QW1 san man. "I worked with him the first day . . . It seemed like we had known each other for years."

Justich kept his grandmother's lawn neatly trimmed, chauffeured her to all her doctor's appointments, made sure she didn't get confused about her medications. When anyone asked about his children, they saw his widest smile. He carried photos of his two small daughters, who always grabbed him around his legs when he came home in the afternoons. He told stories about enjoying an imaginary tea party with his four-year-old, his knees folded to his chin at the tiny table, and showed pictures of himself and his girls dressed as pirates for the younger one's first birthday.

Justich wasn't just visible; he was well loved. But despite his sparkle, despite the affection and respect he earned from those who knew him, he was still not quite visible enough.

On January 26, 2010, he was working his usual Tuesday route. On the corner of Ditmars Boulevard and Thirty-Fifth Street near the Oceano Mediterranean Restaurant in Astoria, he emptied a litter basket and was cycling the hopper, his back to the street, when an eighteen-wheeler turned into the block. The tractor-trailer driver, blinded by sun glare through a filthy windshield, didn't realize that his trailer's turning radius was too tight.

A few minutes before 8:00 that morning, Frank Justich became the tenth New York City sanitation worker in eight years to lose his life in the line of duty.

5. Mongo and Manipulation

It's always been about the body, but it's also always been about the mind. Sanitation workers must master a wealth of knowledge both obvious and arcane. A sample list includes knowing how to troubleshoot equipment problems, decode cartography, interpret intricate departmental politics, translate convoluted regulations, and decipher the up-close and long-range rhythms of various neighborhoods. Many kinds of expertise fall under these elements, like how to work a new kind of vehicle based on experience with an old one, or which detours to take when regular relay routes are blocked, or what the actual trash says about who lives in what parts of the city, on which blocks, with what hardships or triumphs or changes of fortune.

Sometimes workers complain about the day's assignments, especially if they're stuck on house-to-house. Those impatient with such work find it maddeningly tedious, like cleaning ashtrays. They much prefer flats—the Sanitation word for small mountains of trash that, on garbage day, sit outside large apartment buildings typical of New York's high-density neighborhoods.[1] When working flats, a crew can load out in one or two stops. Loading out on house-to-house can take many hours, but such routes have other perks, especially for someone who likes to mongo.

As a noun, "mongo" is Sanitation slang for treasure salvaged from the trash, with an understanding that the definition of "treasure" is both broad and personal.[2] As a verb, "to mongo" is to look for and rescue such wealth. Sal Federici didn't mongo, but he tolerated his partner's predilection for it. Ray Kurtz was not the district's acknowledged mongo king, nor even its second best—his garage mates agreed that he held third-place status—but he could hoist a garbage bag of any size and guess with surprising accuracy whether or not it was worth exploring.

Not everyone mongoes, and technically it's against Department regulations, but the rule is tough to enforce. Locker rooms and lunchrooms in DSNY garages around the city are exhaustively decorated with found lamps, couches, desks, chairs, sports memorabilia, movie posters, magazine cutouts, fish tanks (used for storage, or transformed into terrariums, or occasionally restored to thriving homes for fish). Such collections always include goofy miscellany like a mounted rubber bass that flops back and forth while belting out "Take Me to the River" when you press a button or the foot-tall skiing Santa that sings "Jingle Bells" and gyrates like Elvis.

Many of the pieces Kurtz collected became Christmas or birthday gifts. The white cashmere scarf only needed a trip to the cleaners to be fully restored, while children's toys could be polished up and even electronics and appliances could sometimes be fixed. Once Kurtz found a three-piece suit wadded in a litter basket on a corner near a dry cleaner's shop. While Federici waited, Kurtz took the suit inside, tried it on, had it measured for alterations, and picked it up when he worked that route again two days later.

Plenty of workers disdain mongo. When something has been thrown out once, they reason, it should stay thrown out. But in many parts of the city, it seems foolish *not* to mongo. Because Manhattan 7 serves affluent neighborhoods, some sanitation workers take for granted its rich discards. A worker new to the district came in at lunch one day with a glass tray from a microwave oven. It was unblemished and clean, he told a more seasoned colleague; seemed a shame to throw it out. The older man, his mouth full of sandwich, used one hand to open a deep drawer in the mongoed desk where he sat. It was full of a dozen or more microwave plates in perfectly good shape. He gestured to the drawer and shrugged. The younger san man looked puzzled, then gave his own shrug and added his find to the pile.

Sanitation workers who mongo claim that the street is not just a source of unpredictable bounty but that it takes requests. The second-best mongo man in M7 swore this was true; by way of example, he showed me a pair of air purifiers, fully functional and good as new but for a thin layer of dust. He'd found them on the curb that morning while working one of his regular routes and had diverted them to the mongo bin, a box attached to the side of the truck body meant to hold small tools or other miscellany but most often used for stashing street treasure. He'd recently moved to a new home for which he wanted air purifiers, he told me, so had put his request to the street, and sure enough, three weeks later, he found his loot. "You ask, the street gives," he said with a smile. I thought that meant he asked people who he knew might have such things, but he explained that he simply concentrated on what he needed and eventually found exactly what he was after. There was nothing New Agey about this man, but he sounded as if he were channeling some mystical power.

Kurtz confirmed the seek-and-ye-shall-find approach. He was less discerning, perhaps, than some of his peers, since he took pretty much anything that looked as if it might be worth keeping after at least a spit shine. Some of his trinkets—a necktie, a beaded bracelet, a Christmas ornament—briefly became part of the truck, tied to the hopper handles, though they never stayed long (such adornment is not permitted). Other mongoers preferred to specialize. The guy with the air purifiers focused mostly on electronics and had built a small but steady sideline business selling refurbished computers.

His customers never knew that he'd found the goods on the curb. One man told me he looked for clothes and shoes that were in reasonable shape, had them cleaned, and then donated them to his church's rummage sales. Sometimes workers will sell their mongo on eBay or at a yard sale, then donate the proceeds to a colleague going through financial hard times because of medical bills or family problems.

Even though Kurtz had worked out of M7 for his entire career, he was still mildly incredulous that the district's residents consistently threw away so much good stuff. Once we discovered a flimsy pair of black-and-gold women's stretch pants by Armani. They were in good shape—no stains or tears, no odd smells—and still bore their tag. I went slack-jawed when I saw their price. "Guess," I told Kurtz. From my face he deduced that they cost more than he might expect and aimed for the low hundreds. I shook my head. His bid rose. Finally, his own jaw dropped when I showed him the tag: $1,325. Yes, one thousand three hundred and twenty-five dollars. And we had found them in the trash.

Kurtz said I should keep them and was surprised when I pointed out that they were several sizes too small. ("Are you sure?") We toyed with the idea of taking them to an Armani shop and claiming that they'd been a gift we wanted to return—we would've split the money—but neither of us had quite enough gumption. Kurtz finally decided to give them to the waitress at a diner where he sometimes stopped on his way home. He said they made her very happy.

While Kurtz was well-known for his mongo abilities, his real talent was his job knowledge. He had mastered the subtle but essential skill of knowing how and when to do the job by the book, which is not to be confused with doing the job as efficiently as possible. These are contradictory strategies that an experienced worker can use to his advantage.

The relationship of the workers to their route is one example.

Most supervisors will instruct their crews to work the routes as written on the backs of the 350s distributed at roll call.[3] Each supervisor needs to know more or less where his trucks and his mechanical brooms are at any given moment, and a crew working the route as written is easier to track. It also lets the supervisor estimate how much work is left in the middle and at the end of the shift, when he must relay that information to his superintendent.

A supervisor who knows his district well can write routes that accommodate things like alternate side parking regulations, which mandate specific times on different days of the week for cars to be off the curb so the mechanical brooms can sweep. Those can also be good opportunities to get a truck in and out of a street with fewer obstacles than normal, but not always. Special events (a big funeral, a street fair, a school parade), the time of day (how bad is traffic at what hour on which streets?), knowledge of a crew's general work ethic (are they runners? do they walk backwards? are they union hard-liners, or do they not give a shit about 831?) are among the variables that an experienced supervisor will measure.

Kurtz and Federici enjoyed some immunity from heavy-handed management because their supervisor knew that however the pair decided to tackle them, the routes would be clean by the end of the shift and they would meet their target weight. They could take breaks and lunch only during approved time frames, the foreman had to be able to find them when he looked for them (this was before the Department installed GPS in every truck), and they had to service all the stops on that day's schedule, but within those constraints they could mostly work their routes as they liked.

For instance, when their route included the huge luxury apartment buildings along the far west side of the 1 section, they rarely made it their first stop but instead used it to top off their load when the truck was nearly full. They did the same with The Oval, a fenced area at the end of a cul-de-sac in the middle of a multibuilding housing project. Even if it had been diligently collected on the night shift, by the time the day crew arrived, The Oval looked as if no truck had visited for a long time. That by itself wasn't so bad—plenty of flats filled almost as fast as they were picked up—but The Oval was an exception to the section's reputation for clean garbage. Its vast quantities of food waste made it a four-star dining location for clans of rats. No crew liked to spend time there.

Their reputation for reliability only suffered occasional dents, like when they were late to get out the door because Kurtz's name came up for a PAP. The acronym, for "policies and procedures," is shorthand for the Department's random drug-testing protocols. When the PAP wagon, a small RV outfitted with an office and a bathroom, shows up before roll call, a few sanitation workers looking for their assignments on the operations board will find their name cards standing vertically, like the spine of a book, which means they must take a Breathalyzer test and pee in a cup.

The Department's policy on drugs is uncomplicated. If a new hire is within his first eighteen months on the job and thus is still on probation, a finding of drugs or alcohol in his system is the end of his employment. This is drummed into new hires over and over, yet a surprising number of them don't fully grasp how serious it is, or maybe they think that they won't get caught. There is no second chance, no possibility of appeal, no advocate, no union intervention. If a probationer comes up dirty, he goes down.

Even a single instance of bad judgment can derail what might have been a solid career. A normally clean-living worker has a few tokes off a joint at a bachelor party, say, but otherwise never touches that or any other kind of drug. Doesn't even drink. But the next day his name is up when the piss wagon arrives, he breathes or pees enough residue of weed to test positive, and he's finished.

Sandy McCaffrey, a tough-talking, big-hearted nurse who worked with the DSNY for more than twenty-five years, had to deliver the bad news. She told me once about a young man so proud to have the job with Sanitation, so relieved to be earning a solid wage to support his new wife and their small baby, who wept like a child when she sat him down in his seventh month on the job to tell him that he was through. Another man was three days from the end of probation when he decided to celebrate early, but the next day at work he grazed the entrance to the garage with the fender of his truck. It qualified as an accident. As per DSNY policy, any sanitation worker in any kind of accident, no matter how insignificant, must be PAPed. The fellow came up dirty—and that was the end.

His downfall was cocaine, but even stale beer will do it. Whatever happened on a weekend or in the previous few days, there better not be a trace of it in you by roll call. It's easy to imagine the chill that must go through a worker, especially a new hire, if he arrives at his garage still tipsy from a party the night before, or a little high from those last snorts early in the morning, or only a day past a drunken weekend tear—and there's his name straight up, practically bristling. The same chill will run through him if he's been on antihistamines or muscle relaxants or painkillers and he didn't tell anyone. Anything more than aspirin, basically, and you'd better inform your supervisor, who alerts the Sanitation clinic. If the clinic deems it necessary, you'll be pulled from the truck and given a tissue—that is, an assignment in the office or around the garage—until you're no longer taking the drug that the Department's medical personnel feel might jeopardize your ability to drive safely. If you didn't give the clinic a chance to make that decision and the substance shows up in your breath or urine and you're new, you're done.

Once a sanitation worker passes probation, he is less vulnerable to instant termination for drugs or booze; he now has three chances before he gets fired. The first positive drug test brings a suspension of up to thirty days without pay (which means a loss of benefits until he's reinstated), counseling, and strong suggestions to get help, specific sources of which are recommended. He's also subject to testing every time the PAP wagon shows up at his garage for the following year. If he fails the test a second time, he is suspended for forty-five days without pay (or benefits) and receives even stronger encouragement to seek serious help, like maybe at The Farm, as rehab facilities are sometimes called. He must also sign a document known as the Last-Chance Agreement, which says that if he tests positive for drugs or alcohol once more, he will be fired.

If he does come up dirty a third time, that's it. In some cases the union will fight for him—if, for example, his second infraction was early in his career and his third happened after twenty otherwise unblemished years. But the Department will argue that the union can't prove the man didn't manage to get away with behavior that should've been caught long before. Management does not want to risk putting him behind the wheel of a nineteen-ton garbage truck.

Some workers take creative steps to prevent the chemical enhancement of their social lives from damaging their professional lives. One who was found with dirty urine for the third time went to his disciplinary trial, prelude to losing his job for good, insisting that the urine sample was not dirty. This is not an unusual claim, but he was particularly adamant. When the judge finally asked why he was so certain that the urine wasn't tainted, he exclaimed, "Because it wasn't my piss!"

There's also a strong social incentive not to come up dirty. Partying hard, holding one's liquor, and "taking it like a man" have a certain cachet—among some workers, drinking hard and drugging with abandon are expected behaviors—but it must never jeopardize the job. A man who comes up dirty is only masquerading as a man; getting caught reveals him to be little better than a child, an irresponsible failure. No matter how quiet the person tries to keep it, word spreads. When the PAP wagon shows up and someone's name is drawn and then he disappears for a month, it's not hard to figure out what happened.

To be clear, the fault, according to this perspective, is not in the use of alcohol or drugs but in getting busted. There are not many ways to lose the job once probation is finished, but failing a drug test for the third time is a guaranteed ticket out the door, and why would anyone be so stupid as to lose a pension (only twenty-two years before retirement with half pay and full benefits for life), chances at promotion (a big carrot for some), and often a tight group of friendships?

Drug-testing policies, instituted in 1995, are cited by some old-timers as one of the ways the job has changed for the worse. But before testing, drinking and drugging on the job were big problems. I heard stories about guys carrying six-packs of beer in the truck with them, or stopping at a bar on the way to the start of the route (even on the day shift), or never being fully sober, at work or anywhere else. But then Congress made it mandatory that anyone driving a truck over a certain tonnage had to carry a state-issued commercial driver license, or CDL, and that anyone holding a CDL who drove a truck on roads constructed or maintained with federal dollars—which is basically any road or street in the nation—was subject to drug testing, and the DSNY complied with the law by instituting the PAP wagon. The union fought it, citing invasions of privacy and undue pressure, but to no avail.[4]

There are few ways to delay the test if your name is standing up when the PAP wagon arrives. The Breathalyzer is straightforward, but urinating can get complicated. When collecting urine, the supervisor is supposed to observe it go from person to cup. For some people, however, peeing while being watched is uncomfortable, and even if no one's watching, it can be difficult to pee on demand.

The union has a provision for this situation. Sanitation workers whose names come up for a PAP are allowed three hours to fill their bladders and to overcome any urinary hesitation. Kurtz knew this rule well and could foil a morning's worth of collection for himself and Federici by meandering around the garage with a half-empty water bottle, sipping from it frequently, and shrugging his shoulders when the district superintendent glared at him. "Sorry, boss," he'd say with his sweet half smile, "I'm trying. Anytime now. Won't be long."

I liked working with Kurtz and Federici. Their comfortable rapport with each other made them easy to be with on the street. Both had enough time on the job to be bemused in situations where more junior men might get tense. An irate supervisor could yell all he wanted, but neither man would get ruffled. Though Kurtz occasionally pulled capers like water-bottle PAP delays, for the most part they both just climbed into the truck, did their work, and called it a day.

As much as I enjoyed their company, however, and as much as I appreciated the many opportunities I had to learn about the DSNY, I was still just an observer, not a participant. How could I know what it was like to survey the city from behind the wheel of my own truck? To get up so stunningly early every day? To be in the public eye while wearing a uniform with my name on it?

The answer came from the Department of Citywide Administrative Services, the agency that acts as the bureaucracy for the bureaucracy of New York City government and that manages, among thousands of other responsibilities, civil service exams. Registration for sanitation worker tests, announced a DCAS flyer, was about to open.

6. Being Uniform

The rules are simple. Anyone with a high school diploma or its equivalent who lives in the city of New York or in one of the six nearest counties and who is at least twenty-one years old at the time of employment can apply for the job. Becoming a sanitation worker does not depend on anyone's goodwill or open mind, or on the applicant's postsecondary schooling, her age, sex, religion, prior criminal record, or political connections. To get the job, I only had to follow the required steps and meet whatever standardized measures awaited me.

The rules might be simple, but the journey to become a sanitation worker turned out to be circuitous and fraught with uncertainty: there were a hundred ways to wander or be thrown from the path and so lose the chance at the job, perhaps forever. When sanitation workers claimed, as they often did, that getting hired was like winning the lottery, I didn't understand what they meant, but I was about to find out.

I mailed my application in February and several weeks later received a notice with details about the test. On a colorless Saturday morning in early May, I headed to Seward Park High School on the

Lower East Side. The sky was taut above litter-strewn streets (this section of the Manhattan 3 district has been one of the city's perpetually dirtiest neighborhoods for more than a century). The building was framed by two lines that started at its western entrance and wound down the sidewalk to the north and to the south like a bifurcated army of ants communicating news back to the queen. Barred windows and graffiti-streaked walls suggested that the school's best days were past, but the steps were worn to gentle smiles, and classrooms had polished wood floors that gleamed in the light pouring through tall windows.[1]

My fellow test takers and I settled into our desks. The men around me (I was the only woman) had blank faces and hunched shoulders. Everyone wore dark clothes despite the warm day, and no one looked anyone else in the eye. The exam proctor, in shirtsleeves and khakis, informed us that we had two hours to answer seventy-five multiple-choice questions.

"At the curb in front of an apartment building, you see a sack of garbage, a torn beanbag chair, a plastic pickle barrel, and a wooden box," stated one. "Which of these items is easiest to roll to your truck?" But . . . how big are these things? Is the beanbag chair in a frame or in a heap? Are its innards spilling onto the sidewalk? Must I roll any of these objects? Can't I carry or drag or throw them? What a shame the pickle barrel is plastic; a wooden one might be worth keeping. Come to think of it, could that wooden box be good mongo?

"You are picking up garbage in a residential neighborhood when a man walks up to you and tells you he thinks sanitation workers have no right to be in unions because if they did their jobs right they wouldn't need to organize in order to be treated fairly. He then adds a bag to his pile of trash and goes back into his house. You are a union supporter. What should you do?"

It would feel satisfying to egg the house, but that's not among my choices. I can "ring the man's bell and explain politely to him why unions are necessary." Yeah, right. I could "call [my] supervisor and ask to have another worker assigned to this street." Not if it's in a section known for clean garbage and Christmas generosity and I finally have enough seniority to get this exact assignment. I'd walk away from all that because I don't like the politics of some of its residents? Fat chance. I could certainly "ignore his comments and pick up his trash as you would anyone else's," obviously the sensible response, but I know that many sanitation workers of a certain temperament would "refuse to pick up the trash the man put out, in order to teach him a lesson."

I wondered briefly what would happen if I answered the test questions according to the reality of the street. It could make for a revealing and creative portrait of the DSNY, but I decided that it would not be prudent.

A month later came the news that I'd passed, though I missed two questions. ("What's wrong with you?" snorted a Department acquaintance. "That test asks things like 'What color is George Washington's white horse?'") The test results combined with five extra points for living in the city (residency credit, it's called) earned me a list number of 896, a numerical marker that governed every detail of my progress toward getting the job. It meant that of the forty-five hundred people who scored well enough on the written test to advance their candidacy, I was within the first thousand eligible for the next steps. I had priority over everyone with list number 897 and higher but waited behind everyone with list number 895 and below.[2]

The physical exam was scheduled for the following January at a cavernous warehouse in Queens. The space set aside for Sanitation was filled with litter baskets, burlap sacks, and a variety of wooden structures. The monitor explained that the test, done against time, was about moving weight. The first part involved dragging, lifting, dumping, and returning litter baskets. For the second part, a series of increasingly heavy bags were to be carried or dragged between and around various obstacles and tossed over a barrier set at the height of a truck's hopper.

After he explained the bags, the man paused. "Watch out for the fourth one," he said, his voice dropping. "It's sixty-five pounds. I don't care if you have to burst into tears or scream out loud, you do whatever you need to do to get it in the truck." Surprised, I assured him that I'd give it my best effort.

He asked if I was ready, then set the clock and said go. I finished the baskets with time to spare. Then came the bags. Some I could carry in a straight line from start to truck, but others had to be maneuvered around obstructions. When I met the fourth bag, I squatted, wrapped my arms around it, and exhaled as I pushed up with my legs. I looked ridiculous, but the bag was off the floor, I hadn't so much as grunted, and I got it to its destination without a stumble.

The test monitor congratulated me with a handshake and a smile. I asked if many women had taken the physical exam, and he said he'd seen six so far. The day before, he told me, one girl was bested by that sixty-five-pound bag, which is why he gave me the heads-up. She cried, he said. Sure she did, I thought. Her DSNY future was over before it started.

Would-be Sanitation hires have had to endure a physical assessment of their abilities since 1940, when that year's written test drew nearly eighty-five thousand Depression-weary applicants—at the time, the highest number for a civil service exam in the city's history and the second highest ever in the United States. About forty-five thousand did well enough to qualify for employment, far too many for the twenty-five hundred openings that the Department anticipated. To shorten the list, a series of challenges was devised by a professor of physical education at New York University.[3]

Perhaps he had a sadistic streak. The commissioner of sanitation himself called the new physical exam severe, and it was soon nicknamed the Superman Test. Applicants had to lift eighty-pound dumbbells straight overhead while lying on the floor, scale a seven-foot fence, vault a series of obstacles, hoist a set of hundred-pound cans to a waist-high platform, and sprint a hundred yards while carrying a fifty-pound weight in each hand.[4] Few of these activities resembled any activity required on the job, but they certainly disqualified many men.

Some adjustments were made over the years—applicants didn't have to scale fences, leap over barriers, or run the hundred-yard dash—but the physical test remained relatively unchanged until the 1980s, when it went through the first of several alterations. Men hired off the older test could point to its rigors as proof that they were genuinely strong, but newer hires could make no such claim. "It used to be a *man's* test," explained the more senior men. "Now it's a joke."

And whose fault would that be?

The women's, naturally.

For men of a certain disposition, a woman "garbageman" is just . . . wrong, like a talking dog or a dancing bear. It is so obvious to them why women should not be on the job in uniform that it pains them to have to explain, but when I could convince them to make it clear to me, their logic went something like this.

The work of Sanitation is intended for men—*manly* men. Physical strength and muscular prowess are paramount. A real sanitationman (*sic*) earns his membership in the Sanitation brotherhood with bawdy humor and coarse language, while his confident virility, his stamina, his ease with the truck, and his unwillingness to flinch before even the rankest trash prove his competence on the street.

A woman's role, ideally, is to tend hearth and home while the manly man ventures forth to face the dangers of the world. If she must work, she should choose teaching or nursing or a similar profession that suits her inherently softer touch and sweeter nature. But here come female sanitation workers, thinking they're equal to the kinds of men who have done the job since the beginning of time. Gimme a break. Their arms are so weak that they can't swing a hammer properly or throw a ball with any force, but they're supposed to pick up how many tons of garbage every day? Sure. Women know nothing about the noise and grind of the machinery; can they even change a tire? A woman's sensibilities are far too delicate for the ribald banter of the garage or for the horrors that lurk within the garbage, but she wants to be one of the guys, face the trials of the street? Please. What will happen the first time a rat runs up her pant leg or maggots fall in her hair?

These stereotypes about ability and character are matched by prejudices about behavior. A manly-man sanitation worker won't shirk a tough assignment, will always do his share, will take the hit to protect a friend, will even suffer certain forms of injustice without protest. A woman in the same role will request desk jobs or other easy assignments that once were, and should still be, given to men recovering from injuries. Her mere presence in the garage makes a formerly comfortable hangout as tense as a church. She will be useless for several days every month, guaranteed. She will let her male partner carry her. She will invent charges of harassment as revenge against any imagined slight, against any man who spurns her advances, against any man who does return her flirtations but then somehow offends her.

Even for men not burdened with such attitudes and who recognize that women are as likely as men to be solid workers, loyal colleagues, excellent equipment operators, and unflustered by strong language or off-color humor, the mere fact that a female can earn a place among the Department's ground troops transforms the image of every male who wears the uniform. The tough sanitationman is gone, replaced by the bland sanitation worker. Now it's a job for anyone. Even wusses.

This is a cartoonish account of perspectives that are no longer as prevalent as they used to be, but those who still hold such beliefs cling to them tightly. Like many cultural assumptions, understandings about "proper" roles for women belong to more encompassing beliefs about "proper" arrangements of life and of the larger world. Men who object to women sanitation workers aren't expressing mere disgruntlement or irritation; they're objecting to a fundamental flaw in the order of the universe. They haven't noticed that the order of the universe has been in flux for several decades.

Cultural transformations that swept the United States and much of the rest of the world in the 1960s and early 1970s had many catalysts, but among them was the rage of various groups long denied access to the full bounty of the nation. Women were on that list. They demanded equal access to jobs, equal pay in those jobs, and basic privileges like the right to have bank accounts in their own names. In other words, they wanted the citizenship that was already supposed to be theirs.

Their detractors called them radicals, but lawmakers couldn't ignore them, and the Equal Employment Opportunity Act, passed by Congress in 1972, mandated that previously all-male job titles admit women. In 1974, the Department scheduled a test for the job title "sanitation worker" and begrudgingly allowed women to take it. The commissioner at the time promised that if any were actually hired, he'd have them wear white pantsuits and sweep the curbs.[5] One woman passed both the written and the physical components, but before she could take the job, the city was seized by a fiscal crisis, and the DSNY issued a hiring moratorium. There wasn't another test for many years.

In the early 1980s, Sanitation started the transition from three-man crews to two-man crews. It took many negotiations across several years, but in the end both sides were pleased: the san men ended up with extra pay while the city secured unprecedented productivity savings. The workers were lauded for their concessions, and the reputation of the workforce was at a high point, which turned out to be an important factor when women finally arrived.

Its long hiring freeze meant that Sanitation was the last of New York's uniformed forces to admit females, but the Department's leadership had learned a few choices to imitate and many mistakes to avoid by watching closely as the Fire and Police Departments went coed. When a test for the title of sanitation worker was finally announced in 1986, DSNY Commissioner Norman Steisel set up training sessions to help female candidates prepare.[6] The written format stayed the same, but the physical exam was amended (applicants still had to move more than a ton of weight in a short time). He hired consultants to lead sexual harassment workshops for the brass, who then organized similar sessions for officers working under them, down to the supervisors, who were to pass along their newfound sensitivities to the san men. And he reached out to the workers themselves. He reminded them that the three-man-to-two-man program had earned them a lot of goodwill; did they really want to lose that by making a stink about the women?

Of the 45,000 people who took the written and physical exams that year, 44,000 passed, including 1,357 women. The Department used a lottery to put together a class of 137 new workers. Two were female. The union cried foul. A success rate of more than 98 percent, argued officials of Teamsters Local 831, meant the test was "too easy and degrading to the abilities and productivity of the current workforce."[7] They sued to block hiring off the list. They also objected to new female-only locker rooms and bathrooms under construction in two garages, arguing that male san workers around the city, many of whom had put up with decrepit facilities for years, also deserved new digs. While the cases made their way through various courts during the summer and fall of 1986, the Department went ahead and appointed the first two uniformed women in its 105-year history. Carlen Sanderson, a twenty-one-year-old from Queens, and Gloria Pabon, thirty, from Brooklyn, became local celebrities.

By the time I came on, women had been in Sanitation's uniformed ranks for many years. There were even women in chiefly titles. Most men were fine with women on the job. But every now and then, some man was a jerk.

Several of us were sitting in the lunchroom near the end of a shift. I was the only woman present—I might've been the only woman in the entire garage at that moment—and I was trying to decide what to do.

Every locker and cabinet in the motley assortment lining the walls had been thrown wide open, and taped inside every door were pictures of mostly naked women offering the viewer their voluptuous asses and luscious bosoms and pouty, succulent lips. It wasn't the hard-core variety, but it was definitely porn, aggressively on display.

One centerfold pullout was especially striking. The model, her blond hair blowing softly away from her face, wore nothing but red stilettos and a black motorcycle jacket, unzipped and pushed back from her shoulders a little so that it framed her perfect breasts. She was squatting low over the shoes, her knees open, and gazing at the camera in frank surprise—or perhaps alarm. I understood why. Her crotch was as bald as a baby's. Here was an obviously mature human female adult who lacked a secondary sex characteristic basic to normal human female development. I had never seen anything like it. I had to will myself not to stare.

Most of the men in the room were quiet, but one guy I hadn't met before was talking loud and fast. I didn't want to be surrounded by pictures of naked women, but I also didn't want to give any indication that they bothered me. I went outside for a while; when I returned, the locker and cabinet doors were closed, and the guys were back to normal, except for the former loudmouth. He was sitting in a corner, alone, silent, and looking sour.

A sure but awful sign of female integration into the DSNY came in January 2004. Eva Barrientos, nine years on the job, had climbed atop her E-Z Pack to clear some debris. Her partner didn't know she was up there and raised the truck's mechanical arm. When it caught Barrientos in the head, she became the first woman sanitation worker to die in the line of duty. Her funeral filled a huge Roman Catholic church in Red Hook, Brooklyn. It included the mayor, the commissioner, the DSNY Honor Guard, the Emerald Society Pipes and Drums, a flag-draped coffin, a bugler playing taps, and a police helicopter flyover. Her coworkers, male and female, wept openly. Several months later, the Brooklyn North 4 garage became the first named in memory of a woman.

Part Three

SPECIES OF REFORM

7. Tubbs of Nastiness

Perhaps sanitationmen wouldn't have objected so strenuously to women on the job if they'd had a better idea of who did the work and how it got done—or rather didn't get done—in earlier days. Clean streets and effective garbage pickup were seemingly impossible achievements for most of New York's history, even while rubbish literally shaped the geography of the city.[1] Politicians and other moneyed interests considered the ever-dirtier thoroughfares an unavoidable consequence of the city's growing power, an attitude that made New York precarious for everyone and downright deadly for many. It also meant that those charged with the work of managing the city's wastes were always overlooked.

In 1624, when 110 or so men, women, and children arrived from Europe to settle some of Holland's claims in North America, they established themselves on western Long Island, in the Hudson Valley, and at the southern tip of Manhattan Island.[2] In 1626, they were joined by another group of immigrants, but the eleven men from Dutch holdings in the Caribbean and along the west coast of Africa did not come by choice. They were the first of the colony's many slaves.

Working sometimes alongside but mostly at the behest of the Europeans, Africans filled the role of municipal laborers by clearing forests, draining swamps, laying streets.[3] They dug two canals, the Heere Gracht and the smaller Bevers Gracht, and cinched the island with a wall that, centuries later, defined the path of the world-famous street. Their chores included mining vast shell middens left by generations of indigenous inhabitants, then burning those shells and limestone to use in outhouses and graves.[4] And they took care of the garbage.[5]

The town's first street-cleaning law was enacted in 1657, when householders were forbidden to throw "any rubbish, filth, oyster shells, dead animal [sic] or anything like it" into the streets or into the canals. In a preview of much later efforts to site municipal solid waste facilities, the law also specified that garbage could be dumped at one of only five locations designated for that purpose.[6] These included "the Strand [of the East River], near the City Hall [Pearl Street and Coenties Alley today], near the gallows [Pearl Street and Whitehall], near Hendrik [Willemen] the baker [northwest corner of Bridge and Broad Streets], near Daniel Litsco [Pearl Street near the wall]." One wonders how Hendrik the baker and Daniel Litsco felt about their new proximity to official town dumps.[7] Those who dumped elsewhere were punishable with fines that went up for each successive offense.[8]

This edict must have seemed odd; it was so easy to just toss rubbish into the water. The mighty currents of the North River (not yet called the Hudson) on the settlement's western shore, along with easy access to swampy and low-lying land near the East River, provided ready repositories for anything Nieuw Amsterdammers wanted to chuck. And the dross wasn't always merely waste; it was also a readily available construction material that allowed the town to fill the shoreline, build bulkheads, and stabilize pier foundations. The Dutch never grew far from the island's southern tip, but they started a trend that was enthusiastically imitated for centuries. They grew land outward, especially into the East River. Pearl Street in lower

Manhattan got its name from the lustrous shells that marked it when it was the city's eastern shore. Today it is two and three blocks inland.[9]

Even if colonists had followed the new sanitary codes (evidence suggests that they did not), there was another, equally prevalent source of street debris. After the settlement's director general, Peter Stuyvesant, discovered that marauding pigs and cattle had torn up his garden *again* and had destroyed new improvements to the fort, which also happened to be his home, he ordered all livestock penned. His edict met apathetic enforcement. It's possible that not everyone understood it, since by then the town's inhabitants "were men of eighteen different languages."[10] Despite Stuyvesant's reported fury, the pigs were soon afoot once more.[11]

Nasty streets and rampaging hogs were problems that only got worse, but by now the Heere Gracht and the Bevers Gracht were also headaches. Almost from their inception, they proved tempting dumps.[12] Legislation forbidding citizens to toss into the street or the canals any category of waste—particularly the ubiquitous "tubbs of odour and nastiness," as chamber pots and privies were called—was regularly ignored. At low tide, the stench of sewage, rotting offal, and decaying rubbish emanated from the grachts. These were periodically cleared out, almost certainly with slave labor, but the effort proved useless. Work would end in an evening, and when the laborers returned the next day, they'd find fresh deposits where they had cleaned the day before.[13]

In April 1664, when one of the town constables asked what to do about several dead hogs "here and there on the street"—he wanted to "prevent the stench, which proceeds therefrom"—he was told to use "the City's Negroes to collect and bury the same."[14] But labor assignments and street cleanliness were not to be Dutch concerns much longer. When four British warships showed up in August and aimed their cannons at Nieuw Amsterdam, Stuyvesant was outnumbered, outgunned, and didn't even have enough potable water to endure a siege.[15] He intended to go down fighting, until he received a petition from the town's merchants, his own son among them, urging him to please just surrender.

The originally neat village, still clustered south of its wall and continuing to draw settlers from all over Europe, was no longer neat, and now it was no longer Dutch. England named its new port after the king's brother James, Duke of York.

Nothing in the historical record suggests that the residents of Nieuw Amsterdam or New-York were more slovenly than their counterparts in other colonial American towns (that came later). "Casting rubbish and refuse of all kinds into the street without let or hindrance" was common practice.[16] The British paved some streets, which helped keep down dust, and dug more wells, though the water was only suitable for firefighting.[17] No doubt to the relief of anyone who lived downwind of them, the Heere and Bevers Grachts were filled in 1676, likely with slave labor.[18] Complaints about the "noisome smell" emanating from slaughterhouses and tanneries were answered by moving those trades out of town, just north of the wall.[19]

Then as now, transporting garbage was a challenge. A guild of carters was granted a monopoly on moving any kind of freight on condition that they stop using "ill and bad Language" and that they agree to take rubbish.[20] This included the sweepings that residents were supposed to clear from in front of their homes at least once a week, though the carters would only take the stuff "provyded the dirt be throwne & Loaden uppon the Cart by the owners or tenneants of the howses in the said streets."[21] In other words, in contrast to contemporary practice, you had to load out the cart yourself, or the guys working your block wouldn't take it. Garbage collection wasn't a popular chore, because it paid much less than what a carter could earn doing work for local merchants, so the guild members organized a schedule that divided the burden among them.[22]

In 1684, a constable assigned to each ward was directed to enforce street-cleaning laws, thus formalizing police involvement in public hygiene, an arrangement that has endured, with various permutations, ever since. The year 1694 was significant in the annals of New York's sanitation history: for the first time, a tax was levied specifically to pay the annual salary of a street-cleaning supervisor. Ten years later, scavengers showed up on the city payroll, with different individuals given jurisdiction over specific blocks.[23]

New Yorkers had been strictly forbidden to let privies overflow or to dump chamber pots into the streets for decades (though they could dump into the rivers after 10:00 at night in the winter and after 11:00 in the summer), but the frequency with which such laws were passed suggests that night soil, as the contents of the vessels were called, was always a problem. And despite earlier edicts that slaughterhouses, tanneries, breweries, distilleries, and rendering plants stay far from crowded neighborhoods, they were constructed wherever their owners wanted to put them, which meant they shared the block with homes, pubs, and churches. Dyers, starch makers, shoemakers, and tallow chandlers joined the list of so-called nuisance trades that tossed detritus in the streets, along shorelines, into waterways.

By the close of the seventeenth century, nearly five thousand people were squeezed into the bottom of Manhattan. Ever greater quantities and ever more unusual categories of urban refuse—human and animal, solid and liquid, poisonous and innocuous—seemed always beyond the capacity of householders, cartmen, constables, scavengers, enslaved or indentured laborers, aldermen, or mayors. By this time, whether or not city fathers recognized it, public health and the cleanliness of New York's streets and byways were inextricably linked. The city's inability or unwillingness to keep itself clean was about to become the catalyst for more than a century of tragedy.

It started with yellow fever. The disease made its first New York appearance in 1702. Victims felt unwell and took to their beds, seemed better in a day or so, then succumbed to the jaundice for which the sickness was eventually named. When violent "black" vomiting started shortly thereafter, death was quick. In keeping with conventional wisdom, the devastating illness was understood as proof of God's divine wrath toward those guilty of great sin. The alleged sinners were usually the newest immigrants, the poorest citizens, the already stigmatized. They brought this scourge upon themselves, went the logic of the day, but even upstanding citizens certain of their own guiltlessness, and thus their presumed immunity, fled the city in droves.

Streets that had been ringing with life grew desolately quiet. Famine threatened when farmers dared not come into the city. Panicked families tossed stricken mothers, children, grandparents, into the gutters; carts passed several times a day to collect the dead and the soon to be dead. Gravediggers filled potter's fields with dozens of bodies at a time, the victims' souls unshriven. Before it was over, the epidemic had claimed the mayor, several members of the Common Council, and 570 others.[24]

Yellow fever made more visits throughout the eighteenth century, as did malaria, smallpox, whooping cough, and measles, which ravaged adults as well as children. The city tried to respond. More streets were paved. The contents of privies (the same privies that weren't supposed to be dumped on the streets), along with assorted excrement from hogs, dogs, cattle, chickens, goats, and horses, as well as the usual glut of miscellaneous crud, lingered in the avenues whether they were dirt or paved, so in 1703 gutters were cut down the middle of newly cobbled roads. The cuts were intended as conduits to help the variety of city wastes make their way to the rivers and then out to sea, but the debris didn't wash away with the tides. Instead, the worst of it floated indefinitely between pilings and surrounded docked vessels with a soup-like foulness.

A doctor-politician named Cadwallader Colden did a survey of the town in 1740 and pointed out that disease hit hardest in the vicinity of slimy ground and near swampy areas known for their filth and dampness. He published a treatise in which he argued that the way to protect New York from illness in general, and from yellow fever in particular, was to remediate these conditions. The provincial legislature and the Common Council, in dread of future epidemics, took Colden seriously by passing the city's first comprehensive sanitary codes.[25]

Tired street-sweeping regulations were strengthened, reintroduced, and finally enforced, as were rules against improper disposition of night soil (again). Noxious businesses were banned from residential neighborhoods, a kind of proto–zoning measure (they joined other trades already clustered north of town near the deep and formerly sparkling Collect Pond, thus hastening that water's unhappy end), and were prohibited from dumping their wastes into city streets during warm weather (it was still accepted practice in the winter). Slips clogged with sewage slop were dredged or filled. Meat markets were moved and their old locations cleaned, while butchers and fishmongers had to adjust to new requirements about the quality and sale of meat, fowl, and fish. Strict quarantine was imposed on all foreign vessels (since perhaps not every illness was locally grown), while swamps, bogs, and marshes were filled and pools of standing water were eradicated. Hogs, cattle, horses, and goats were ordered penned (again); dogs were to be tied (again).

Just as Colden had predicted, yellow fever and other diseases were less virulent than in prior years. His sanitary reforms stayed in place and were followed, more or less, for a few decades, but there were still problems. Ashes, offal, sewage, and other unpleasantries still filled the streets; drainage ditches under Broad Street (the filled-in Heere Gracht) and other places regularly backed up, causing appalling smells and drawing hordes of flies.[26]

The Revolutionary War brought the city to a standstill. When the British finally left in 1783, New York was home to about twelve thousand people, roughly half its prewar population. This lessened some chronic sanitation stresses, but a postwar population surge soon overwhelmed whatever remnants of urban infrastructure remained.

In 1784, three commissioners were appointed to enforce street-cleaning laws, but they had little effect. In 1788, the mayor complained about private contractors who used "Criminals & Vagrants" to clean the streets, thereby "depriving the industrious Poor of the Means of Subsistence."[27] That year, and again in 1792 and 1795, the stagnant gutters, festering cellars, piles of unattended street dirt, mounds of manure, abattoir emanations, and rotting animal carcasses inspired grand jury indictments against the Common Council, but little changed.[28]

Yellow fever remained a terrifying if erratic motivator, claiming hundreds of victims across several summers.[29] Then came the epidemic of 1798. To the city's horror, it rivaled the devastation wrought almost a hundred years before. Surely, wrote one witness, this bout of the fever was "a homebred Pestilence. The inhabitants have really poisoned their city by the accumulation of Excrement, putrid Provision and every unclean thing."[30]

The situation was made worse by the lack of clean water. Other cities used water for all manner of tasks, including flushing their streets, but not New York. Its last sure source, the privately owned Tea Water Pump, had drawn from springs deep below the Collect Pond for decades, but even that water had become "foul with excrement, frogspawn, and reptiles."[31] One source called it "very sickly and nauseating" and warned that "the larger the city grows, the worse this evil will be."[32]

Sixty thousand people lived in New York in 1800.[33] Homes, businesses, and ambitions stuffed into the bottom of Manhattan Island strained against closely packed buildings and labyrinthine streets, which were dirtier than ever. Because much of the city's refuse included manure and other organic wastes that could be sold to farmers, street cleaning was intended to be a financially self-sufficient enterprise. Opportunities for mismanagement were many, however, and the city had trouble keeping the streets clean or the money honest. The superintendent of scavengers exemplified the problem. The position, created in 1803, was held by a former grain measurer named Stephen Hitchcock. He managed to cheat the sweepers who collected the manure, the boatmen who transported it, the farmers who bought it, and the officials who were supposed to keep tabs on him.

New Yorkers still created land on the rivers' edges, but not everyone appreciated the practice. A group of citizens opposed a plan to fill lots on Greenwich Street and Beaver Lane. "Fatal experience has proved that a crowded population on *made ground* uniformly increases the malignancy and ravages of disease," argued the petitioner Marshal Wilkings in 1804, who wanted to prevent a recurrence of "the malignant fever which hath so dreadfully scourged us." The lots were filled anyway.[34]

The city was also pushing north. City authorities were glad for the trend, but they wanted such expansion to be orderly. How better, they reasoned, to foster a stable and prosperous economy? They also believed that rational growth would surely help to organize, perhaps even discipline, the minds and spirits of a citizenry that seemed in perpetual disarray.[35]

Manhattan's many hills, valleys, rocky outcroppings, and slender cliffs were laced with streams, underground springs, marshes, meadows, and forests. A thoughtful street plan would take those into account as much as possible—or so early collaborators assumed. Politicians thought differently.

After several years of careful surveys that documented the island in precise detail, a proposal was unveiled in 1811 on a map more than eight feet long.[36] The orientation puts Manhattan on its side, the southern tip of the island a stubby finger pointing left. That section is shown in red, as if the finger and its adjoining hand were inflamed by the stress of too many inhabitants jammed into too little space. Just beyond the island's widest expanse, twelve horizontal avenues that slashed north were crossed by straight vertical thoroughfares all the way to a distant place labeled 157th Street.[37] These lines described more than two thousand blocks across eleven thousand acres in a relentless grid of evenly spaced, right-angled boxes that allowed no obstacle or geographic particularity.

In its audacity and in its scale, the Grid Plan, as it came to be called, was magnificently bold, but even to its supporters it bordered on the outlandish. It proposed a metropolis that must have seemed an unattainable fiction to citizens living atop one another in the crowded, narrow bump of lower Manhattan.[38] But that vast and unlikely city came into being faster than anyone could have predicted because of the second daring project of the era.

When the Erie Canal opened in 1825, New York's fortunes were radically changed. A ton of flour worth forty dollars in Buffalo tripled in price during the three weeks it took to reach New York by overland routes, but on the canal, that same ton of flour arrived in eight days, at a cost of about six dollars.[39] As raw materials and agricultural products moved from west to east, so people moved from east to west, settling towns all along the canal and beyond— and they flocked to New York. The city grew so fast that it was building out ten miles of streets a year (with guidance from the Grid Plan). As the streetscape expanded and the economy boomed, so did the foulest problems of urban life. By the early 1840s, New York's stench was so gaggingly rank that sailors claimed they could smell it six miles from shore.[40]

8. A Matter of Spoils

By 1850, more than half a million people lived in New York—a nearly tenfold increase from 1800, almost all through immigration. Newcomers staggered off ships or delivered themselves from the slaveholding South only to discover that paid employment was a rarity, conditions when they could get a job were inhumane, and basic necessities like wholesome food and clean water were luxuries beyond their grasp. Many arrived too sick even to look for work or housing, but private hospitals refused them.[1] The unluckiest ended up dead on the streets, where they were sometimes hard to discern amid the pervasive rot and muck that had come to be called "Corporation Pudding."[2]

A study done in 1851 concluded that fully a third of the city's deaths that year could have been prevented if basic sanitary measures had been in place.[3] A grand jury investigation in 1853 tried to discern why the streets remained so filthy, especially because there was plenty of money to get the work done, but street cleaning had already been discovered as a source of easy and thus irresistible plunder. Its managers created no-show jobs and enjoyed an apparently bottomless pot of funds that was used for many purposes, but not so much for cleaning or sweeping. Street cleaners themselves were understood to be political loyalists first, sweepers second, if at all. The results were catastrophic: by 1860, New York's annual mortality rate of one in thirty-six was among the highest in the world.[4] Even as the city's filth proved fatal to countless victims, it made many businessmen very rich.[5]

Some among the humbler classes also made good use of the limitless debris, though at far more modest scales. For those who knew how to see and where to look and who had the stamina, gleaning enough bits and oddments on enough days provided a steady income, more or less. Scavenging was one of the few labors that had always included women; for those caught in deepest poverty, their skill in finding, assessing, and fencing flotsam kept them out of the almshouse—or an early grave.[6] Their children learned similar proficiencies, some while they were still toddlers.[7] New York's wealthier denizens, who had no affection for these youngsters, called them rag fairies, guttersnipes, dock rats, river thieves, and street urchins.[8]

Working together and on their own, women and children from Five Points, Ragpickers Row, and other slums in the east-side wards scoured the streets, "hook in hand, basket on the arm, and sack over the shoulder, moving through the gutters and searching in the ash-barrels and boxes and overhauling garbage vessels" for bones, fish heads, rags, paper, wire, lengths of string and thread, strips or laces of leather, nails, horseshoes, cord, bottles, tufts of cotton or wool, lengths of rope, chunks of wood, metal scraps, shards of coal—in short, "whatever there is that is not utterly worthless, or that was not destroyed when once used."[9] They frequented the entrances to lumberyards, slaughterhouses, mills, dairies. City dumps were fair territory, though women and children had dibs only after the piles had been searched by men with contracts for the work.[10] Some women found a more stable life as partners of the men who trimmed the garbage scows. While their husbands stood in the boats, dodging debris that rained down from rubbish carts tipping loads off the piers above them, the women sorted and bundled the scraps that the men recovered from the piles.[11] Entire families devoted themselves to this work, sometimes living under the docks. Conditions were miserable, but "still there are people who get used to them," noted one cynical commentator, "just as eels are said to become accustomed to being skinned."[12]

The women sold their wares to middlemen, often Irish immigrants who had come to dominate the city's carting business.[13] More carters than ever plied the streets of the city in the mid-1850s, but four-wheel wagons and other large conveyances were also becoming common choices for hauling freight around town. These needed more power to move them, so they were drawn by two or more horses, which in turn required men with sufficient skill and strength to master the animals.[14] These drivers came to be called teamsters; unlike carters, whom they soon displaced for most jobs, they were not exclusively white.[15] Neither their knowledge nor their abilities earned them much respect, however, and like carters they were considered low-class (their detractors said it was because they stank of horse).[16] The teamsters found steady work in the thriving economy of the city, but carters didn't disappear completely for many more years; their modest wagons were still the best choice for household garbage collection.

At the other end of the social spectrum, the U.S. Sanitary Commission, formed to improve conditions at Union army camps and hospitals during the Civil War, saw firsthand that basic hygiene and simple sanitation made a real difference in soldiers' recovery and health.[17] Many of the commission's members were from New York. If sanitary improvements could happen in army camps, they reasoned, they could happen in city slums—but just how bad were those neighborhoods? The Citizens' Association of New York set about finding the answer with the most ambitious sanitary survey ever organized.[18] The city was divided into thirty-one districts. Each was assigned a physician, who went block by block and building by building to ask every family the same battery of questions. Artists accompanied the doctors to sketch what they saw. The findings filled seventeen volumes (and the condensed version ran five hundred pages).[19]

Report of the Council of Hygiene and Public Health of the Citizens' Association of New York upon the Sanitary Condition of the City was scathing. It showed that wholly preventable diseases like smallpox (more than thirty-two hundred cases) and typhus (two thousand cases, though that was probably only half the real number) were rampant. There were approximately twenty-eight cases of illness for every death; in some tenements, between 50 and 70 percent of the residents were ill at any given time.[20] The authors pointed out that these ailing people were workers who could not show up to their jobs, a fact meant to awaken the city's business interests to the urgency of the problem.[21] They also wanted to make clear to upper-class New Yorkers that disease did not respect boundaries between poor and wealthy neighborhoods.[22] The city, they argued, must have "an efficient Health Board" staffed by people with "a profound knowledge of disease" as well as those "accustomed to the dispatch of business." Above all, it had to be free from political or partisan influence. "We trust that this species of reform will be appreciated," they added sternly.[23]

Officials were prepared to heed none of it, until a ship whose passengers were stricken with cholera arrived from Europe in November 1865. Physicians and politicians alike knew that winter's cold weather would hold off the disease only temporarily. By February 1866, the state legislature both authorized the Metropolitan Board of Health and gave it real power. Police enforced health and sanitation codes. Entire neighborhoods were scoured: apartments, streets, alleys, and privies were cleaned and disinfected. Some tenement dwellers were even removed from their homes and sent to dispensaries. When cholera did strike the city that spring, it claimed only a few hundred victims—many fewer than expected, and fewer than were killed in other cities.[24] The nation's first municipal board of health was soon imitated in cities around the country. Unfortunately for New Yorkers, the board's creation coincided with Tammany's most rapacious years.

When it was founded in the late eighteenth century to counter Federalist (mostly aristocratic) New Yorkers, the Tammany Society had the markings of a fraternal organization.[25] Its original aims might have been brotherly, but by the end of the Civil War, the Ring, as its inner circle was called, wielded unprecedented power. Tammany controlled nearly all facets of New York government, from the city and the county up to the judiciary, the governor, and the board of audit, which rather conveniently had oversight for city finances.[26] A significant portion of the perpetually ballooning budget earmarked for street cleaning found its way into the pockets of local officials, and street-cleaning jobs were choice sinecures; the ersatz sweepers gave their bosses and ward captains regular kickbacks. Businesses paid big-money prizes for insider information and rigged contracts. Citizen protests about such shenanigans were met with winks (from insider politicos) or with shrugs (from resigned observers), while the deplorable streets became a national scandal. Public health reformers watched the gains they made in the 1860s disappear while the city stayed squalid and the poor died in droves; infant mortality rates were 65 percent higher in 1870 than they had been in 1810.[27]

It was a disgruntled minion who helped loosen Tammany's grip. The accounting books that he turned over to *The New York Times* in 1871 and that revealed the extent of the Ring's fiscal venality were too damning to ignore, and the press didn't hold back. The arrest of the Ring's leader, William "Boss" Tweed, and the subsequent melodrama of his escape and capture were sensational news.[28]

Empowered by its success in unseating Tammany's kingpin, the press took on other causes, like the state of the streets. It seemed that the more funds the Bureau of Street Cleaning received, the less work it did. Merchants in many neighborhoods, pointing to reeking piles of evidence, grumbled that they had not seen street sweepers or carters in months. In April 1874, after a series of newspaper stories provided proof of graft and other abuses, the state legislature intervened, but the practical changes it suggested for the Bureau of Street Cleaning were ignored.[29] "The feeling among most experienced citizens of New-York in regard to the possibility of cleaning its streets properly," sighed *The New York Times*, "is of resigned hopelessness."[30]

When the independent Department of Street Cleaning was finally established in 1881, it had little power.[31] Contracts could be awarded or canceled at any time, with no oversight or review. Several agencies—Street Cleaning, Public Works, Health, Police— and the mayor's office were responsible for street cleanliness, with the unsurprising result that nothing was well or often cleaned. "The whole street-cleaning movement of this spring," wrote one commentator, "is a forcible illustration of the myriad mischiefs of treating every public work as a matter of spoils."[32]

"The people of the city ought to have some means of knowing why it is that they cannot have tolerably clean streets when considerably over a million dollars of their money is spent every year by a department devoted exclusively to that object," sputtered another source, who laid blame on "a department without an intelligent system, without adequate authority or support, and with the rot of local politics sapping all its energies."[33]

"Are you aware that the downtown streets of this great city over which you preside are and have been for a long time in a disgustingly foul and dirty condition?" an angry resident wrote to the mayor in 1890. "What is the reason for such a barbaric, pig-styish state of affairs? Are there not brooms, hoes, sweepers, horses, and carts enough to be had and men enough to operate them, or has the Street-Cleaning Department been bought off by a soap and laundry trust?"[34]

Battle-fatigued sanitary reformers were beginning to think that neither ardent complaints nor the unflagging efforts of New York's most dedicated citizens would ever make a difference. The cause was in desperate need of fresh inspiration, and it came from a surprising source.[35]

By this moment in urban American history, the wives and daughters of New York's prominent families were familiar with "domestic hygiene," a field first proposed decades earlier and freshly propagated by new publications like the *Ladies' Home Journal*, which debuted in 1883.[36] Why not take the managerial acumen they had honed in their homes and direct it toward the greater common good?[37] Concern about the streets, they reasoned, could be construed as an extension of a woman's natural responsibility for her family. "It is, indeed, an eminently proper thing," asserted one genteel matron, "for women to interest themselves in the care and destination of garbage, the cleanliness of the streets, and, in fact, everything that constitutes the city's housekeeping."[38] With this aim in mind, the Ladies Health Protective Association, one of many sanitary societies organized by privileged women around the country, was formed in New York in 1884.

Educated, confident, and savvy, the Ladies drew attention to their causes by framing them as problems of aesthetics and cleanliness rather than of science or politics.[39] The group's first target was a vast mound of manure that had been fermenting for several years at the foot of Forty-Sixth Street and the East River. Despite laws forbidding such accumulations, and despite the fact that the pile poisoned the air for a thirty-block radius, the dung heap's owner had political connections that insulated him from compliance with the law and from heeding his neighbors' many complaints. It took the Ladies six years, but eventually they succeeded in getting the stable owner indicted and the forty thousand tons of decomposing excrement removed.[40]

They and their cousin organizations in other cities were soon acknowledged powers in a host of urban reform efforts; New York's in particular became one of the nation's most influential civic groups.[41] Their cause was bolstered when an extensive investigation into municipal corruption revealed depths of vice that amazed even the most jaded observers.[42] The scandal broke during an election year. Tammany leaders, fingered by witness after witness, could not salvage their power, and their mayoral candidate was trounced by a former bank president and pedigreed member of the city's Republican Protestant elite named William L. Strong.

Strong delivered on his promise of an honest administration in part by choosing commissioners who were not beholden to anyone within Democratic or Republican political organizations.[43] One candidate in particular had the endorsement of the Ladies Health Protective Association; they urged the mayor to name Colonel George E. Waring, Jr., a Civil War veteran and self-styled sanitary engineer, head of the Department of Street Cleaning.

Strong met with Waring and asked if he would consider the post. Only under one condition, the colonel replied.

"I get my own way."

"The law gives you that to a large extent," Strong replied.

"I do not mean the law; I mean you." He needed this point to be clear. "You can remove me, but you must not interfere with me."[44] Strong gave his word, and Waring took the job. The mayor could not have known the significance of the appointment. When Waring assumed command of the beleaguered DSC on January 15, 1895, vowing to clean the streets and keep them clean, New York was never quite the same again.[45]

9. Apostles of Cleanliness

It's easy to imagine some New Yorkers dubious about Colonel Waring. His pledge to turn things around could only come from a foolish outsider. His indomitable confidence sounded more like brashness and naïveté. Never mind that Philadelphia had succeeded in cleaning its streets years earlier and that cities throughout Europe had long ago conquered the same problem. Anyone could see that the situation was different here, even without Tammany's empty excuses. The city was too big and too crowded with too many different kinds of people. Waring, the naysayers muttered, could not succeed.

The naysayers were right on one account. Waring was brash, sometimes infuriatingly so. But his occasionally excessive self-assurance had earned him notable mentors, including Frederick Law Olmsted, his boss when they worked together building Central Park in the 1850s.[1] Waring's boldness won him fast promotions during the war, and afterward it helped him build a profitable career.[2]

The colonel relished predictions of his failure, most particularly when he confounded them. Ignoring the Department's legacy of fraud and purposeful inefficiency, Waring made clear to DSC employees that any worker willing to actually use his broom, fill his cart, dump his load, and go back for more would keep his job.[3] "I have hit upon a plan for street cleaning which has proved effectual," he told the city's Good Government Club three months into his tenure. "It is to put a man instead of a voter at the end of the broom handle . . . The men have learned now that it doesn't matter what their politics may be; if they attend to their work they will be kept."[4] He estimated that five-eighths of the workforce stayed.[5]

Waring drew on his wartime experience to codify the Department's hierarchy and to establish strict military-style order. The city, already divided into districts, was further divided into sections. Sweepers and carters attended a daily roll call where they were assigned specific streets within those sections. They reported their progress, or any problems they encountered, to their foremen. Foremen reported to their district superintendents, and the supers reported to chiefs higher up the chain of command. Anyone with a rank above sweeper or carter was considered an officer and therefore was expected to make decisions, give orders, and be obeyed.

To show that he was serious about cleaning the entire city, Waring started in one of its worst neighborhoods. "I said we would take up Five Points as a test and if we could not clean that district we might as well give up," he recalled later.[6] "I put two young men in charge of the Five Points District, with instructions to do whatever they thought necessary to clean the streets there."[7] It took two weeks, "but now they may go there alone day or night, and they are received with open arms. The people there now take great pride in keeping the streets clean themselves."[8]

Waring believed that the city's waste problems were serious enough to deserve the best minds of the day, so he tapped recent college graduates for leadership positions, including as mechanics and supervisors. His superintendent of final disposition (the old name for waste disposal) was twenty-five years old. Methods of sweeping and collecting rubbish were refined. It used to be that sweepers made piles along the curb and carters followed to collect them, but sometimes with a lag of days. Waring had carts follow sweepers immediately, and no piles of dust or debris lingered. His wife made her own contribution to the cause when she devised a metal barrel set on a small wheeled platform, propelled by a handle and big enough to carry brooms, bags, and shovels. This contraption, called a can carry, was used in New York until the mid-1980s and—like many of Waring's innovations—was copied by cities around the country.[9]

Snow had confounded all his predecessors. When the fetid streets, shin-deep in ashes, manure, offal, and all other manner of rubbish, suffered the addition of snow, even the most robust travelers were stymied. "There was mud galore," went one typical account after a snowstorm, "mud that blended itself with the slush and rain, and seized every opportunity to cause profanity and injure clothing."[10]

Barely two weeks into Waring's term, four inches of snow fell during the night. By 5:30 the following morning, workers were clearing it from the streets; when the full force was deployed, thirty-eight hundred men were shoveling, tossing, and hauling it away. "So early were the employees of the Street-Cleaning Department sent out to attack the snow," marveled *The New York Times*, "that not a little of it was caught as it fell on the shovels of the laborers."[11] Over time Waring came to brag that more snow was taken away in the first five weeks of 1895 than had been removed in five *years* prior to his arrival.[12]

There was more. The requirement that workers wear uniforms, on the books since the DSC was established back in 1881, had never been taken seriously. Waring insisted the men adhere to it, but in a most curious way. With a showman's zeal for publicity, he had his troops sweeping streets, emptying ash barrels, and carting rubbish while dressed in white trousers and jackets made of heavy cotton duck, and tall white helmets. He knew that clean streets meant an immediate boost to public health, and he wanted that public to associate the DSC workforce with hygiene and cleanliness—thus the white suits.[13] They also had authority to do what was necessary to get the streets clean—hence their tall helmets, which imitated those of the police. And any worker who felt like sneaking off for a beer or taking a nap under his cart would find it tough to do in his dazzling duds.[14] "The white suits . . . served to make every man realize that he was being observed," Waring explained to an audience in Brooklyn.[15] His wife called him crazy, but it was a brilliant move: the men were no longer invisible, and the public could no longer avoid seeing them.

To a modern sensibility, some of Waring's reforms sound like simple common sense, but in New York's gaslight era they were almost revolutionary. He kept DSC workers on the streets long enough to finish the job and demanded tools and equipment of usable quality. He insisted the Department's horses be the appropriate breed and that DSC stablemen keep them healthy. He renovated or built necessary infrastructure like stables and dumping piers and attempted to renegotiate contracts with scavengers, tugboat owners, and scow companies. This kind of effort cost money, and Waring didn't hesitate to spend it. One source estimated that nearly 8 percent of the city's budget was devoted to the costs of street cleaning. "The present authorities spend as much money as the old Tammany regime," noted the writer, "with this difference: A large sum is used, but the streets are clean; Tammany spent as much and left the streets dirty."[16]

A clean city, Waring believed, required cooperation from the entire citizenry, and he initiated a program aimed at the youngest New Yorkers. Juvenile Street Cleaning Leagues were formed as clubs that taught children how to be the eyes and ears of the DSC in educating a public sometimes slow to break old habits like littering. By the end of Waring's tenure, there were forty-one leagues involving nearly a thousand children throughout the city.[17]

To foster loyalty among his workers and to prevent potential labor agitation, Waring established a review board to hear complaints and the Committee of Forty-One to adjudicate grievances. The committee, named for the city's forty-one street-cleaning districts, was made up of a representative from each. He raised wages to

sixty dollars a month—nearly twice the salary of unskilled laborers—
and mandated an eight-hour workday, considerably shorter than the
norm.[18]

The result of all these initiatives was close to miraculous. "New
York has long had a street department," observed *Harper's New
Monthly Magazine*. "It was an original discovery of Colonel Waring's that this could be made and used to clean the streets."[19] For the
first time in memory, New Yorkers could see, smell, and walk through
what must have felt like a city reborn. Streets were no longer buried
from curb to curb with sometimes knee-deep piles of moldering
vegetable rinds and blowsy wood shavings and festering oyster
shells and oozing fish bones and stuffing-popped mattresses and
staved-in furniture and fluttering rags and overflowing barrels of
ash and heaps upon heaps upon heaps of horse manure marinated
in millions of gallons of horse urine (and often mounded around
the maggoty carcasses of dead horses, dead dogs, dead cats, who
might lie where they fell for days or weeks), all mashed into an in-
choate mass of shifting berms and ruts by passing carriages, wagons, omnibuses.[20]

Pedestrians no longer had to say their prayers and trust their
luck just to cross an avenue after untended snow lay in gutters long
enough to become slippery, malodorous ooze. Householders no
longer had to keep their windows clamped shut all day, even in the
worst heat of the summer, against the nauseating dust that billowed
from the streets. (In the rain that dust became an unctuous mud
with a repulsive smell. God help the man or woman who found it
adhered to shoe soles or skirt hems; the stench permeated forever
anything it touched.)

Instead of these many horrors, New Yorkers witnessed men in
white uniforms actually sweeping the streets—*all* the streets, not just
those of the wealthy—several times in a single day, with carts following close behind. They saw ash barrels emptied with on-the-clock
regularity. Crisp curb lines and elegantly laid paving stones revealed themselves for the first time in decades.

To celebrate, Waring organized a parade. On a sun-filled afternoon in May 1896, the entire Department of Street Cleaning workforce, more than twenty-two hundred strong, marched down Fifth
Avenue in those startlingly white uniforms. The sweepers kept a
tight formation, brooms over their shoulders like rifles, while the
carters were at the reins of ash and hose carts drawn by horses
groomed to gleaming. The animals looked so fine that they seemed
fit for private carriages, not for lowly rubbish wagons. Covered steel
carts, a significant improvement over the leaky wooden contraptions that had been the norm, glinted in the light. Interspersed
throughout were ten marching bands, including that of the famous
Seventh Regiment, to rouse the onlookers' spirits and to keep the
men in step.

When the parade was in full procession, marchers and floats
and bands extended from Sixtieth Street to the turning point on
Twenty-Third Street. It took an hour and twenty minutes for the
entire procession to pass the reviewing stand, built in front of the
massive walls of the reservoir on Forty-Second Street.[21] At the ends
of the stand, snapping in the breeze, were banners that would serve
as prizes for districts with the tightest marching formation, bright-
est uniforms, best-groomed horses. Waring led the column from
astride a tall brown filly. He wore his military dress uniform and
the same white helmet that crowned his sweepers. "The barber who
waxed his moustache," remarked one source, "was an artist."[22]

On some blocks, the crowd watching the parade was seven- or
eight-deep. Many of them "did not seem to be frequenters of Fifth
Avenue. Nearly every one that stood on the curbstones had some
friend in the procession."[23] These particular parade-goers had reason to be proud. The spruced-up husbands, sons, and brothers of
the spectators had accomplished a Herculean task. Onlookers
who greeted the men with catcalls and raspberries at the start of
the parade soon realized that their scorn was outdated. When the
marchers that day heard those initial jeers turn to cheers, they understood why.

Waring's tenure lasted barely three years before the Ring engineered a return to city hall, but his successors could never again claim that the DSC's budget was insufficient or its manpower inadequate. No Tammany hack would dare argue, as so many had before, that the streets could not be swept several times a week or that a metropolis as large as New York could not be kept clean.

"It was Colonel Waring's broom that first let light into the slum," wrote the journalist and photographer Jacob Riis. "His broom saved more lives in the crowded tenements than a squad of doctors. It did more: it swept the cobwebs out of our civic brain and conscience."[24]

For all his accomplishments, however, there was one promise that Waring didn't keep. When he took office, the city was dumping much of its garbage in the ocean. It was a lousy waste disposal choice for many reasons, and the colonel said he'd put a stop to it, but he never came up with a viable alternative. Perhaps he would have made it a bigger priority if he'd talked with the men who actually took the trash to sea. They had plenty of harrowing tales about their work, such as that time six garbage boats left the harbor and only one came back.

10. An Angry Sea

Late on a Monday night at the end of January 1892, a cluster of men at the Street Cleaning docks on East Seventeenth Street worked to get two tugboats and four garbage scows ready to sail.[1] The tugs— the *H. S. Nichols* and the *Edwin Webster*—carried about twenty tons of coal and plenty of water, along with food and coffee for their captains, mates, and deckhands. Each of the four scows, known by numbers (3, 5, 16, and 17), held several thousand cubic yards of trash and would be manned by a captain and a mate.

The tugs were to pull the scows down the East River, across the Upper New York Harbor, through the Verrazano Narrows, and out to sea. In warm weather, their destination was supposed to be seventeen nautical miles from the Rockaways, but this time of year they stayed closer, maybe ten or so nautical miles off Breezy Point. The exact distance, a source of acrimony between the city and her neighbors, depended on the weather, on the mood of the tug captains, and on the harbor master's fluctuating desire to keep the captains honest. Whether seventeen miles or ten (or fewer), the men were to empty the scows' cargo into the ocean, and the tugs would pull them back to the docks.

It was a familiar assignment. For centuries, the city had consigned her waste to her waters. From the earliest European settlement, garbage was tossed along the shoreline, first with casual disregard but soon with the deliberate intention of building land. Eventually, the port's slips were so filled with garbage that ships couldn't berth. In 1857, the state ordered dumping moved farther into the harbor.[2] Debris floated ashore in New Jersey. The dumping zone was moved again, in 1872, to an area off southeastern Staten Island. The foul loads killed what had been profitable fishing grounds and oyster beds, and trash that didn't sink still found its way to shore—exactly as increasingly irate citizens in New Jersey and Staten Island had predicted.[3] Waste that did sink started to choke shipping channels. In 1883, more than nine ocean steamers ran aground when they were arriving in or leaving New York. Garbage, declared some, was becoming "the ruin of a noble harbor."[4]

Dumping was pushed still farther out, beyond the Rockaway Peninsula. Surely that was enough distance to prevent the detritus from returning, or from blocking ships, or from killing shellfish, but neither currents nor winds cooperated.

"Contact with the bodies of dead animals and decayed vegetables has been so frequent at the most accessible beaches," fumed one irate swimmer, "that many fastidious persons have long abandoned the practice of bathing in the surf at Coney Island, Rockaway, and the neighboring resorts. Certainly it is not pleasant while swimming to be borne down upon the floating body of a dead horse, or to have the carcass of a cat strike the bather in the face while diving beneath a breaker."[5]

Officials recognized the problem even as they despaired of a solution. "The method now in vogue for the disposal of garbage and street refuse is . . . crude and primitive in the extreme," declared New York Mayor Thomas F. Gilroy. "Under any condition a system which involves the taking of refuse from the streets of a great city to throw it broadcast upon the water contiguous to a great harbor is simply intolerable."[6]

It was also illegal: the federal Supervisory Harbors Act of 1888 made final disposition at sea a crime. New York skirted, flouted, or got exemptions to the law when its other means of disposal proved inconvenient, inadequate, or too expensive, which was often. The ocean answer was temporary, claimed city managers, but water disposal had been going on for so long that their assurances sounded hollow. Though ocean dumping was suspended now and then, serious alternatives always presented serious problems, and the city turned again and again to the sea.[7]

At the Street Cleaning docks in the early hours of Tuesday, the men cast off with the ebb tide under clear skies, the air a moist thirty-six degrees. The *Edwin Webster*, captained by George Clark, was pulling scows 5 and 17, one behind the other. Her partner tug, the *H. S. Nichols*, with Captain A. E. Gove at the helm, mastered scows 3 and 16. Their cargo was mounded in gentle pyramids, and a light northwest wind played with bits of it as they moved through the dark waters.

The scowmen counted themselves lucky. Their vessels were Barney self-dumpers, a newfangled scow made of six compartments with hinged bottoms. To unload trash from a Barney boat, the men released a chain, a compartment bottom fell open, and the rubbish slid into the sea.[8] Self-dumpers needed a crew of only two. On a conventional flat-bottomed garbage scow, by contrast, dozens of laborers had to climb and slip and claw their way over heaps of debris while they spent hours with pitchforks and shovels flinging the stuff overboard. Wind and waves often threw it back at them. Their balance was unsteady on the shifting slopes of trash, and not a few of the men themselves went over, their bodies lost forever in the waste-strewn water. Such tragedies didn't happen so much with the new dumpers. Rumor had it that the Barney company charged the city top dollar to lease its fleet, but the scowmen were glad that their work was less perilous and that each scow's deckhouse had bunks, a stove, and coal.

When the boats arrived at the dumping grounds, the wind had started to pick up, clouds dulled the morning light, and the air felt colder, but the sailors weren't worried. Most of them had years of experience on the sea and were accustomed to sudden shifts of weather. After the scowmen finished dumping their loads, the little armada turned toward home, but by then the weather wasn't just shifting; it was mutating. The mercury had plummeted more than twenty-five degrees since they'd left Manhattan (a change so dramatic that it made front-page headlines the next day). The winds were ratcheting up to gale force, and then the clouds released blinding flurries of snow.

A trim vessel would have struggled in such conditions, but it was particularly daunting to tugs pulling empty dumpers that rode high in the water, their eight-foot freeboard like stiff sails.⁹ The *H. S. Nichols* was making slow progress, but not the *Edwin Webster*, which pulled and groaned. Her engines roared and her funnel blew fat plumes of steam, but she seemed to be pushed backward. She was off Sandy Hook in sixty-four-mile-an-hour winds when the hawser that held her to her scows snapped. The errant line flailed in the water for a moment before it snarled around the propeller, bringing the boat to a dead stop. Then the lines that bound scows 5 and 17 to each other also came apart.¹⁰ George Clark, the *Edwin Webster*'s captain, sounded a distress call.

Captain Gove, on the *H. S. Nichols*, had his scows—3 and 16—anchor in the lee of the Rockaway Shoals and went to Clark's aid. He made pass after pass, letting his own coal and water run dangerously low as he and his crew struggled to get a line across to their comrades, but the convulsing seas made it impossible, and finally he had to give up. When Clark realized that the rescue attempt had come to naught, he dropped anchor. It didn't reach bottom.

The men on Gove's scows expected him to return for them;

instead, to their amazement, he steamed past. They thought maybe he yelled something about going to Staten Island; they didn't know he needed more fuel, or that he wouldn't be able to return. Gove didn't know that his tows were in trouble. The anchor of 16 had caught bottom, but 3's anchor had not. Then 16's anchor chain broke. The boats were still tied to each other; scow 3's dangling anchor gave it some stability, but now 16 had no comparable weight helping to steady it in the angry waves, and the two boats started pitching and slamming together. The pair drifted toward the *Edwin Webster* and her dumpers, and for a time it seemed that the five boats would collide, but wind and currents carried the pair away from the others and out to sea; by noon, they could no longer see the shore.

None of the men could have known it then, but they were being assaulted by one of the most violent storms in recent memory.[11] Ships all over the northeastern seaboard and the North Atlantic were getting thrashed. The *Harry and Aubrey*, a British brigantine, foundered off the Blue Point Life Saving Station near Fire Island and was lost (though her crew was saved, and her cargo of coconuts delighted the residents of nearby Patchogue, Long Island). A fishing boat with a crew of five went down near Sandy Hook (the men were rescued). In the Long Island Sound, three barges of corn dragged anchor and were driven aground at Sea Cliff, where pounding waves destroyed them. The German steamship *Fulda* "looked like a ship of glass, so completely was she shrouded in ice" when she reached the Sandy Hook Lightship on Tuesday afternoon. The *Andes*, a steamer from the West Indies, was smacked around so violently that all her cargo shifted to starboard; she came into port listing like a drunkard. The Cárdenas-registered steamship *Cuba* saw her rails and decks smashed, while the steamer *Hopetown*, from northeast Brazil, had all her lifeboats destroyed. Ferry passengers coming from Brooklyn, New Jersey, and Staten Island were tossed about like popcorn.[12]

There are conflicting accounts of how and when officials at the Department of Street Cleaning learned that five of their vessels were lost, but by Tuesday afternoon several tugboat owners had answered the call for help. No doubt these would-be rescuers wanted to save their fellow sailors from a dreadful fate, but their motives were more than humanitarian. A salvage fee of half the boats' value went to the finder. The scows were worth between $12,000 and $15,000 each, while the tugboat was valued by some sources at $25,000.[13] Even if a search party only found a single vessel, it would reap a hefty reward.

The *William H. Vosburgh*, an oceangoing tug significantly bigger and sturdier than the *Edwin Webster*, headed into the Atlantic on Tuesday afternoon. Her captain and crew intended to stay as long as their supplies lasted or until they found one of the DSC boats, but they were back by late Tuesday night. Her crew had seen no scows, nor the *Edwin Webster*, but her captain reported ice packs running fast in fierce winds and punishing breakers that nearly swamped them. Salt and ice were caked up to the top of the tug's funnel.

Another formidable ocean tugboat, the *Dasseni*, joined the search and traveled east by southeast nearly thirty miles before she, too, was bested by the storm. Hanging with icicles, her starboard bulwark "battered into kindling," and looking "as if she had been wintering in the Arctic," she limped back to the Seventeenth Street docks after midnight on Wednesday, where an anxious crowd of more than five hundred awaited news.[14]

"I have had an experience such as I hope never to have to go through again," said the *Dasseni*'s exhausted captain.[15] "The weather was fearful, the cold intense and the wind terrible. The water broke over the decks of the tug and froze before it could roll back again into the ocean. The ice on the head of the boat began to get very heavy, and she began to settle in the water. We began to fear for ourselves, so decided to turn around and get back to port."[16]

Families of the lost men had reason to expect the worst, especially if they glanced at the front pages of the daily newspapers. "All persons in a position to give an opinion on the subject unite in saying that the chances of escape for the storm-driven men are as one out of a thousand," *The Evening Sun* proclaimed. "No news from the drifting flotilla from the Street Cleaning Department!" wailed the *New York Evening Telegram*. "This is the latest word from the cruel sea, and in this case no news is very bad news indeed." *The World* ran an interview with a supposed expert. "The scows, being light, are in great danger of being swamped," he declared. "It is also likely that their deck-houses will be swept away and then the men who are in them will be exposed to this awful weather. Without shelter they can not live very long. They will freeze to death."[17]

A wreck with no survivors was reported strewn across Rockaway Beach. It was thought to be one of the scows. Another wreck was seen off Fire Island; knowledgeable sources guessed it might be the *Edwin Webster*. Neither report could be confirmed.

By dawn on Wednesday, the five drifting DSC boats had long since lost sight of one another, but they were sharing the same fate. Waves lifted them on steep walls of water, threw them into frothy gullies, and drenched them incessantly, sculpting them in ice that grew thicker and heavier by the minute, while winds as strong as a hundred miles an hour pushed them farther out to sea. Tempests of snow cut visibility to a few yards. Mini-icebergs battered the hull of the *Edwin Webster*, and soon she was taking on water; all hands took to the pumps and bails. On scow 5, the captain and mate secured a line to lash themselves to the boat itself in case their deckhouse actually did wash away. The scowmen on 17 traded ten-minute watches, the most they could endure in the cold.

The crews on dumpers 3 and 16, their boats still linked, set their flags Union down and shouted and waved at passing ships. Their deckhouses seemed to be secure, but the men on scow 3 made preparations to move to the hold—though soon they began to wonder if the scow itself would stay intact. They knew that the ominous shriek-like noises sounding every time the two boats rammed together meant the vessels were starting to break up.

Then, on Wednesday afternoon, approximately fifty miles from Sandy Hook, the watch on a tug called the *Luckenbach* spied scows 3 and 16 "driving along in a heavy sea and apparently bound for a trip across the ocean."[18]

"When the four castaways on the scows heard the hail from the tug they rushed from their deckhouses to the slippery decks, and when they saw the big 130-foot tugboat a short distance away they sent up a cheer which showed how great had been their despair," reported *The Evening Sun*. Crewmen from the *Luckenbach* tossed over sacks of food, then a lead-weighted line that was followed by a ten-inch hawser, and the men on scow 16 affixed it to their vessel's bow.

The trip home took thirteen hours. They traveled through the Coney Island Channel, which afforded some relief from the still-fierce wind, and came into the Upper Harbor unobserved, arriving at the Atlantic Basin docks in Brooklyn very early Thursday morning. Much rejoicing greeted them, but fourteen men and three boats were still unaccounted for. The *Luckenbach* replenished its provisions and returned to the sea in predawn darkness.

Around 10:00 that morning, a hundred or so miles off the Sandy Hook Lightship, one of the *Luckenbach*'s deckhands saw a single vessel on the horizon. It was scow 17. The reunion went much the same as with the previous rescue, and the shivering men were delivered to the Atlantic Basin docks just before 1:00 on Friday morning. They could not quite believe they'd survived their ordeal. "Every thump of the waves against the sides and stern of the scow seemed to me like the falling of a clod of earth on my own coffin," said 17's captain.[19]

Only the tugboat and scow 5 remained lost.

The *Edwin Webster* had been built in Baltimore in 1865. She was a solid boat when she was young, but by the time she was towing garbage, her seaworthiness was in doubt. Critics claimed that she wasn't up to the task of moving scows in any but the tamest weather, and she certainly couldn't survive "in the trough of such waves as those of Tuesday night."[20]

In fact, the crew's desperate efforts with buckets and pumps had kept the tug afloat through Tuesday and through Wednesday, but just after midnight on Thursday morning the water started rising faster than they could bail it. "One of the men cursed," went an account written later. "Another threw his pail to the deck and said, 'Good by, boys; I've dumped my last bucket' . . . The man's voice seemed to strike a death knell in every heart. Somebody gave a choking sort of sob and began to pray."[21]

But then a deckhand noticed a light.

"It rose and fell indistinctly," Captain Clark remembered. "I jumped to the pilot-house and waved a lantern. Then the vessel veered and bore right down on us . . . They saw that something was wrong with us and pretty soon we saw them drop a boat from the davits and away it came to our rescue." The ship, a three-masted schooner out of Philadelphia, was bound for Boston. Her captain said later that he'd chanced upon the *Edwin Webster* only because the storm had forced him to alter his course. Less than an hour after the last man was off, the doomed tug went down. Her owner, Mr. William Hennessey of Brooklyn, had let the boat's insurance expire three days before.

There still was no sign of scow 5. An official at the Barney Dumping Boat Company doubted it would sink, but the men aboard had supplies for no more than a day or two. If they weren't dead of hunger, he said, they were surely dead of cold. Searchers continued to ply the waters, but Friday and then the weekend passed without any news. By Monday, it seemed certain that the scow and her two crew had been claimed by the sea.

But on Tuesday morning, a full week after the misadventure began, a steamer carrying iron ore from England to Philadelphia came upon the lost boat, her captain and mate frostbitten and dehydrated but still very much alive. They had drifted 160 miles. Their rescuers delivered them to the City of Brotherly Love, where the Maritime Exchange fed and boarded them for the night. The Reading Railroad gave them free passage home the next day.

When they arrived in New York, one witness mentioned casually that the two men "showed no signs of having suffered from the exposure. [They] seemed to belong to a class which is used to hardship."

Flavio Canale's wife would have disagreed. Canale was the mate on scow 5. When he was finally reunited with his family, he caught his wife in his arms, and both fell to the floor weeping. He embraced each of his three children in turn, and then each of the neighbors who had crowded into the family's tiny one-room apartment on Franklin Street in lower Manhattan. "A bottle of whiskey remained undisturbed until Flavio seized it, and then he cried for beer," said *The Evening Sun*. "His face was badly swollen and his eyes were red and bloodshot. His ears were blistered and raw from frostbite. His hands were powerless and swollen. He moved with difficulty."[22]

Canale had only been employed on the scows for two weeks. He said he would not be going back.

Part Four
SENDING IT UP

11. You Are a San Man

The single hardest part of the job is not the trash—its weight, its smell, its relentlessness, its perils. The hardest part is not working in miserable weather, or rarely getting two days off in a row, or bouncing around the clock (sometimes for years), or driving relays forever, or working nights, or being sneered at by the public you serve. The hardest part of the job isn't even the occasionally senseless fulminations of departmental bureaucracy, which can make you nuts.

The hardest part of the job is much more straightforward.

The hardest part of the job is getting up.

Maybe it's because the day starts so early and demands such brute labor. Maybe it's because the human animal isn't meant to get up every morning in the middle of the night. Maybe it's because the work is so often routine, even monotonous.

You'll never decide why it's so tough, but even after all these years it sucks. Your curse at the alarm clock is always real.

You find jeans, a T-shirt, your hoodie; you brush your teeth, pull a comb through your hair, leave the house, climb into your car.

On the road, you think about the only time you ever bounded out of bed to go to work, and you think about the story of Flavio

Canale. You're glad you never faced the tribulations that he and his mates endured those many years ago, but you understand the impulse to quit almost before you've really started.

It was your first day. Nervous, cocky, glad for the job, you hit the streets as if you wanted to go after all the trash in New York. Your partner, a senior guy, cautioned you to slow down a little, but you ignored him. Late in the morning, you were still feeling strong and moving fast when you gave one particularly heavy can a good tug. It sloshed. That was odd. You heard your partner yell as you turned and saw that it was full of dead pigeons floating in maggot-laced water. You let out your own yell as you tried to jump clear, but you had pulled too hard and reacted too late and gallons of reeking liquid, along with a few bloated pigeon carcasses, slopped all over you.

You danced away from the mess and tried to hold your breath, but you also started to retch. The smell—sharp, sweet, cloying—was worse than anything you'd ever encountered, and you were saturated with it. Your partner tried to be sympathetic and suggested that you pull off your T-shirt and wear his sweatshirt, but that didn't help with your sopping pants, and besides, he had trouble talking at first while he was doubled over laughing. He warned you that nothing would get out that stench. Your clothes, your gloves, your boots—all were ruined. After a few minutes gagging with you next to him in the truck, he started to say that he couldn't bear your fragrant self the whole day, but then he laughed again so hard that tears ran down his cheeks. Finally he banished you to the running board and wouldn't let you back in even when it started raining.[1]

That evening, after you'd thrown out your entire uniform (so new that the T-shirt sleeves were still creased) and borrowed temporary replacement pieces from your coworkers, and after you'd taken a shower almost hotter than you could bear at the garage and another at home for so long that the hot water ran out, you tried to lie down on your bed and discovered that you couldn't. The horrific smell lingered in your nostrils, which was bad enough—you thought about trimming all your nose hair in case that's where its molecu-

lar remnants were lodged—but now you discovered that you couldn't
lie flat. Your back muscles seemed deformed. Your spinal column,
normal that morning, felt torqued. Aches that you thought the hot
shower might ease were only beginning to assert themselves. You
rolled over on your stomach but still couldn't lie flat. You tried a
position on your side; that didn't work, either.

You said out loud to the empty room, I can't do this. I don't have
what it takes. I'm going to fail as a fucking garbageman, for chris-
sake. Your voice was thick with despair. You were glad no one could
hear you.

You were going to get up and tell your wife—right after you took
a deep breath (even that hurt), composed yourself a little. You
needed to close your eyes for just a moment, then you'd go to the
next room, face her, blurt it out. You were not going back to that
fucked-up job.

But you fell asleep—your wife told you later that you slept so
heavily you didn't move all night—and the morning came too hard
and fast for you to remember that you couldn't cut it. You stumbled
to work, where you were called Birdman for a long time.

Over the next weeks and months you learned a few necessary
tricks, like lifting with your legs instead of with your back (you'd
have sworn you already knew how to do that), how to wait for your
partner instead of being macho with a heavy load, how to pace yourself across the route and across the day. You developed a healthy
distrust of every bag, pail, and can left out for collection. You still
declared at least once a week that you were going to quit, but no one
took you seriously. The senior guys just smiled and said sure you
were going to quit, just as they'd been going to quit every day for
years. They told you to hang on awhile longer; they swore it would
get better. You told them their brains were addled from inhaling
diesel fumes for too many years.

But once you were through that first year, you thought you
might be able to stick it out for a second year, and a third, until five
had passed without your noticing. By then your back had returned

to something like normal, you'd found real friends, and you never
again encountered Dead Pigeon Soup.

You pull into the district, back your car into an empty space, and
step into the cool darkness. You notice that one of your fellow san
men has added whitewall tires and spinner hubcaps to his SUV.
Your own car is a recent model. You've been on the job long enough
to earn top pay, and you always make the truck, so your paychecks
have room for occasional extras.

You couldn't quite believe it when you first learned that the city
would pay you extra for doing your job, part of an agreement ham-
mered out in the first half of the 1980s when the three-man crew
became a two-man crew. Savings to the city were significant, and
the incentive to the union was the agreement to pass some of the
productivity gains back to the workers who helped bring it about.
The reasoning behind it was sound, but it still came as a surprise
that you could sometimes earn extra money on top of your regular
salary. You calculate for the umpteenth time that this year, with
your regular pay, truck money, the night diff you got when your
section was split last winter, and then the snow overtime, you'll
probably pull down somewhere around $80K, maybe close to $90K.
It's not an unusual year's pay for a senior man; most of the guys who
came on about the same time you did earn in the same range.

Most people believe this is exorbitant compensation for a mere
garbageman, as the public still calls you. You've often thought that
the city should start a "Sanitation Worker for a Day" program, in
which every New Yorker is required to spend one day accompanying his or her local san men, riding the routes, negotiating the traffic, hefting the trash. You're pretty sure that if the average citizen
had a clue what the job takes, no one would begrudge you or your
coworkers a nickel. Your buddies assure you that the public will
never be happy paying decent salaries to those who lug away its
trash. And besides, they reason, your "San Man for a Day" dream

will never materialize, because can you imagine the liability waivers the city would have to come up with?

You're still thinking it would be an idea worth trying when you walk into the lunchroom, where the usual posse is around the table. You've brought doughnuts and coffees for whoever wants them, and the guys hassle you good-naturedly—"Why the sudden generosity, you tightfisted bastard?" and "Hope this didn't break you!" and then one that makes you smile: "What's wrong with you? I take mine with milk! These are all black!"

Once, years before, you were working as the garage clerk and had an RO super.* Having an RO was usually like having a substitute teacher in grade school. It almost always meant a long, difficult day. But this one knew the job and seemed like a good guy, so when you went to the back to fix yourself a cup of coffee, you asked if you could get one for him. Sure, he said; thanks. You asked him how he wanted it; he grinned, looked at you kind of sideways, and said, "Just like me."

You were taken aback. The RO was black. Did he want his coffee black? Or—he wasn't dark-skinned, but you couldn't call him light-skinned, either; he was of medium build; he wasn't a pushover, but he wasn't a hard-on. So did he want his coffee . . . dark? light? large? small? sweet? some combination thereof? You were too flustered to just ask, so you brought him three, each different. He asked why. When you explained, fumbling for words and feeling like an idiot, he laughed pretty hard. He'd meant regular, he told you.[2]

You're wondering if that super is still around or if he's retired when you step into the locker room and are immediately distracted by Sanitation Worker Cogliandro, who is leaning over Sanitation Worker McPhee and shouting, "You cocksucking motherfucker, don't you *ever* do that again!"†

"Go fuck yourself" comes McPhee's quiet reply.

---

*Rotating officer; someone who fills in for another supervisor or superintendent.
†These names are pseudonyms.

They are resuming an argument started the day before. Though both Cogliandro and McPhee have twenty-two years on the job, their work styles are completely different. They aren't exactly enemies—or they weren't before yesterday—but they've never been friends. Cogliandro, a large white guy with thick hair and a big mouth, is a master of walking backwards, while McPhee, a small and muscular African American, always runs it up.

When a slow man and a fast man work together, the slower one sets the pace unless the faster worker is willing to carry them both, but that choice means that the faster worker picks up far more than his share of the day's weight. Usually, san men like Cogliandro and McPhee never worked together, because the super's clerk and the garage foreman, who make assignments for upcoming shifts, knew their different styles and didn't pair them up. When an out-of-town clerk put them together on the board for yesterday and then the super refused to reassign them, the rest of the garage immediately laid bets on how soon the fight would start.

Everyone knows that Cogliandro, who threatens to deck people at the slightest provocation, won't actually throw a punch. McPhee is more even tempered; indeed, he's famously slow to anger. Yesterday he had displayed not the slightest bad temper. Instead, after watching Cogliandro drag his ass and generally do his best to ruin the day, McPhee made what everyone agreed was a creative decision. He got in the truck and drove off. Alone. Cogliandro had to walk fifty blocks back to the garage, fuming more with each step. The ribbing that had greeted him on his sweaty return only made him madder. McPhee was gone already, so Cogliandro had to wait until this morning to vent his fury, and his voice caroms off the locker room walls.

He reminds you of an old-timer you met while you were still on probation. You'd been sent out of town, to a district on the far side of Staten Island, and were partnered with a senior guy who made a show of walking backwards. At first you thought he was just a pain in the ass, but then you realized that he was a scumbag.

It was your first time on house-to-house. Before that day, you'd only worked neighborhoods in Manhattan and the Bronx with such huge piles of bags that trucks were loaded out after finishing routes of no more than eight or ten lines. Here in the suburbs, a single route was pages long and every street looked like every other street. One place gave you a particularly bad moment. You backed the truck up a short dead end and worked both sides down to the corner, then drove a block and backed up another dead end identical to the first, worked your way to the corner collecting what looked like the same trash you'd just picked up on the previous street, then drove a block and backed up what you swore was the exact same dead end. You were starting to wonder if you'd fallen into a space-time warp and were doomed to work the same little street, with the same piles of the same garbage in front of the same houses, for ever and ever. It was so disconcerting that you started to ask your partner about it, but he didn't give a shit about anything you had to say.

On a street of ritzy homes, you watched in the side-view mirrors while he leisurely sifted a plastic garbage pail for mongo. He didn't keep much—he told you he didn't even like mongo—but he was glad that it slowed him down. Then you saw him open the mailbox at the curb and look inside. At the next house he did it again. You realized with a start that he was investigating every mailbox on the street.

You jumped out of the truck. "What are you doing?"

He shrugged. "They leave me envelopes."

"What?"

"You know. They leave me . . . envelopes."

During training, the speaker from the inspector general's office had been booed out of the room, but not before you and all the hundred-some other new hires had understood his very clear and very simple point. If any sanitation worker takes any form of tip, bribe, graft, or other compensation while on the job—even a cup of coffee from the deli guy or a bottle of water from a pretty girl—that sanitation worker can lose his job. Furthermore, if a sanitation worker is getting a payoff of any kind and his partner is *not* getting any payoff but knows about the payoff to the first guy, the second guy must speak up or be considered equally guilty. If he's a probationer and is discovered to have kept knowledge of such illegality to himself, he'll be fired. Guaranteed.

"You saying we have to rat out our partners?" The worker asking the question from the back of the classroom sounded incredulous.

"You must abide by the law, your partner must abide by the law, and if you know your partner is not abiding by the law, you must report him." The IG fellow was implacable. "If you do not report him, you will lose your job." The class hissed.

"What about the Green Wall of Silence?" someone yelled.

That day on Staten Island, working the house-to-house route from hell, you saw your partner for a day grub for a tip, thought about how long you'd been chasing trash that could've been collected in a couple of hours, and remembered another lesson from training: don't assume that senior guys will watch out for new guys.

"You asshole," you said evenly. "You're driving."

He just laughed at you as he climbed into the truck. For the rest of the route, you cursed him silently while you ran it up.

Cogliandro has stopped shouting, and you turn your attention to getting dressed. Time to transform from a regular schmoe into a sanitation soldier.

The DSNY is proud to call itself a quasi-military organization (you especially like it when someone says it's "paramilitary"; you picture yourself and your buddies wearing face paint and urban camo gear as you stalk bags of garbage with night-vision goggles or leap from helicopters, wielding your hand brooms like rifles). You're certain that Sanitation is the unlikeliest "army" ever assembled, and in what military do the privates have a strong union? But when san workers wear their button-down shirts and new jackets for a parade cleanup or—God forbid—a Department funeral, they look sharp. So do the officers in their Class A dress uniforms, though more than a few, displaying the gut morph that seems their fate after they're promoted off the street, severely test the limits of their jacket buttons.

You consider your fingernails and glance at your hair in the mirror inside your locker door. It still rankles you that the Department now regulates these details, a rule supposedly inspired after the commissioner pulled up behind a san man who had pierced ears, nostrils, lips, and eyebrows (with each telling of the story, the number and location of the piercings grow). His entire face and shaved head were inked with tattoos (or maybe not; in early versions, he only had a single tattoo on his forearm). The man's appearance, whether the exaggerated version or the real one, was said to have so angered Doherty that shortly thereafter, in the autumn of 2002, a new set of regulations called the Personal Appearance Code showed up in every Sanitation facility citywide. It spelled out, in embarrassing detail, specifics like fingernail length, limits on earring choices, and permissible hairstyles.

The rank and file went nuts. Suddenly san men who'd had long hair since they'd been hired years before were told to cut it, make it disappear under a hat, or take a rocket. Older guys with DAs were personally affronted. Wannabe rednecks with mullets were up in arms. Guys with 'locks they'd been growing for decades tried to bring charges of religious discrimination. Women had to leave their bling at home.

The whole thing would have been amusing if it weren't so irritating. It's not as if New Yorkers are going to run out of their homes and stop you from picking up their garbage because your hat's on crooked. And who sees your fingernails? You're wearing gloves from the moment you step out of the truck; heck, plenty of guys wear them while driving (the steering wheel is pretty grimy). After your boots, gloves are your most important gear.

It took you a while to figure out the right combination. First you wore latex ones like from a hospital, over which you pulled fifty-cents-a-pair knit cotton numbers with blue or red rubber-painted palms. But your hands sweat too much in the latex, and the cotton didn't give enough protection and were useless in the rain. One wet morning you put on a pair of those bright orange rubber gloves that so many fellows liked in wet or cold weather. They must've been made for some Gigantor because even size small was too big; they kept your hands warm and dry, but they made it difficult to get a firm grasp on the ear of a bag. The last time you wore them was the day you gave yourself an extravagant black eye. It was an on-the-job injury of the most embarrassing sort (and it was another occasion, like with the maggot juice, when your partner laughed so hard that you thought he might wet himself), and it earned you your new nickname: Rocky.

12. Road Worthy

Sanitation workers must hold a Class B commercial driver license, or CDL. These allow us to drive single vehicles (as opposed to combination vehicles such as tractor trailers) that weigh more than twenty-six thousand pounds gross. The license must have no L or L2 restrictions (meaning we must know how to work air brakes) and no K restrictions (so we can drive out of state), and it has to include an N endorsement so that we may drive tankers, or trucks that carry liquid (collection trucks qualify as tankers in some states).

Regardless of all these requirements, we had to be capable of piloting large, loud, heavy trucks through city traffic, down narrow streets, on highways, through toll plazas, over bridges. For most of us, this meant we'd need driving lessons, which the Department provided (for a fee taken from our first several paychecks). But before the driving lessons, we needed our CDL permits, and to get those, we had to pass three written tests. That meant studying the *New York State Commercial Driver's Manual*, a task I put off for weeks. When I was offered a spot in a spring CDL class with the first batch of new hires, I had to defer to the next round because I hadn't yet cracked the book.

When it finally lay open in front of me, my ignorance felt bound-less. I stared at a list of suspension-system parts, circling terms I didn't know: gearbox, torque rods, cell caps. I was supposed to be able to look at various mechanisms under a truck—there was an incomprehensible line drawing—and know if a leaf spring or U-bolt was cracked. The exhaust system might have missing vertical stacks or mounting brackets; this would be bad.

The manual did have some straightforward text. Before driving a truck, I was supposed to do what's called a pre-trip inspection, making sure that all parts (see the partial list above) were in good working order. A thorough inspection would require me to walk around the vehicle, which might happen while I was parked on a street with oncoming traffic. The text was stern: "Pay attention so you don't get run over." I underlined this.

There was also reassuring advice written fortune-cookie style, like "If you are blocked on both sides, a move to the right may be best" and "Always be prepared to take action based on your plans." Said action was meant to be in response to hazards, of which there are many. The manual informed me that children were dangerous (I *knew* it!) as were talkers (talkers?) and workers (all of them?). Ice cream trucks had their own listing, with the caution that "someone selling ice cream is a hazard clue" (maybe Mister Softee, finally driven mad by the incessant jingle, would start creaming cars with geysers of vanilla/chocolate twist). Shoppers were perils (no sur-prise). Confused drivers, slow drivers, fast drivers, impaired drivers, and conflicts concluded the list, conjuring images of intersec-tions gridlocked by a melee of motorists acting like a cross between Keystone Kops and Dirty Harry. Hazards, indeed. When I finally sat for the permit tests and passed them all, I was amazed.

The job was still not within reach.

Before the city of New York would let me serve the public from behind the wheel of a truck, it needed to confirm that my person did not pose any unusual risks or conditions. The time had come to face the clinic. It's on a street that used to be a small stream and then was the Bevers Gracht, one of those modest canals filled in when the good people of colonial New-York wouldn't quit ruining it with offal and excrement. Today it's a short, single-lane passage through lower Manhattan, lined with multistory office towers that give it permanent shade.

In the clinic's dreary waiting area, fluorescent lights made everyone look mildly jaundiced. We were there to be probed, quite literally, and the results of the tests we were about to undergo would determine our immediate future. If anything was amiss, we'd get no further than this place. If we made it through the medical gauntlet, the city would be assured that our irritatingly individual, unpredictable, and unknown selves were of minimal menace to the public and of adequate health to do the work, and we moved a step closer to actual employment.

For the next several hours, we filled out forms, waited, breathed into a tube, peed into a cup, filled out more forms, waited. Our vision was tested. We lay flat on a table and were hooked up for an EKG. We filled out more forms. A doctor tapped my knees, asked me to squat, to reach way up, to touch my toes. We were sent elsewhere for yet more tests, more forms. Some of us schlepped to Brooklyn so that a psychiatrist could verify our mental stability, necessary for those on any kind of antidepressant; this group included many veterans. We traipsed uptown to have our blood drawn, then to the East Side for a hearing test. Still more forms, then X-rays at yet another doctor's office, where a nurse saw me waiting with other DSNY job candidates and told me gently that patients needing mammograms should be in the seats over there, in that quieter corner. She was perplexed when I reassured her that I was in the right place.

I was eventually given clearance, which meant I could advance to the next rounds of paperwork. These were scheduled across several sessions at the Department's personnel offices in 346 Broadway.[1] The elegant lines of the McKim, Mead & White building were still evident despite the construction shed that has wrapped the lower floors for years. Metal detectors dissecting the lobby couldn't obscure the sweeping stairs or cathedral-like ceilings, but when I stopped to admire the marble detailing, security guards barked at me to keep moving.

We waited for instructions on the tenth floor in a small room with metal folding chairs under the ubiquitous fluorescent lights. A thirties-ish man with sallow skin and greasy hair said loudly to no one in particular that no woman could last on this job. "Sure, they get hired," he declared, "but they can't hack it. None of 'em lasts." I was sitting near him, the only female in the room, unsure why he was mouthing off. "The women who've been on since 1986 might disagree," I said quietly. He didn't reply.

We were soon distracted by the day's chores, which involved forms of proof. Our utility bills, passports, Social Security cards, most recent diplomas, were photocopied, verified, and the copies tucked in our files while we pushed through more paperwork. "Only use ballpoint pens," an elegantly dressed staffer told us about one set, "and press hard. These forms are carbonated."

When we lined up in the hallway to be fingerprinted, a different woman held our hands and pressed each digit onto an ink pad and then onto the little squares of—what else?—a form, for which privilege we had paid a hundred dollars (money order only, please). Everything about Fingerprint Woman was short—her hair, her stature, her temper. I empathized—if even two thousand or so job applicants got this far, she had to manipulate twenty thousand fingers—but I jumped when she yelled at me to relax my hand. She pulled it, yelled at me again, gave another tug, and finally turned, purple with frustration. "What is *wrong* with you people?" she shouted in my face. "RELAX YOUR HAND!"

After that day we went back several more times to face yet more thickets of paperwork. I wondered if maybe Vogons had taken over New York. They wouldn't save their own grandmothers "without orders signed in triplicate, sent in, sent back, queried, lost, found, subjected to public inquiry, lost again, and finally buried in soft peat for three months and recycled as firelighters." According to *The Hitchhiker's Guide to the Galaxy*, Vogons are among the most intimidating monsters in the universe.[2]

But just when I assumed my quest had fizzled to an end in some obscure file drawer, the notice arrived telling me to report for driving lessons. Big horizons, big skies, and big engines beckoned.

"Good morning," yelled a loose-limbed man in a sanitation worker's uniform. Mo Ragusa could be a tall Mickey Rooney. He was standing before us in a long cinder-block classroom, its yellow walls made yellower by the usual wash of fluorescents. When we muttered an anemic reply, he looked at us with contempt.

It was just past 6:00 on a soft Monday in early summer. Our class of seventy-seven men and two women sat alphabetically in rows of nine tables, simultaneously sleepy and tense. If we had been in a room with windows, we might have felt the gentle breeze blowing off Jamaica Bay. When we went outside, we could look across the water to Kennedy Airport, where planes rose and descended all day.

Floyd Bennett Field was an airport itself once.[3] Though the concrete runways are cracked and in some places gone to grass, the empty straightaways and wide practice areas are excellent venues for Sanitation students attempting to master various pieces of heavy equipment. Before it was an airport, the land had been part of Barren Island, home to the world's largest concentration of rendering plants, where the carcasses of horses and cattle were processed into various commodities. It seemed fitting that the DSNY training facility stood where laborers in another era had also worked with city waste.

"Let's try that again," Mo said, then bellowed another, heartier "Good morning!" We shouted back at him, and he smiled. "You're nervous?" he asked rhetorically. "Good! I'm nervous, too. I've never seen so many ugly people in one room." We laughed weakly.

One of a team of Department personnel assigned to Safety and

Training, Mo taught both Class B and Class A commercial driver license courses, wrecker classes (wreckers are tow trucks, and learning to operate them includes tipping over and then righting a collection truck), snow school, and mechanical brooms. Everyone who teaches at Safety and Training is handpicked; before anyone is considered for an instructor slot, it must be understood that he or she brings to the work a certain patience and clarity of intention.

Because Mo was an instructor, therefore, I assumed he was good at his job, but that didn't give the whole picture, which was this: Mo Ragusa was one of the two or three best teachers I'd ever seen in front of a class, in any subject, in any context. His energy was unflagging. He listened closely, all the time. Mo exhorted, berated, admonished, in timeless New Yorkese. "I'm not gonna baby none o' yuz," he warned. "If you think you're gonna put *your* bags on *my* back, fuhgeddaboudit." With his mirrored sunglasses and slight swagger, he was our Patton, and within hours of meeting him, we would have followed him anywhere. We feared his gaze but sought it out. We wanted to please him. We volunteered answers to his questions, even though we knew that, at least in the beginning of the week, we would get it wrong. "That answer sucked" was his standard reply, but later, when we were on the field chocking tires or releasing our air brakes, we'd get a squeeze on the shoulder and his quiet reassurance that our mistake had taught the whole class not to ever again mess up that particular detail.

We trained on dump trucks known as cut-downs, not on collection trucks—supposedly, DMV examiners didn't tolerate driving around in collection trucks—and had only a week to learn so much. We had to know all the parts checked in a pre-trip inspection, which included lights, reflectors, brakes, and mirrors, mirrors, mirrors. "Take my mirrors away," said Mo, "I can't drive that truck." When we were actually driving, we had to learn how to move what felt like unfathomably large vehicles on crowded highways and around tight corners, but each separate skill was broken down into small, careful steps. When you back up, we were told, just feather the wheel. "Trust your hands," Mo told us, "just a little push-pull. No pizza making." On the highway, *here* is where you place the road lines in relation to your windshield, and you've done it right if you see them appearing behind you just outside your rear left tires. Occasionally mangled words—"nomenclature" became something like "normal culture"—didn't obscure the precision of the lessons.

I was feeling sorry for myself because I lacked the intuitive knowledge of engines and motors that I assumed inherent to males (and never mind that I understood how ridiculous was my thinking) when I realized that I was surrounded by young men and women who grew up in New York City. When would they have needed to drive? While I was nervous to command a truck, the act of driving wasn't new to me, but many of my younger colleagues, even those in their twenties, got their regular driver's licenses only a week or so before getting their CDL permits. Driving *anything* was entirely new to them. My jitters were nothing compared to theirs.

A week or so after CDL training finished, I met seven of my classmates back at Floyd Bennett. We piled into a DSNY van and two of our instructors drove us to the Bronx for our road tests. Chiefs at Safety and Training boast that Sanitation's CDL success rate surpasses that of any private company. It's so good that employees of other city agencies who need CDL training come to Sanitation for lessons. But bragging rights fluctuated with each set of road tests. If we passed, our instructors would be pleased, and we would have overcome the last obstacle between us and the job. If any of us failed, all the instructors would catch hell, and that potential new hire would be cast from the path just at the moment when the prize was closest. The Department taught us to drive a truck and delivered us to the road test, but anyone who failed that test was on his own. He was welcome to take more classes with a private company and attempt the test another day, and if he passed then, the chance at the job was revived, but he had to make his own arrangements for the extra training and second test.

We arrived in the Bronx and waited all morning as a stern DMV examiner called each of us to join him in a Sanitation cut-down. One by one we disappeared around the corner, our faces tight. One by one we reappeared a little later, looking visibly more relaxed because we'd passed. By the early afternoon almost all of us had finished, and we were beginning to feel jubilant when we noticed a commotion across the street. A young woman stood on the sidewalk sobbing while a young man paced back and forth near her and two DMV examiners stood talking in quiet tones a little ways off.

One of our instructors stepped away for a few moments, then came back with the story. The young man had taken Sanitation's CDL classes but had failed his road test. He took more lessons from a private company, and had returned today for his second road test, but had failed again. No doubt this was discouraging, but it didn't have to qualify as a disaster—until he had offered the DMV examiner a crisp hundred-dollar bill to fudge the results. It was a big mistake. He lost the chance at his CDL, but worse, he would now have his regular license revoked and face criminal charges.

The weeping woman was the young man's new wife. The man himself looked very angry. I wondered what circumstances had compelled him to make such a foolish choice, but I knew that when my classmates and I passed the road test and the doors to Sanitation finally swung open for us, we were stepping into a situation available to fewer and fewer workers in New York or anywhere else in the United States. Our salaries, though meager at the outset, would be relatively secure. We'd have benefits, a pension, and a union with real muscle. The middle-class life that we'd been taught all our lives was supposed to be our objective was suddenly a possibility.

I would never know why the young man thought a bribe was a good idea, but I understood why his wife was crying.

This cover of an 1891 issue of *Harper's Weekly* sums up sentiment toward the city's Department of Street Cleaning in that era. (Courtesy of HarpWeek)

A sweeper from the Department of Street Cleaning in the late 1890s. The white uniform was meant to indicate public health and hygiene. The helmet, which mirrored the style used by police in that era, signaled authority. The workers were nicknamed "White Wings." (Courtesy of the Department of Sanitation, City of New York)

Colonel George E. Waring, Jr., Commissioner of New York City's Department of Street Cleaning from 1895 to 1898

NEW YORK CITY'S STREET-CLEANING DEPARTMENT ON PARADE.—[See Page 559.]
1. Going through Thirty-fourth Street.   2. Passing the Metropolitan Club, Fifth Avenue.   3. Colonel Waring.   4. Ash-Carts that competed for the Prize.
5. Platform Trucks to show the Processes of Street-Cleaning.

The inaugural White Wings parade in 1896 traveled down Fifth Avenue from Central Park to Madison Square. (Courtesy of HarpWeek)

Street Cleaning Commissioner George Waring made a dramatic difference in a short time. The photographs on the left were taken in 1893; those on the right were taken two years later in the same locations, just six months after Waring took office. (Courtesy of HarpWeek)

This 1896 patent for a mechanical street sweeper hints at contemporary mechanical broom design.

Tandem plowing, back in the day
(Courtesy of the DSNY)

Department of Street Cleaning White Wings in the 1920s. The foreman on the right is holding a time book. Similar ledgers were used to track time and to calculate payroll until the end of the first decade of the twenty-first century.
(Courtesy of the DSNY)

A DSC White Wing sweeping in city traffic, 1920s (Courtesy of the DSNY)

Sweep magazine, a DSNY quarterly published between the 1950s and early 1970s (Courtesy of the DSNY)

Working a basket route. Notice the step on the truck. These were removed in the mid-2000s. (Photograph by Michael Anton, courtesy of the DSNY)

Working a basket route in Brooklyn (Photograph by Michael Anton, courtesy of the DSNY)

Bag stops like this one are called flats. (Photograph by Michael Anton, courtesy of the DSNY)

House-to-house collection (Photograph by Michael Anton, courtesy of the DSNY)

Loading out with recycling in Harlem (Photograph by Michael Anton, courtesy of the DSNY)

Christmas trees are collected by the DSNY and mulched by the Department of Parks and Recreation. (Photograph by Michael Anton, courtesy of the DSNY)

A cavalry of plows heading into the Christmas Blizzard of 2010 (Photograph by Michael Anton, courtesy of the DSNY)

Plows passing through Brooklyn's Grand Army Plaza, December 2010 (Photograph by Michael Anton, courtesy of the DSNY)

Tandem plowing, December 2010 (Photograph by Michael Anton, courtesy of the DSNY)

Basket routes are suspended during heavy snowstorms, but the public doesn't stop generating litter. (Photograph by Robin Nagle)

The Manhattan 8 garage is inside a building originally built as an incinerator. (Photograph by Robin Nagle)

Accidents involving these trucks killed their drivers. According to figures released by the Bureau of Labor Statistics in 2012, sanitation work is the fourth most dangerous job category in the nation. (Photograph by Robin Nagle)

Frank Justich was killed on the job in January 2010. The Queens West 1 garage was named in his honor a few months later. (Photograph by Robin Nagle)

Ticker tape parade cleanup (Photograph by Robin Nagle)

Ticker tape parade cleanup sometimes involves equipment designed for snow. (Photograph by Robin Nagle)

After the parade (Photograph by Michael Anton, courtesy of the DSNY)

13. Bumper Cars

When I was finally called to start the job two months later, I joined a class of 120 other new hires for three weeks of training back at Floyd Bennett Field. Early on our first day, Mo poked his head into the classroom, where he was greeted with a burst of spontaneous applause and chants of his name. We sought him out at break, at lunch, asked his advice about which garage we should try to land in, which assignment we should aim for, which chief we should propitiate with what kind of plea. Mo was a natural and charismatic leader. And when he had first come on the job, he had been assigned to the Department's mechanical sweepers. In other words, Mo was a broom man.

I was astonished to learn this. According to those who prefer to work behind the truck, broom men are not very smart. Who would take a job as arduous and thankless as that of sanitation worker and not try to earn truck money? And how can broom men (or broom women) really know the job? The guts of the job are on the street. Broom men only ride the street; they don't *work* it.

Broomies smile at these charges. They point out that it's called the Bureau of *Cleaning* and Collection—notice which comes first?

They claim that their truck-working cousins are the ones who don't really know the job and aren't quite intelligent. You drive a truck, they point out, but you *operate* a broom. Which is more difficult?

Truck men say that broom work is for sissies because more women have broom routes than truck routes. Real men don't go for brooms. Refuting this assertion are the many manly men who are happy to be broom qualified.

Truck men say that more chiefs come from brooms, which proves (as if more proof were needed) that chiefs don't know jack shit about the job. Quite the opposite, counter broomies: the greater number of broom alumni in chiefly ranks merely proves the original assertion that broomies are smarter.

I was thinking about the trucks and thinking about the challenge of lifting my share of ten or thirteen or eighteen tons of trash (depending on the target weight of the garage and on the conditions of the moment). I'm fit, but I had few illusions about the strength and stamina required to load out a truck. I secretly wanted a broom assignment. I mostly knew people who worked the truck, however, so believed that no self-respecting sanitation worker would request a broom.

But *Mo* was a broom man. That changed everything.

An effective mechanical sweeper has been something of a holy grail for municipal sanitation efforts. Patents dating back to the nineteenth century show elaborate contraptions that look preposterous to a modern eye but that offered creative and potentially useful solutions to the intractable problem of street dirt. In that era, such inventions were also seen as portents of unemployment. When the draft riots erupted in New York in the summer of 1863, the four days of lynching, murdering, and destruction were motivated by several factors, including an effort by the city to replace men on hand brooms with machine sweepers. Today workers on hand brooms still have a place in the DSNY's mission, and certainly some tasks can't be accomplished with any other tool, but mechanical brooms are the go-to answer for a host of needs.

Access to the cab is up three ladderlike steps built into the front bumper. The single door opens from front to back on what would be the passenger side. Riding in a broom feels like being in a tall Volkswagen Beetle, the old model, with the intimate black-upholstered interior, similar chugging hum to the motor, and sometimes lurching starts and stops. The governor limits maximum velocity to thirty-five miles per hour, but even at such breakneck speed a broom can do a neat little shimmy of a fishtail when stopped too suddenly on a wet street.

New York's machines, manufactured by Johnston Sweepers, use a trio of brush mechanisms. Those on port and starboard, called gutter brooms, are bristle-laden disks the size of large pizza pans and set at an angle. They swing out to sweep, either singly or in pairs, and when they're not in use, they hunch up under the chassis like shoulders stuck in a shrug. They spin with various amounts of pressure at various RPMs, depending on conditions and on the operator's expertise, and are responsible for moving debris from the vehicle's edges to its underbelly.

Once there, flotsam is met by the pickup broom, a kind of oversized, coarsely textured lint roller. Trash from the gutter brooms is carried by the pickup broom onto moving steps, called flights, that hang at an angle between a pair of cambered conveyor belts. The flights deliver debris to the hopper, which sits directly behind the cab and holds about a ton of litter. The whole process is aided by nozzles that spray water slightly ahead of the front bumper, dampening dust and litter and thus, ideally, making the sweep more effective.

The gutter broom's bristles are secured in four pie-shaped segments (and, in fact, bristles aren't called bristles, they're called segments). The actual bristles themselves wear at different rates, depending on the pressure and angle at which they're used and the condition of the streets they clean. Dividing them into interchangeable quarters lets mechanics replace only what's worn instead of having to pitch the whole part. When gutter brooms are balanced right, a broom idling at a stoplight will leave marks on the asphalt that look as if someone has drawn a pair of mirror-image crescent moons, each about the width of a dollar bill.

Brooms are on the city's streets every day, but they play an especially vital role in cleaning up after big celebrations like the New Year's Eve ball drop at Times Square. The evening's many corporate sponsors want to leave pieces of themselves in the hands and minds of revelers, who are strategically corralled during the hours before midnight. The partygoers, for their part, are happy to leave those pieces on the street after the ball drops.

In the olden days, streamers and noisemakers and similar trinkets were sold by vendors on street corners around the city. Now, in carefully branded shapes and colors, such geegaws are handed out by the hundreds of thousands to the trapped multitudes. Red-jumpsuit-clad Times Square Business Improvement District workers give away hats, boas, pom-poms, balloons, eyeglasses ("with special optical effects for viewing the lights of Times Square"), each bearing the name of a different corporate sponsor. Other sponsors shower the assembled with regular releases of confetti; sometimes that includes small metallic red cards printed with words of the season (Hope! Peace! Joy!).

One recent New Year's Eve relied on a two-part cleanup campaign, a strategy often used after large public events. A contingent from the south moved toward Times Square about an hour after midnight in a loose caravan of mechanical brooms, collection trucks, officers' cars, and a white bus that carried everyone assigned to hand brooms and backpack blowers. Another team with the same configuration headed down from the north.

On Seventh Avenue just below Times Square, the corners held thick knots of people who watched us languidly, as if from a distance. They'd had the streets to themselves for several hours and were in no hurry to relinquish control. We rolled forward, over bags, paper cups, playing cards, bottles. The bottles concerned me.

When they are sent spinning by the gutter brooms but not caught by the pickup broom, they can fly back out from under the vehicle and launch toward the curb at considerable speed. A long strip called a dirt shoe drags parallel to the broom body and acts as a fence to contain such potential projectiles, but not all bottles obey. As we came close to the most crowded corners and our noise became harder to ignore, people turned their faces toward us again, but they looked slightly dreamy, unconcerned. Perhaps if they did get knocked by flying bottles, they'd be too relaxed to notice.

Times Square, in a fine example of New York braggadocio, has been nicknamed the Crossroads of the World. The actual crossroads are the intersection of Broadway and Seventh Avenue. The former, which runs the length of Manhattan from northwest to southeast, slices Seventh at Forty-Fourth Street. The result is a pair of triangles called the bow tie, defined by Forty-First Street on the south and Forty-Eighth Street on the north. This is the heart of the New Year's Eve action and where we'd spent most of our night.

The bow tie was bathed in flat white light from the dozens of fantastical billboards that adorn this patch of the city and that made the streets as bright as day. The normal chaos of neon competed with light packs mounted on tall portable poles glaring down onto makeshift stages that roadies clamored to strike. At Forty-Fourth Street and Broadway, news flowed a word at a time across the golden-orange Reuters zipper, with sports scores running in green on the zipper below. The air smelled of cigars.

Crumpled streamers, paper bags, plastic bags, plastic bottles, glass bottles, the shiny red cards with the seasonal words, all united in drifts of confetti and buried the street ankle-deep. Bursts of wind sent errant swirls of more confetti off nearby rooftops and windowsills, while whooshes of air from subway grates created momentary confetti tornadoes on the ground. A clutch of black and white balloons, late for the party, rose slowly from an office building. Police officers stood in clusters near the curbs. The background tension at occasions like the Times Square ball drop is always palpable, but now that it was just cleanup, the cops were more relaxed. One stood off by himself to practice his nightstick swing unobserved.

It was easy to spot the new broom operators. Their gutter brooms, which were soon festooned with color, rode the sidewalk, which bends the segments out like an old toothbrush. They drove too fast, tried to sweep up too much at once, and soon the solid *lub-dub* of their engines changed to less steady rhythms as their flights tangled with streamers and plastic bags. They opened their hoppers, slashed at the jams, pulled out trailing clumps of dead balloons and mangled plastic novelties. Seasoned operators moved more slowly and made modest swipes, peeling back the litter a little at a time. Their brooms eventually jammed, too—the quantity of debris made it inevitable—but not so fast and not so thoroughly.

A drizzly rain had made the work a little easier, but when it became a downpour at about 3:30 in the morning, it plastered the rubbish to the sidewalks. Workers on hand brooms mostly just scraped across it; those wearing backpack blowers fared better. Blowers are awkward machines with pull-cord starters, like lawn mowers, that belch gasoline fumes and make tremendous noise. They were soon the only tool that still moved the mess from sidewalk to street.

There, however, progress stopped. The mechanical brooms were churning the wet litter into a thick soup dyed pink by the metallic red cards that had long since disintegrated into the mash. It looked like oatmeal made with Pepto-Bismol. Mechanical brooms don't do oatmeal. Workers with hand tools moved it into the gutters, but then the brooms trundled past and sprayed it back onto the sidewalks. The hand sweepers and blowers pushed it into the gutters once more; the brooms splattered it back. All over Times Square, mechanical brooms and sanitation workers were having the same exchanges of pink spray. Our boots and pant legs and jacket hems started to look like Jackson Pollock had been experimenting with them as canvases. The equipment wasn't up to the conditions, but short of a large sump pump I'm not sure what would have worked.

The next day, chiefs in charge of the effort faced harsh criticism from higher-ups because the side streets weren't completely clean by the end of the night and because the shift that started at 7:00 on New Year's morning had to finish up the bow tie. But I had watched all of us on the night crew give our best. If the bosses wanted to get upset, I thought, they should be angry because of the rain, or because the stages and then the tractor trailers brought in to move them had kept us away from long stretches of curb until late in the shift, or because there was more confetti and litter than anyone anticipated, or because the rain had melted all that into glop, or because the glop was like glue. Did I mention? Brooms don't do glue.

To learn the nuances of the broom and the details of their routes, new broomies train with seasoned operators. The good ones know the districts they serve like a village mayor knows his town. I trained mostly with Gil Bailey*, a quiet, elegant woman who had been on the job since 1990 and who worked out of the Bronx 6A broom depot. She didn't request it, but nearly everyone addressed her as Miss Bailey. There was something regal about her, something calm and still. And as I quickly discovered, she was an excellent teacher.

By the time I got to 6A, I understood that broomies have a much more complicated relationship with their vehicles than a regular sanitation worker has with a truck. When a san worker takes out a truck at the start of the six-to-two shift, he loads it, maybe dumps it, and then brings it back to the garage, where he fuels it and parks it. Before he actually gets it on the road, he's supposed to pre-trip it (that is, give it a once-over inspection) by checking the tires, the brakes, the mirrors, the lights and reflectors, the oil levels. If he skips that step and a problem comes up that a pre-trip would've revealed and that therefore could've been prevented, he'll take a hit. The guy on relays from a garage on the far side of Queens East to

---

*This is a pseudonym.

dumps in New Jersey—a journey so long that only two round-trips fit in an eight-hour shift—didn't check his oils (or anything else) before he set out. His engine seized on the Jersey Turnpike in the small hours of the morning. His rescue took a long time, and the truck engine had to be rebuilt from scratch. Because he hadn't noticed that the truck was oil-less before he left the garage—something he should've checked—he was banged for destroying the equipment. He was also in trouble for not finishing his work.

When the truck is fueled and parked, the sanitation worker who drove or loaded or dumped it is done with it. It will get a PM—periodic maintenance—once every two weeks, when mechanics make sure the air brakes are in good shape, the hydraulics are functional, the grease points are lubricated, and the engine is sound, but no mechanic will touch it until it's been cleaned. That happens when a san worker assigned to the garage uses a power washer to blast the truck inside and out with a concoction of 180-degree water and soap. The power washer, a swordlike pipe with a trigger at one end and a bell-shaped opening at the other, doesn't have the force of a fire hose, but what comes out of it is more focused and a good deal hotter, a sort of watery version of a light saber. A good garage person will do a thorough job with the power washer, even climbing inside the truck body to get at the crags and hidden spaces. But the sanitation worker who drives the truck cares not a whit for the thoroughness of the power wash, and the person doing the power wash isn't concerned about how the truck drives.

A broom operator's interaction with her broom is much more involved. For starters, she can't skip the pre-trip. There are too many parts that can and often do malfunction. She must confirm the usual—that the motor oil and hoist oil tanks are full, that the hopper lifts, that the brakes grab and the brake lights light. But she must also see that the left and right gutter brooms drop, swing out, rotate, stop, swing in, retract, rise. She must make sure the pickup broom also drops, rotates, retracts. Inside the cab, she must know how to interpret and adjust an array of gauges. There are so many dials and switches on the dashboard that when I sat inside a broom for the first time, I felt as if I were in the cockpit of a small, albeit very slow, plane.

She must make sure she has a reflective triangle and flashing hazard lights on the back of the broom and a yellow strobe light on top. She must have her tools—a hand broom, a shovel, a hydrant key, and a hose are required; an experienced operator will also carry a knife and a rag. If the broom happens to have heat in the winter or air-conditioning in the summer, that's nice, but you can't down a broom for lack of either. If the broom doesn't have such amenities, the operator can open her windows while she's moving, but I know of none who'd be willing to do such a thing even when just traveling to and from the route. The dust that brooms gather complements the dust they send aloft. Even with the windows closed, the inside of the cab is always gritty.

A single broom depot serves many districts, so when she's on the road, a broomie must know many more streets than a sanitation worker assigned to a conventional garage. On any given day, the operator will be in completely different sections of the borough, and she must know all of them well because her routes are carefully timed. She has to be on the avenues when the SCR—street-cleaning regulations—have forbidden cars to park there, usually for a window of as little as half an hour, and then she must be on the side streets while those are clear. If she's late, especially on the commercial strips, she's lost the day; the cars are back on the curb, crunching debris under their tires.

When we were together, Miss Bailey tolerated me sitting next to her in the jump seat of the broom's tiny cab and patiently taught me how to get from the broom depot to the routes we were working each day. She took pride in doing her job well, especially when her broom was humming at its best, but she put the less well-kept vehicles to good pedagogical use by teaching me how to tease stuck gauges back to life and how to coax reluctant gutter brooms into positions that best suited a given block or condition. Heavy dirt that had collected against the curb after rain, for instance, didn't do well with the gutter brooms' full force. Better to use a lighter touch and make several passes. She showed me the best angle of the broom's many mirrors so that I knew my segments were on the street and not riding the curb.

She also taught me that mechanical brooms are finicky. They can't pick up anything really heavy, like bricks or stones, or bulky, like lumber or cardboard boxes. Cloth confuses both the gutter and the pickup brooms. Clothes hangers, electrical wires, hazard tape, plastic bags, dead umbrellas, and rope or thick string can disable a broom in a hurry. When the operator sees these obstacles, she's supposed to stop, get out, and hand carry them into the hopper, but plenty still find their way into the broom's guts, where they cause problems.

Sometimes it wasn't objects that troubled the broom but the broom troubling the larger world. Especially on dry days in the winter, when it's too cold to fill the water tanks, the brooms seem to disturb more dust than they collect. I was in my own broom driving behind Miss Bailey one afternoon when we traveled a street that had a berm of dirt against the shoulder. Though not a hundred yards ahead of me, she was soon completely obscured in a dense cloud of dust. I half expected that, like in a dark fairy tale, when it dissipated, both she and her broom would be gone.

When I was sweeping by myself, I most enjoyed coming into a commercial avenue clotted with litter but free of cars. If alternate side parking regulations were in effect and the curb was clear, bits of trash were like targets in a video game. I adjusted the speed and force of my gutter brooms, making sure I wasn't riding the curb or using too much pressure. If the street did have cars at the curb, I used a technique called sniping, where the broom moves around the vehicles in supple arcs to get as close to the curb as possible. It felt kind of like a waltz. Whether the block was car-less or had to be sniped, it was thoroughly satisfying to move from one end to the other and leave nary a stray napkin or paper cup behind.

Once the routes are cleaned, the broom is dumped, the 350 is signed, and it's time to wash.

When I learned that washing the broom is a mandatory part of the day's labors, I assumed it was just a token gesture meant to get salt and muck off the wheels and rotating parts, a make-work chore that would take a few minutes at the most. At Floyd Bennett Field, our instructors demonstrated the best technique for being thorough, but by then I suspected that many teachings from Floyd Bennett were meant to reflect ideals, not actual practices. On the street, when I helped fellow broom operators wash, I saw that it actually took time and required meticulous attention, but I assumed that my coworkers were being extra careful because I was tagging along. I wanted to learn the real way to wash, the secret, insiders-only knowledge that would get me back to the garage and done with my workday just a little faster.

But then I had to wash my own broom for the first time. I was following Brian,* another broomie. When we left the garage where we'd dumped our afternoon loads, he promised to show me two new things. The first, he cautioned, was against the rules, but it was useful, and if you could do it without getting caught, it saved you a headache.

He took us to a street that was a bumpy washboard of loose tar and gravel. Apparently, it had been in such condition for a while. It was lined with auto-body shops and tall, beat-up fences. When we were about halfway down the block, I heard the deep-noted drone of Brian's pickup broom and a moment later saw a fat stripe of mashed-up crud lying in the street behind him. I had only seen brooms sweep stuff up and set dust whirling; I didn't know they could excrete as well.

Later he explained that the easiest way to clean the pickup broom is to run it backward against a rough street surface. It's the same logic as scraping a lint brush against its nap. The problem was

---

*This is a pseudonym.

that it left a pile of crap in the middle of the street. We should've gone back over it and swept it up, but since it was the very stuff that had caught on the pickup broom in the first go-round, it would likely catch on the pickup broom again. The trick was to find a street that was difficult to really get clean, like a stretch with torn-up asphalt, in a neighborhood that wouldn't notice. Broom operators kept their eyes out for such blocks and used them strategically—never the same place two days in a row or even twice in a week, if possible.

After he'd used the street as a rasp, Brian rounded the corner and went to the far end of the block, where he did a U-turn and pulled to a stop in front of a hydrant, which was the second thing he was showing me this afternoon. He had brought me to one of his favorite places to wash. No one else used this spot, he said, which meant he never had to wait for his turn at the water.

Brian tipped up the body of the broom—imagine the lid of a kitchen wastebasket that opens when you step on the pedal at its base—then used his knife to clear plastic cord and lengths of un-spooled cassette tape from the flights (the steps that carry debris from the street to the broom's hopper) before he flipped a switch to set them cycling. He screwed the fire hose to the hydrant, set the hydrant key against the cap, and started working it open. After a few tugs there was a spurt, the hose swelled and tensed, and water exploded from the nozzle. It blasted with almost equal force from a large hole created by a split in the hose.

Brian explained that he'd clean his broom and then wait while I cleaned mine. I assumed that since he'd brought me to his secret hydrant, now he'd show me the shortcut real way to wash.

He started on the outside, where grit cascaded in watery sheets. Then he turned to the innards of the machine, aiming high on the wall behind the belts to dissolve an impressively thick layer of dirt. When he trained the water on the belts themselves, they gradually transformed from mucky black into an iridescent blue-green, like the scales of a fish flashing in sunlight. Gunk flew as he hit each flight with water many times while they rolled up and back down. Water pounded onto the pickup broom.

He was quick and efficient, and it still took quite a while to extract the debris caught in the flights and segments, to wash out all the dirt, to get the congealed gunk out of the many grease points. The elusive broom-cleaning technique I had been waiting to discover didn't exist. Cleaning the broom took time.

When it was my turn, we shut off the water while Brian backed up his broom and I moved mine into place and tipped up its hopper. By now the leak from the hose had created an ankle-deep pond impossible to avoid. Brian turned the hydrant key again, and the hose leaped to life, its weight and liveliness knocking me back a step. I felt its power as I aimed the spray at the flights and sent the dirt streaming. The blue-green of the belts glimmered when a weak sun glanced off them for a moment. Washing the broom was a chore, but it had unexpected pleasures.

Except that my aim wasn't quite what it should've been. I was nearly finished when I adjusted the spray to hit the top of the belt, a corner where debris tends to lodge, and instead sent a bower of water over the back of the broom's cab and into the street. I didn't see the woman who had gone around us to the street so she could skirt the impassable lake we'd created across the sidewalk. Water from the fire hose hit her directly.

She howled. I pulled back the hose, and Brian scrambled to turn off the hydrant as I ran around to the front of the broom. The girl, maybe in her early twenties, was drenched. She also seemed stunned. I apologized profusely. She looked at me, slowly shaking her dripping head. I apologized some more. I offered to get her a towel (then thought better of it, since anything I might find in the broom would be smeared with grease), to call for help, to give her my jacket. She didn't speak, just shook her head a moment longer, then said she would go into the store down the block to dry off. Though it was a cold day, she wasn't warmly dressed, and now she was wet to the skin. I felt awful.

I also felt wary. If she'd had her wits about her, she should have noted my broom number and my name embroidered on my sweatshirt. She should have asked what garage I came out of. She should have called 311, and perhaps even called the garage, the borough, and downtown. She had every right to be livid and to get me in very deep trouble.

As she opened the door to the store, I thought I saw her stagger a little—just how hard had I hit her? Brian suggested that we leave. Immediately. He had already packed up the hose. My broom wasn't perfectly clean yet, but we decided that it was clean enough. When we got back to the garage, neither of us mentioned my mishap.

14. Getting It Up

Specialized fields of knowledge are marked by phrases, abbreviations, and slang that develop over time as a way of verbally concentrating complex detail. Civilians are often surprised to learn that Sanitation is no exception. First-time visitors to a garage are likely to hear dialogue that they'll understand very little, if at all. To more fully understand the life and ways of the DSNY, it helps to be familiar with the language. Here's a quick lesson.

SANITATION WORKER: Where's the 57?

DISTRICT SUPERINTENDENT: Redlined.

SW: Already? C'mon, boss—you're not really looking to bang me, are you? Yesterday I gave you a good load, dumped it, and then went back out for a piece. You know I always get it up, I always get good weights.

DS: How long you on?

SW: Sixteen this week.

DS: Then why am I explaining this to you? You guys are walking backwards right now. I know *you* always get it up, but I

have orders. I don't wanna give you a rocket, but I gotta
cover my ass.

sw: Okay. No more full loads, no more dumping, no more
going back out. Or how about I swing a piece.*

ds: Then I'd have to do a lot more than just light you up.

sw: So can I just sign the sheet?

ds: You got your 350?

sw: I was hoping you might put me on the FEL. And you know
I'm broom qualified, right?

ds: You don't want your truck money?

sw: You know I'd make the truck if I wanted. I do FEL, I'll get
schranked.

ds: Not if you volunteer for it. Besides, I thought you'd want to
work on the arm.

sw: My ass!

The district super and the san worker are exercising their different forms of power. The super or the foreman can only redline, or
close, a sign-in sheet at the official start of a shift, and usually workers are allowed a few minutes' grace. By redlining it exactly on the
hour, the officer played strictly by the rules, but now he has made a
routine task difficult.

The san worker can't necessarily get his signature on the sheet
after it's been redlined, but he can try to convince his boss to give
him a break by reminding him of his exemplary record. The super
doesn't want to alienate one of his best workers, but he can't set a
double standard. If this one is allowed to sign in a few minutes late,
why can't everyone else? When it seems as if the super will hold
the line, the superlative worker threatens to become what officers call a slug. This could directly hurt the super, since he counts

---

*This is an anachronism. Since the Department started exporting all the city's
municipal waste, anyone even attempting to swing a piece would get in serious
trouble.

on men like this to help pick up slack for other, less dedicated individuals.

The super asks the worker about his assignment card—the 350— as a way of defusing tension, thereby proving he's tough enough to stay firm, but also that he's not unreasonable; he hasn't yet ruled out the possibility that he'll let the man sign in. At the end of the conversation the super jokes that either the worker will lose the extra pay he gets for working on the truck or he's willing to work for free, both of which are ridiculous notions.

If an officer or a chief is going to bang a worker, light him up, or give him a rocket, it means he's going to file a complaint against him. A long and detailed list of possible infractions includes signing in late (or not at all), not finishing the route, coming in from the route too early, or filling a truck with less than the required weight.

Weight requirements, or targets, vary considerably. The citywide goal right now is 10.6 tons per day per truck, but that's an average. To reach it, each district agrees to targets established through negotiations between the Department and the union. Targets differ according to population density, the variable nature of garbage in different neighborhoods, and the seasons. Garages that serve affluent neighborhoods come up lighter in the summer because more residents are away, while suburban districts pick up more weight because of yard waste.[1] If a sanitation worker fails to reach the weight established for his garage, he may or may not face a reprimand, but if he fails to finish his route before the end of his shift, he risks getting a complaint.

A "load" refers to a single truckload of trash and is the measure of the work at hand. Each day in the mid-morning and mid-afternoon, supervisors must tour the district and report to their superintendent how much garbage still needs to be picked up. If a supervisor (also called a foreman) radios the garage and says, "I'm calling out three loads," it means there is enough garbage left on the streets to fill three trucks.[2]

Miscalculating such estimates, or giving a bad call, gets a foreman and his super in trouble. The number of loads out tells chiefs at the borough level, where district resources are coordinated, how many trucks to send from which garages throughout their jurisdictions for the next shifts. If I were a district superintendent and I called six loads out on the day line, meaning the day-shift workers left that much trash on the street, then the borough might have me send out extra trucks and extra men on the next shift. Say those trucks came up short, or maybe the crews on those trucks brought them in too early but had cleaned the backlog. It would be obvious that fewer than six loads had been left out. My miscalculation would have cost the Department resources, wasted money, misdirected manpower, and squandered time. Similarly, if I called out six loads and had underestimated, the truck allocations wouldn't be sufficient to get the entire district clean by the end of the night shift. A bad call in either direction would earn me a complaint.

The obverse is never true. If I call out exactly the right number of loads day after day, I won't earn a pat on the back from my superiors. Let's say that I actually have my entire district completely clean by the end of every day shift, month after month. That would be an admirable accomplishment. It still wouldn't earn me any kudos, or even a stronger chance at promotion.

I learned about these dynamics from Thomas Lyons, who has worn the DSNY uniform for a long time. When I first met him, I spent a few moments trying to reconcile his appearance with his thoroughly Irish heritage. His dark hair, broom-bristle mustache, and sharp nose make him a cross between Friedrich Nietzsche and Mark Twain. But Irish he is; his parents, who met in New York, were both born on the Emerald Isle.

Unlike his straight-arrow older brother, Tommy had always played fast and loose with any rules he encountered. After eighth grade he abandoned the parochial school around the corner so he could attend the public high school, one of the largest and most storied in the city, to play basketball. But "attend" is a strong word. He made an art of finding ways not to be in class. In the front door, out the side door; in the front door, out the back door; walk straight past the front door and keep on walking. Truant notices stuffed the mailbox. His father lectured, yelled, pleaded. His mother wept. After much imploring from the family, an uncle with a graduate degree from Trinity College in Dublin agreed to work with Tommy, but not for long. "There's no teaching this boy," he declared, his brogue thick and his judgment final.

But Tommy could shoot a basket. He played varsity from his freshman year. After practice, he'd find his way to the park and play some more. He played on weekends, played at night. He played well enough to overcome his dismal grades and earn a slew of basketball scholarships. He chose New Hampshire, but it was too cold and too far away. The junior college in Arkansas was even farther away, both on the map and in his mind. After less than a year, he dropped out for good.

A nineteen-year-old with a New York City public high school diploma, a mean jump shot, and no marketable skills has nothing to push him to the front of any job line. His parents breathed easier when a combination of family connections and lucky breaks helped him get a membership card and an apprenticeship in a trade union local, but his father also urged him to take city civil service exams. One of those was for Sanitation. By the time he was called for the job, Lyons was recently married and about to move to a tony suburb outside the city; he was getting steady work through his union, and his future looked secure without the city job. His mother, his brother, most of his friends, and especially his wife all urged him not to take it. When he ignored them and signed on anyway, only his father congratulated him for making the right choice. His new wife was furious. She forbade him to tell their neighbors.

Many years and a couple of promotions later, Lyons is a "white shirt," a designation within the city's uniformed forces that signals a position of command—in this case, of a Sanitation garage. He has a reputation among Department brass for being a street-savvy officer who always gets the weights required of his district, while the workers who report to him know him to be unflappable but not unreasonable.

Lyons's attitude toward his day-to-day job and toward his over-all career typifies the ambivalence expressed by many of the Department's uniformed employees. He claims that the men and women of Sanitation are not of the same character as those who work for Police or Fire, but he is also quick to point out the injustice of media attention given to a sanitation worker killed on the job compared with coverage for the death of a cop or fireman. Police officers and firefighters receive front-page banner headlines and often several days on television news. The san man gets a few inches on a back page and maybe—though not always—brief airtime on a local TV station.

Lyons commonly refers to the place where he works as "this shit hole," but he has not taken a single sick day in nearly twenty years. If asked to contribute any uncompensated time to a job-related cause—for the DSNY's annual Family Day gathering, say, or for a community event that happens off-hours—he refuses on principle, but he arrives at work every morning a full hour before his shift starts so he can get a jump on the myriad demands of the day.

When pressed, he will admit that he considers himself a failure because he has spent so many years with the Garbage Department, as he calls it. In that same conversation, however, he will point to the stability it has provided him and his family and how it let him build a life rich with social, educational, and professional opportunities for his children.

He and I had a few conversations in which I tried to explain why I believe Sanitation is the most important force on the streets, but Lyons—not his real name, by the way—always had the same reaction.

"Aw, bullshit," he'd say, dismissing me with a wave of his hand.

Even after decades on the job, he still hasn't told the neighbors what he does for a living. His wife is happier that way. So is he.

Part Five

LOADED OUT

Part Two

LOADED OUT

15. Lost in the Bronx

Bart's collection truck moved steadily up the street, its many back lights and reflectors bright against the dark evening.* I was directly behind him in my own truck, the doors folded open for the warm breeze. We were on the Grand Concourse, one of the city's celebrated thoroughfares and a defining landmark of the Bronx. Once-grand movie theaters and stately apartment buildings with the bold grace of Art Deco aesthetics suggested the optimism of an earlier time, while their boarded-up windows and graffiti-streaked walls told a more troubled story. Usually, I'd be intrigued by such details, but not right now; not tonight.

Pedestrians crowded the sidewalks, their arms heavy with shopping bags or schoolbooks. Thick traffic slowed our pace. Bart signaled a left turn and I did the same; a short block later, he signaled another left, heading us back the way we'd just come. Again. A trip that normally took about twenty-five minutes had already lasted more than an hour, and we were no closer to the garage than when

---

*This man's real name was not Bart.

we started our journey. Or maybe we were closer to the garage. I had no idea. I was thoroughly lost.

Only a few hours earlier, we'd signed in for our four-to-twelve shift, ready to run relays. Except for traffic jams, or long lines at the dump, or discovering too late that a particular truck had mechanical trouble, or losing our paperwork, or breaking down on the highway, or forgetting to weigh out (not possible when dumping garbage, but I'd done it at the paper dump), there wasn't much that could go wrong. We usually finished our target of five or six round-trips by the time our shift was done.

I was working out of Bronx 7, known as the House of Pain because of its punishing weights. Workers in Bronx 7 pick up the neighborhoods of University Heights, Jerome Park, Fordham, and Kingsbridge. The garage itself, at the tip of northern Manhattan, was built in the 1960s, with the barren lines and bland details found in many city structures of that era. Today the Department's architects design more inviting spaces, but at least the workers assigned to Bronx 7 didn't have to change into their uniforms or take their showers in the defunct incinerators that were home to two other garages down the street.

By the time I met Bart, I preferred traveling to the dump on my own. I'd discovered Mona the Chanting Truck on one of my many solo runs, and I was glad to gawk at the fecundity of the place without any coworkers nearby thinking I was weird. That night, however, someone from the borough office was watching garage operations more closely than usual. Because I was new, I was supposed to be following an experienced person, so I'd been assigned to Bart. He had seventeen years on the job. Why was he stuck on relays? It was an unusual task for a senior worker; unlike the labor of loading out a truck, relays include no extra pay. And was it my imagination, or did he and our garage foreman exchange a few hard looks?

Workers and managers throughout the DSNY walk a line between orthodox obedience to the Department's many regulations and relative indifference to them. The resulting variations of attitude and behavior shape so-called house rules that create slight but distinct variations in the cultural mores of each of the city's Sanitation garages. Knowing and following the house rules helps the day go smoothly. A crew that regularly takes too long at morning break, for instance, is mostly immune from punishment if they always finish their route. A worker slow to provide a doctor's note explaining an illness receives a few extra days' grace because he never protests any assignment. But it's a fragile harmony. If a supervisor writes the late-from-break crew a complaint for lingering over their coffee, or if a loud coworker broadcasts the favor given his colleague who is slow to turn in paperwork, the accord created by house rules can fall apart and rebellion ensues.

An outsider won't necessarily see signs of trouble, but an insider will recognize that when a rough-talking crew suddenly speaks in extra-polite tones, or when normally animated workers become models of studied nonchalance, something's up. Or when frosty glances pass between a worker and a supervisor. Unlike an outsider, I recognized many unspoken but significant social cues, but unlike an insider, I didn't yet know how to read them. Bart was no help. When I asked him why he was on relays, he just shrugged, and when I asked if he was angry with the supervisor, he gave *me* a hard look but said nothing.

We found our trucks, dumped them, brought them back, took another two. Between dumping our third pair and returning to home base, we stopped at a Dunkin' Donuts for our break.

I am not a student of the chain's design schemes, but this particular franchise was starker than most. There were no chairs or tables, just a scuffed bare floor and a counter in front of the wall of doughnut choices and coffee machines. Security cameras recorded a good gauge of our heights as we passed the inch marks running up the doorjamb, the same kind used by banks to tell cops the size of fleeing crooks. I wondered how many times the store had been robbed before that innovation was introduced, or if Corporate had considered it a prudent addition to this neighborhood's franchise right from the start.

Break was fifteen minutes. Getting food used up much of it, and I climbed back into my truck to eat fast so we could get back on the road. Bart, uninvited, joined me. Steam from our coffee scented the air while we made small talk and I watched the time stretch to twenty minutes, then thirty. I couldn't just drive off with Bart sitting in my truck, and I didn't want to be rude and kick him out, though I wondered at my timidity. I drummed the steering wheel, cleared my throat, jiggled my knee, said vague things like "Okay, then!" a few times. Bart seemed not to notice.

Finally, to my relief, after forty minutes, he crumpled his doughnut bag and started to get out of my truck. "Follow me back," he said. Well . . . duh. I'd been doing that all night; obviously I'd follow him back.

Then he paused and looked at me.

"Never trust a senior man."

I felt a quick rush of gratitude. Here was a guy with years on the job imparting to me, a brand-new sanitation worker, a key insight that I could add to my collection of Essential Sanitation Knowledge. And he knew this bit of wisdom because . . . he was a senior man.

"Wait," I said, "you mean, never trust a senior man besides you, right? Never trust *other* senior men?"

Neither his voice nor face changed. "Never trust a senior man."

I nodded uncertainly.

The normal route from the dump to the district took us down a few dark blocks, under an overpass, and onto the interstate. We started out the usual way, but when we skipped the entrance ramp to the highway, I felt even more appreciation for this generous man. What an excellent partner! Bart was teaching me a shortcut!

But this new route, with its double-backs and meanderings and loop-de-loops, made no sense. I wished I'd understood the implications of those looks that had passed between Bart and the boss before we'd left. They had indeed been meaningful, and I should have been wary. He wasn't teaching me a shortcut. He was teaching me that he was a first-class asshole and that I was a first-class fool.

Bart had dragged me into his own individual protest, a private job action, and I had followed like an eager child. Whatever revenge he was seeking or protest he was staging against whatever injustice at the job, real or imagined, I cursed him for including me. The third time past the Bronx County Courthouse I told myself to peel off, ask directions, find my own way, but I had no idea where I was. I recognized few street names, no landmarks but Yankee Stadium.

As the evening wore on and we continued tracing what felt like big, ragged circles, my exasperation faded to resignation. At least I was getting good practice driving at night on busy city streets. When easing to a stop at red lights, I marveled at the waves of pedestrians who stepped in front of me without looking, sometimes while the truck was still in motion. I felt a rush of tenderness toward them as I considered the depth of their unthinking faith. The traffic signal told them that the crosswalk was their right, and they assumed I was competent enough not to run them over.

They had no idea that the immensity of the truck had nearly overwhelmed me. I was sure this predicted my certain failure until a sanitation worker with many years on the job told me that the first time he'd driven a collection truck, he'd been so scared that his partner had had to peel his fingers from the wheel at the end of the shift. Then there was the story of the new hire who went only a few blocks from his garage before he froze at the prospect of making a necessary sharp right turn between the beams of an overpass. His foreman found the poor man blocking the intersection, weeping, both his hands in a death grip on the wheel.

And my complete ignorance of the Bronx was slowly being replaced by a vague sense of familiarity; someday I might know these streets much better, and I would remember the storefront churches and bucolic parks that we had passed so many times tonight. I'd certainly be in big trouble when (if?) we made it back to the district, and because I was on probation, I knew there could be no mercy, but that was out of my hands, so there was no point worrying about it.

And I realized how very much I had yet to learn.

Those who pick up New York's trash, drive the collection trucks, and sweep the streets are classified as manual laborers. The forms of expertise that they must master to do their jobs well are not generally recognized as valuable. Yet just in this one evening I had encountered complexities I didn't understand, like the many languages and techniques of resistance that are central elements of the job (just as they are central to many kinds of work). Until a newcomer knows how to recognize and interpret them, and unless that newcomer has more backbone than I showed that evening, she is at risk for the kind of casual hijacking that I was experiencing with Bart.

When we finally arrived back at the garage, our supervisor was outside his office waiting for us, his arms folded and his face grim. He stayed there while we parked our trucks and walked back to him, then he asked Bart what had happened. Bart looked him square in the eye and said there had been a lot of traffic. The two men exchanged another of the hard looks they had shared so many hours before, then the supervisor turned to me and asked the same question.

I was furious with Bart. I had no idea what game he was playing, with what larger scheme it might have been connected, if he made such choices regularly, or if this was an isolated incident. I also had no idea how much trouble I was in, and I didn't want to lie. But I absolutely knew that except in truly dire and unusual circumstances (and maybe not even then), you don't give up your partner.

So I also looked our supervisor square in the eye, but I didn't say anything. I just gave a small shrug, hands out and palms up (a gesture that, I later learned, is called the San Man's Salute). He considered me for a long moment, shook his head, and turned away.

I never learned why Bart had dragged us both all over the Bronx that night, but I did figure out that, whatever his motives, he had indulged his private rebellion while we were running relays together because I provided cover. Whatever punishment his exploit might have provoked had to fall on both of us, but his seniority protected him from any significant reprimand. As a probationer, I had no such security, and our spontaneous tour had been such a serious breach that it was unequivocal grounds for dismissal. I should have been fired.

Our foreman knew this, and had to choose between banging Bart or letting me keep my job. Bart had guessed correctly which way that decision would go, thereby presuming and simultaneously abusing our supervisor's decency. If there were any consequences at all, Bart knew, they would likely fall on the foreman.

Among their many other responsibilities, garage foremen on the four to twelve make sure that the trucks loaded out on the day line are emptied and ready to go before the midnight shift starts. Bart and I had returned to the garage too late to run more relays, so the trucks we'd been scheduled to dump were still full, which foisted the work onto the next shift—and meant that at least two sanitation workers already assigned to other tasks, such as baskets or collection, had to be put on relays instead. Our foreman would have to explain the discrepancy to his superintendent and maybe even to one of the borough chiefs. Depending on the mood of that chief, the foreman might well get a complaint.

Our foreman had many years in title, and this was hardly the first time he'd been ill-treated by a san worker. He told me he hated the job. No doubt colleagues like Bart didn't help, but perhaps he was just tired of what a supervisor must endure.

16. We Eat Our Own

The DSNY spreads responsibility across all ranks, but more than a few Sanitation folk throughout the chain of command claim that a supervisor's job is the toughest. Because theirs is the position of oversight most immediately engaged with the street, foremen get pressure and pushback when sanitation workers give them trouble. They are also the first interface between the street and the rest of the Department hierarchy, so they get pressure and punishment from their superiors, especially when, as often happens, they are held accountable for a myriad of details over which they have little control. And at the same time, duties like writing summonses for traffic violations and litter conditions draw rebuke from a startlingly rude public. As one chief put it, supervisors are the shock absorbers for the entire system.

That's enough to squash the idea of promotion for many workers. I knew a few who took the supervisor test every time it came around (approximately every four years) just to see how well they'd do. One earned the highest score in the city three times in a row. When I asked him why he didn't take the badge, he said he couldn't think why he would. He worked out of a good garage not far from where he lived, he had a decent partner, he had enough seniority to make the truck regularly and to have the district's best section. His foremen knew that he finished his routes and dumped his truck, so he had his independence. He enjoyed his job just the way it was. And besides, he added, who needs that kind of agita?[1]

He's right. The title of supervisor—a.k.a. foreman—brings a lot of agita.

When he first starts in his new position, a supervisor earns less than senior sanitation workers who are taking home top pay. He's back on probation (though only for twelve months, not the eighteen imposed on new hires). Worse, his seniority starts over, so a freshly made foreman will bounce all over the clock again, just like when he first came on.

These logistical challenges are hard, but far more difficult is the first, most essential lesson of the new rank. Supervisors must recalibrate their relationships with their former colleagues. "Don't think they're your friends," more senior officers caution. They are referring to the sanitation workers whom the new supervisors just left. A foreman can choose a management style that inspires resentment or cooperation (the former is considered a mark of success by some higher-ups, while the latter is thought to be a weakness), but it may take him a while to figure out what works best for him. Some are too hard-assed from the beginning, while others assume a camaraderie they haven't yet earned. Practitioners of either extreme tend to face similar problems with crews that suddenly go slower than they used to or miss stops they never missed before.

The second big lesson a fledgling supervisor must absorb points in the other direction. "Watch your back," warn colleagues. Anyone working within the DSNY even a short time has seen foremen laid flat by vituperative superintendents and by mean-spirited chiefs. It's often easier to punish a supervisor than to go after the san men when something goes wrong. The official explanation is that officers are held to a higher standard. The disparities of power between the two groups may well be another reason. The officers' union, Local

444 of the Service Employees International Union, is smaller than Teamsters Local 831, which represents New York's municipal san workers. An injustice against a supervisor (or against a superintendent, also a member of 444) is not met with the same force of union protest that can be mustered on behalf of a sanitation worker.

A story from a couple of years ago illustrates this. A foreman new to the title and assigned to work on a Sunday was to supervise four basket trucks. He and all eight sanitation workers on this particular detail were told, clearly and repeatedly and in writing, that no one could come in early. When a route was finished, the crew was to go back to the top and start over. It was a logical command, since all four crews were working commercial avenues that had a heavy pedestrian presence on Sundays, and one pass at all those baskets wouldn't be enough to keep them empty.

Two conditions made the supervisor's task more difficult than normal. The four trucks were split between that borough's northernmost and southernmost districts, which meant they were as far from one another as was geographically possible. Travel between them with absolutely no traffic took twenty-five minutes. Leaving one district to check on the other meant that the four sanitation workers in the first would be unsupervised for at least an hour. It was an inconvenience, but it didn't have to be a problem—until the workers made sure it was. They knew they were forbidden to come in early, they knew that their foreman was forced to be far from them for long stretches of the shift, and they knew he was still on probation.

While the foreman was with his northern crews, both southern crews finished a single pass and came in. When he arrived at the southern garage, he found them playing cards. He ordered them back out, but they didn't have time to do their routes again from start to finish, and they ducked back into the garage as soon as he left. Meanwhile (you know where this is going, right?), after he sent the southern trucks back to the street and returned to the northern district, the foreman discovered that those two crews had also finished early and were in the garage.

The borough chief promised harsh punishment for everyone involved. At first the sanitation workers feigned ignorance, claiming that they hadn't known they were supposed to stay out, but finally they admitted that they had ignored the order. They were suspended for several days, but then those punishments were knocked down to mere verbal reprimands—in other words, none of them suffered any real penalty.

Not so for the foreman. Only a strong ally higher up the hierarchy saved him from being demoted.

The situation demonstrates the central dilemma of the supervisory role. Foremen have neither the clarity of their previous title nor the authority granted to titles above them. They shoulder the obligations of management and are simultaneously responsible for the actions of labor, a catch-22 that can create impossible situations. It's as if DSNY foremen are trapped in an administrative purgatory—or a permanently liminal status.

The word "liminal" comes from the Latin *limen*, for threshold, and means "a space between." The anthropologists Arnold van Gennep and Victor Turner suggested that liminality is a central part of all rites of passage, the rituals that bring about status changes for individuals within a community.[2] Such rites vary widely in form and content, but they are found in every culture in the world, and Van Gennep and Turner argued that all of them have the same three-phase structure. First, an initiate is separated from his original cohort; often this includes a symbolic marking of some kind (think of a shaved head or special clothing). In phase two, he goes through a trial that eradicates, or at least amends, his prior identity, and that also proves him worthy of assuming a new self. The third and final phase happens when the community welcomes the initiate back into the group and acknowledges him in his new role.

Of these three stages, the second is the hardest. The person is no longer part of his original community, but he hasn't yet earned the new position that he needs before he can go back. He's caught on a threshold between his old and new selves; that is, he is forced to endure a period of liminality, a betwixt-and-between condition that is ambivalent and stressful.

There are plenty of examples close at hand. When a man joins the military, for instance, he separates himself from his original community, dons a uniform, and has his head shorn, thus signaling affiliation with and submission to his new collective. Basic training, a stressful time, tests his mettle while pummeling him out of his old self and shaping the person he must become. When it's over, he is reintegrated into the larger world in his new identity as soldier. The pattern is similar for people who join holy orders. Less dramatic, more quotidian examples include a bar mitzvah or a first Communion.

Sanitation supervisors don't think about themselves or their work in these terms, but they have long recognized the contradictions inherent to their title. Part of the challenge is the long and eclectic list of their duties.

Until recently, foremen working out of a district on the day line and given responsibility for a specific area were known as section supervisors. They were charged with overseeing as many as seven Sanitation crews—that is, fourteen workers on seven trucks. Foremen handed out routes at the start of roll call, met their workers morning and afternoon to sign the route cards, rode the routes morning and afternoon to make sure they were clean, and gave the district superintendent the morning and afternoon reports on trucks that would or would not be dumped and routes that were finished or that still had work left out.

Foremen also met MLP* and basket trucks to check their progress and sign their route cards; answered 311 complaints by phone or, if circumstances warranted, in person; issued summonses for litter and traffic violations; visited the homes of sanitation workers who called in sick; and responded to any unusual events, like a plow

---

*Mechanized (or motorized) litter patrol, an old-fashioned name for cleaning up various litter conditions or going after bulk collection.

moving a road plate out of place and thus leaving a car-sized hole in the middle of the street, or a truck knocking limbs off a tree in a residential neighborhood, or a LODI (a line-of-duty injury for a worker in the field), or an accident involving a DSNY vehicle.

Each of these chores is accompanied by complex documentation protocols. A fender bender that involves a Sanitation vehicle is a good example. The supervisor arrives on the scene and fills out an 806, in four layers with carbon, and no matter what, he must make sure the worker gets PAPed (if he skips that step, it's a guaranteed complaint). If the worker goes LODI, however, the proper form is the 807, but if he's injured badly enough to go to a hospital or clinic, that's the 807B, and he doesn't get PAPed until after the hospital releases him (which seems especially illogical). If an ambulance or EMS is called, the foreman can't forget to include the name of the medical technicians who respond. He also must not neglect to draw the scene as it looked when he arrived, where the vehicles were at that exact moment. If the accident was caused by mechanical failure, it requires form 240, and the 806 must be included when the truck is towed to the mechanics. When a civilian operator (as in a motorist) is also involved, the foreman must fill out an 808 and an MV104, but if it happened in New Jersey (with a truck running relays to the dump in Essex, perhaps), he'll want an SR1.

Any bureaucracy as large as the DSNY must feed itself with multiple layers of accountability, but even with that in mind it's difficult to imagine the provenance of such convolutions of paperwork. It feels as if many of the protocols were constructed on top of previous regulations that were themselves based on older rules and procedures. A serious study of such documents would have much to teach about how the DSNY's mission has been organized, and about the history of governance more generally.[3] Who created all these forms, and what needs are they intended to meet? What problems do they solve? Who created their many fields? What happens if they're not followed? Are more forms invented to solve the problems created by other forms? Where does the resulting documentation end up? How did the job of cleaning the streets and picking up garbage get so complicated, anyway?

But the paperwork required at an accident is nothing compared with the eye-crossing task of payroll. For decades, it was kept in time books so big they had a wingspan of nearly a yard. On the left side of the left-hand page, each sanitation worker's name was written by hand. Those in blue ink worked the day shift; names in green worked nights. The rest of the two pages was filled with a grid of half-inch squares. Before a foreman could do payroll, he sat with a ruler drawing diagonal lines from the lower-left to the upper-right corner of every square. Stroking the book, it's called. There were hundreds of squares on a page, one for each shift worked by each loader in a section—or, for garage foremen, for every driver in the whole garage. All of them had to be stroked (the squares, not the men). It took about thirty days to fill the two pages. When a fresh page was started, the workers' names had to be written anew on the left side, and all the blank squares had to be stroked and filled in.

A straight eight-hour day with no dumping and no overtime needed only the simple diagonal across the square, but if anything else happened, the number of hours worked went in the lower-right half of the box, while extra information was recorded in codes in the upper left. Red ink meant snow, and it also meant overtime, but for what? Look to the codes! There were codes for working extra hours past the regular shift, for working a chart, a Sunday, a vacation day, a holiday. There were lost-time codes—different numbers for different circumstances (a PAP? an unusual?). There were codes for when a worker was sick or had gone LODI, codes for full or partial truck money, for night diff, for being excused with pay, without pay. There was a code for when a worker normally on the truck was assigned to another piece of equipment and so would be schranked.[4] The lists of numerals—some two-digit, some three, some four—were part of a larger set called cascading codes that indicated a specific time-measurement context, but to supervisors who didn't understand the intricacies of the system, payroll was a nightmare.

In John Steinbeck's version of the King Arthur myth, Arthur's foster brother, Kay, is every bit the equal of the Knights of the Round Table—until he becomes the castle's accountant. "A heart that will not break under the great blows of fate can be eroded by the nibbling of numbers," Kay laments. "Look, sir, did you ever know a man of numbers who did not become small and mean and frightened—all greatness eaten away by little numbers as marching ants nibble a dragon and leave picked bones?"[5]

Kay could have been describing the Sanitation time book, and more than a few supervisors would have been all too familiar with his despair. Over the years, many otherwise capable young officers were so undone by the impenetrable intricacies of payroll that they threw in the badge. Now that the entire DSNY system is done on computer, the complexities have moved from paper to screen.

Payroll is vitally important, but it's office work, and a foreman learns fast that the job is in the field—as when, every workday morning, he must meet the mechanical brooms assigned to major thoroughfares in his jurisdiction. Though it's a routine assignment, it's often emotionally charged.

The streets of the city are swept according to a regular schedule. Signs on all commercial blocks indicate the thirty-minute SCR, or street-cleaning regulations, when there must be no vehicles on the curb (most residential streets have a ninety-minute window). Broom operators have no enforcement power, however, so cars don't move and the street stays dirty if a foreman isn't present, tapping his car horn to nudge vehicles out of the way.[6] The technique inspires most drivers to rouse themselves enough to move their cars or trucks or vans—they can come back immediately after the broom passes— but sometimes the gentle approach doesn't work.

I saw this firsthand one morning with Julio Platero, a soft-spoken, broad-shouldered supervisor in Manhattan with more than twenty years on. Julio knew from experience that he would likely encounter difficulty along a stretch of upper Broadway. The problem wasn't so much the throng of cars and double-parked trucks—most streets with shops were similarly crowded at that hour—but on these few blocks, he explained, the people responsible for all those vehicles never wanted to move. Sure enough, after a few short and then more insistent honks, no one had budged. No one had even looked at Julio or at the broom idling behind him. With a sigh, he pulled over, climbed out of his car, and approached a dark-haired man in a sweatshirt who was unloading a small delivery truck into a nearby grocery.

From inside the car I couldn't hear their exchange, but it wasn't hard to get the gist. As Julio spoke, the man looked at him intently, then frowned, threw up his hands, and started shouting, his mouth wide. Julio listened a moment, then tapped his own chest as he leaned forward slightly, shaking his head as he spoke. The delivery guy, still shouting, swung one arm toward his truck, the other toward the store behind him. His face darkened. Julio's face, impassive at the start, became even blanker as he pulled his summons book from his back pocket and flipped it open. The man bent toward him with a curse. When he started to swing his arm again, I thought it would connect with Julio's jaw, but instead he slammed his truck's back doors, stomped around to its cab, jumped in, slammed the door, gunned the engine, and peeled away from the curb. The other malingerers in cars and delivery trucks, deciding to do the same, disappeared like a school of startled fish, and all at once the street was clear.

The broom pulled forward and snugged itself against the curb, the susurrus of its machinery suddenly loud as it moved from one end of the block to the next. In only a few minutes the street was swept, the broom was on to the next block (where Julio met more recalcitrant motorists), and the displaced vehicles swooped back to their places. The only sign that the broom had even been there was the temporary lack of litter and a broom-width streak of moisture that glistened on the asphalt.

When he returned to his car, Julio's normally calm look was replaced with a grimace. He understood that the delivery guy was just doing his job, he said, but what about our job? How do we sweep if they won't move? Since when do they have the right to prevent that street from being cleaned? And if we don't sweep, what kinds of complaints will there be later, when these bozos are long gone but the litter remains?

Meeting the brooms and verbally jousting with stubborn deliverymen are still part of a foreman's day, but the rhythms of that day changed when the former mayor of Indianapolis came to town and convinced his new boss, the mayor of New York, to let him tinker with the DSNY.

In the spring of 2010, Mike Bloomberg needed a new deputy mayor of operations. Bloomberg, who rewards loyalty in kind, is known to work best with people who have been close to him for a while, so when he announced that he was giving the job to Stephen Goldsmith, a sixty-three-year-old Harvard professor who had never worked inside the Bloomberg administration or lived in New York, more than a few people were surprised.

The mayor's press release bragged that Goldsmith was "the nation's premier expert on innovation in government." After working as a county prosecutor in Indiana for more than a decade, he served as mayor of Indianapolis for two terms in the 1990s. At Harvard he directed a Kennedy School program called Innovations in American Government. He had been chair of the Corporation for National and Community Service and had written or coauthored several books about urban administration.

The deputy mayor of operations was the most pivotal position within Bloomberg's administration, and the mayor showed his high hopes for his new man by giving him its entire portfolio. Goldsmith was to have a major role in managing the Police and Fire Departments, as well as the Offices of Emergency Management, of Budget, and of Labor Relations. He was directly responsible for the Taxi and Limousine Commission and the Offices of the Criminal Justice Coordinator, of Long-Term Planning and Sustainability, of Contract Services, and of Operations. In addition, he was in charge of the Departments of Buildings, of Citywide Administrative Services, of Environmental Protection, of Information Technology—and of Sanitation. In other words, a man who had only ever visited New York, and who would continue living in Washington, D.C., even after he took his new job, was now partly or wholly in charge of every agency that had anything to do with the city's daily functions.

The press gave Goldsmith a cautious welcome. *The New York Observer* interviewed labor leaders who had worked closely with him in Indianapolis and who gave him high marks.[7] The *Daily News* said it would be good to have a newcomer's fresh perspective but cautioned that there would be "a steep learning curve for a Republican dropped into New York without a deep familiarity with it."[8]

Sanitation insiders and others close to city hall were skeptical about the appointment, and Goldsmith's initial comments didn't inspire confidence. "I know a lot about how to run a government," he said. "I don't know nearly enough about New York City. I hope to get up to speed very quickly."[9] Even the mayor justified his choice oddly. "People who've worked here know what can be done," he explained. "We need somebody from outside that doesn't know that and isn't burdened with that."

One of Goldsmith's first mandates was to figure out how to cut costs with minimal impact on city services. Every agency had been ordered to whittle down its budget for the coming fiscal year. Perhaps because he had experience restructuring municipal waste management back in his own mayoral days, Goldsmith took early aim at Sanitation, claiming that he wanted to "reengineer" the DSNY. And perhaps because he was famous for streamlining government by going after middle management, he focused specifically on the title within Sanitation that was the first step up from the street. He went after the foremen.

When Goldsmith arrived in New York, Sanitation's ranks included only fifty-eight hundred sanitation workers—the smallest
the force had been since 1895. Local 831's president, Harry Nespoli,
argued that, come winter, such low numbers left the city vulnerable—
no, worse than vulnerable. With so few workers on hand to respond,
a serious storm could be a genuine disaster.

The new deputy mayor hit upon a strategy that seemed to address the mayor's demand for budget cuts and the union's call for
more workers by eliminating two hundred supervisor positions.
Half would disappear through attrition when retiring foremen were
not replaced, and the other half would disappear through demotions; the hundred most junior officers in the city would be knocked
back to the rank of sanitation worker. At the same time, Goldsmith
told the Department to hire a hundred new san workers. He claimed
that his plan saved the city twenty million dollars in labor costs
while imposing no layoffs and simultaneously beefing up snow-
fighting troops. "This is a win-win for everyone," he told the press.[10]

The "everyone" didn't include the supervisors. Foremen still on
probation could return to their previous posts as sanitation workers
with no loss of seniority, but if officers in title more than a year were
demoted, they would become the most junior workers in the city,
even if they had many years on the job. They would have less seniority even than new hires who would start later in the year. And
for those past probation, what constituted time on the job? Did the
clock start from a person's initial hire date into the DSNY, or from
when he took the foreman's badge? What about those who had been
in civilian DSNY jobs before joining the uniformed ranks? And did
military time figure into the calculations?

Goldsmith wasn't finished. Because there were fewer san workers,
he reasoned, the foremen left standing after the demotions would
have to cover more ground. Their span of control, meaning the
number of trucks they were required to oversee, had been a maximum of seven. Goldsmith bumped it to twelve.

His intervention (some called it interference) in Sanitation's work on the street had far-reaching effects. The Department's geographic divisions had to be reconfigured. A small district with three sections might run only ten trucks on a given day, but where there had been three supervisors to monitor them—one per section—now there was only a single foreman, called a field officer. A large garage that ran thirty-six trucks across five sections would have only three field officers.

It also meant that established patterns of seniority went out the window. Supervisors with many years working days in a particular section of a particular district were suddenly bounced to nights in a different borough because another foreman with slightly more time on the job was assigned to the day shift as the field officer in that district, even though that slightly more senior officer had been based in a distant garage and had little or no experience in the new location.

There is always room for improvement in the managerial structure of a department as large and complex as Sanitation, and maybe Goldsmith's plan looked sensible on paper, but it made clear that he knew little about New York and even less about the DSNY. An exercise meant to enhance bureaucratic efficiency had instead upended a solid organizational structure, and a system that had worked pretty well now worked badly. Foremen all over the city asked how they might follow twelve trucks, many of which were far apart from one another, and still take care of their numerous other obligations. They asked what would happen, for example, if they were doing the paperwork required for an accident or an unusual and some of their sanitation workers left routes unfinished. Would foremen still take the hit, as had been the custom? Were they still to write as many summonses as before? Who would answer the 311 calls, do the sick checks? Would they still meet their brooms and their basket trucks?

Facebook was a place to vent. Goldsmith's mandates didn't improve city government, but they succeeded in pitting foremen against one another.[11]

Supervisor 1:

I hope what happened to me Saturday is an example for all. I was working in a section with 7 start trucks plus 2 afternoon halfs [trucks not completely filled in one section that are moved to another section]. A truck had an accident at 1140. I was at the scene until 1315. Super called up for the report, I told him I didn't know. He asked me to call a crew to get the recycling left out, I said I didn't have cell numbers. The work got left out. I went back to the garage by 1335, did my tickets, set the route up for 4–12 and by this time it was 1355. I wrote in the telephone order book "no time for unusual and accident report due to end of shift." I signed out and walked out. I will never, ever, go above and beyond for this dept again. I suggest you all do the same.

Supervisor 2:

See that is 100% wrong of what you did, maybe that is why the city is fuckin demoting supervisors, if any one had common sense, the Borough would have authorized some over time. Do you know how many times I stay on my own time to get things done? Am I going to bitch because I stayed 20 or 30 minutes on my own time?

Supervisor 1:

And what did u gain by staying on your own time? Nothing. No one knows or cares that you stayed late to do your job, but people would have noticed if you were unable to complete your tasks in an 8 hr day. Thanks for making the city believe we can watch 12 trucks, write ASP's [summonses for blocking the broom] and ECB's [summonses for litter], answer 311's, do sick checks and car re-checks, write unusuals, accident reports, payroll, 350's, evaluations, hold roll calls, talk to the public, etc etc all in 8 hours. Let me know next time u stay late on your own time and I'll get the boro to inter-office you a cookie.

The public doesn't usually know much about the discontent of city workers whose jobs have been drastically transformed. There were occasional stories in the local papers, but dismay within Sanitation's supervisory ranks, their intense resentment of Goldsmith and of Bloomberg, and ongoing confusion within the day-to-day of the job weren't headline-worthy. Nor were Commissioner Doherty's quiet but steady efforts behind the scenes to get the demotion orders repealed. Even Goldsmith himself, despite his power, wasn't often on the front pages.

Then came the Christmas Blizzard of 2010.

17. Night Plow

The Sanitation year has four seasons: spring, maggots, leaf, and night plow. During night plow, which lasts from early November until mid-April, the Department awaits flurries, ice storms, blizzards, and anything in between with a day shift that starts and ends an hour later than usual and one section in each district assigned nights. Night plow ensures that a crew is in place and ready to confront a storm, no matter the hour. If snow does arrive unannounced, despite three different and sophisticated private weather forecasting firms that the Department has under contract, there will be workers and officers on hand to wrap tires with chains, secure plows to trucks, top off spreaders, and at least start working the major roadways.

It's an old legacy. While garbage collection and street sweeping are Sanitation's logical concerns, laborers and managers responsible for those chores in New York have also always had the task of snow removal. In its earliest days, the Department of Street Cleaning leadership titles included a superintendent of final disposition, a superintendent of stables, and a superintendent of snow. The first two are long faded from memory, but the snow superintendent is still around. All seven borough commands have one, as does every garage, and at Sanitation headquarters there are people in every office whose primary duties include snow.

The fundamental importance of Sanitation's snow-fighting charge and its legacy of success in storms large and small made it all the more surprising when a blizzard in late December 2010 crippled the city. Citizens were accustomed to seeing plows and spreaders trawling the streets for hours on end whenever snow fell, but this time plows were absent and streets stayed buried. When a newspaper quoted a Queens politician who claimed he had proof of a deliberate slowdown by the DSNY, public alarm turned into anger and then into a potent mix of outrage and righteous incredulity. News of Blizzageddon exploded across local, regional, and national media. Blogs, YouTube, and even *Saturday Night Live* pilloried and parodied individual Sanitation people, the Department, and the mayor.

Then garbage languished uncollected and the piles grew bigger by the day while the DSNY continued to struggle with the storm's aftermath. A television reporter at the local NBC affiliate, implying that Sanitation work attracted "economic bottom-feeders," revealed the supposedly bloated salaries of several high-up managers who, he suggested, were responsible for the mess.[1] The comments sections on the Web sites of every news outlet bristled with condemnation. Even in Internet forums where postings were often nasty, the vitriol directed at Sanitation was unusually caustic.

The real story is different from the cartoon version offered by most media. Understanding what happened, however, requires knowing more about the role of snow in the Department's history and structure. Snow in New York has been a catalyst for technological innovation, for infrastructural improvements, and for political change, and regardless of rank, duties, or time on the job, snow irrevocably influences the relationship of Sanitation personnel to the job. It shapes their professional lives long before, all throughout, and well after any storm.

Some Sanitation chiefs take snow so seriously that they seem to think street sweeping and garbage collection are merely useful ways to keep the workforce busy during warm weather—that is, when they're not preparing for the coming winter. Every district and bureau in the Department spends part of the summer tending to snow-related chores. For each plow on their premises, garage supervisors and garage utility workers inventory and assess the forty-eight parts that make up a single apparatus. Hinge pins known unofficially but universally as bull pricks, used to affix the two-thousand-pound mechanism to the truck, simmer in barrels of oil, ready for smooth insertion when orders come months hence to plow up the trucks. Ladders of skid chains are untangled, repaired if possible or replaced if necessary, and hung out of the way in heavy curtains. Vats of liquid calcium chloride are topped off. Twenty-two salt dunes around the city are topped off and sculpted into tall cones.[2]

Among the most essential vehicles are spreaders and their more powerful cousins, called flow-and-dumps. These form the city's first line of defense against a winter storm. Spreaders are sturdy orange variations on a dump truck, with a slant-walled body, an internal conveyor belt, a variable spindle at the back, and a pair of hundred-gallon calcium chloride tanks, called saddlebags, on either side. As their name suggests, they spread salt on icy roads. The white flow-and-dumps are amped-up versions of the same thing. Where a spreader sends salt in a four- to eight-foot radius, flow-and-dumps can scatter it across many lanes of a highway or a wide avenue. So important are spreaders and flow-and-dumps that they were the first DSNY equipment fitted with GPS devices, and the operators are given radios (one of the only times a san worker would ever be in possession of that device) so supervisors may deploy them with more efficiency and speed.

Between April and November, this entire fleet receives a

thorough checkup. The long black tongues of spreader conveyor belts are stretched across the floors of DSNY repair shops to be cleaned, inspected, repaired. Replacing broken or missing bolts, chains, chain shackles, curb bumpers, plow shoes, or cutting edges happens at the district. Trouble with pistons, moldboards (the actual plow blades), or semicircles (arched supports that brace the moldboard) requires higher-level intervention, as does serious structural damage to the vehicle. A sanitation worker who came on with me managed to snap two of his truck's three axles when he smashed into a Jersey barrier on the highway he was plowing during his first winter; that truck was towed to the Department's massive Central Repair Shop in Queens for repair. The dry language of the accident report could not conceal a tone of disbelief that the truck could be so thoroughly damaged while Dave, the san man, was unharmed.

Dave broke those axles while he was plowing at night. Such assignments are planned long before winter starts. District officers must know well ahead of time that their strategy for splitting shifts, a mandatory division of the entire workforce into two twelve-hour rotations, will run smoothly when a big storm hits. The other staffing plan that the district works out long before night plow is the designation of one section to go nights all winter. Senior section workers get first dibs on night shifts, but not all of them sign up because they're locked into the schedule until spring. If not enough people volunteer, the rare and dreaded policy of reverse seniority takes effect, and junior-most workers (like Dave) go nights whether they want to or not (it's called being forced).

Among the chiefs who believe garbage is a sideline to the real work of snow are those who feel that records are as much a part of storm readiness as any piece of heavy equipment, and they are not wrong. Forms document hours worked, by whom, in what conditions, for what reasons. They indicate what equipment is up or down, if it's on loan from one district to another, when it's coming back, where it's stored, when it's to be repaired, where, by whom. Forms tell who pays for what part of which storm cleanup chore—

the DSNY? another city agency? Uncle Sam? Forms keep track of outside laborers, among whom might be employees of the Departments of Transportation, or Parks, or Environmental Protection, as well as laborers who hear on radio or TV that they can earn a few dollars as temporary shovelers and so wander into the nearest Sanitation garage, ready to throw their backs into a snow-clogged storm drain or buried bus stop.

Such records also constitute the essential account of who is at fault, or at least who will shoulder the blame—not always the same person—when something goes wrong. It is the unofficial but all-important policy of CYA (Cover Your Ass) that anyone who works inside a complex bureaucracy is wise to learn sooner rather than later. In a snowstorm, the DSNY paper trail can hang an ass or two from the nearest metaphorical tree, or make a particular officer or an entire garage look heroic.

As in most large institutions, some people are more capable than others with the finer points of paperwork. The super's clerk or foreman or superintendent who is good with such details earns grudging respect from peers; the one who is good with paperwork in the wake of a big snowstorm is held in considerable, if sometimes temporary, esteem. That person can provide valuable ass coverage for the less bureaucratically ept (a favor for which some individuals charge a tidy sum) and thus save his paperwork-challenged colleagues from a mess of woe.

Sanitation workers don't have to worry so much about snow paperwork. When they start on the job, their first snow-related responsibility is to appreciate the seriousness that it inspires. It's woven into all their lessons at Safety and Training, where the instructors are blunt. "When it snows," they tell us, "this Department *owns you*." They know that we have no idea what they're talking about and that we won't learn this truth until the first real storm of our new careers.

Training includes Snow School. It sounds rather grand, as if new sanitation workers spend time in simulator booths learning to maneuver a loaded spreader backward up a steep hill in a blizzard with the spindle set to maximum coverage and the usual challenges of traffic, pedestrians, and lousy visibility adding suspense to the task (this is a real scenario in hilly parts of the city, such as some districts in the Bronx, but it goes to senior sanitation workers blessed with equal measures of experience and rock-solid confidence).

The real curriculum isn't so fancy. New hires are put through the tasks they'll need to master when they're in the trenches of a snow battle, like how to "dress" a truck with a plow. The moldboard is balanced on the tines of a Hi-Lo (what the lay public calls a forklift), moved into position at the front of a truck, and raised to the plow jack protruding from the truck's snout. In an ideal world, the jack fits easily into the moldboard brace and the bull prick is sledge-hammered neatly into place. Especially as the winter matures, however, when jack components can become dented and bull pricks warp slightly, dressing the plow becomes a fight. Or maybe the person doing that task moves a little too fast, or isn't as sharp as she was before working more than forty days in a row (with no break in sight), or is inexperienced, and she raises the moldboard from the wrong angle, or it wasn't balanced when she lifted it with the Hi-Lo, so she has to back up and start again. The process of plowing up a fleet of trucks can take a while.

Tire chains pose their own challenges. They're kept neat and organized during warm months, but in the winter, when they're put on and taken off the trucks as often as several times a week, they wind up in tangled heaps. An experienced worker can look at a pile of chains and sort the most confounding mess in a few movements. He looks as if he has some kind of clairvoyance, but he's reading the knuckles of the cross-chain hooks to know how to twist which ends into or over which segments.

Untangled chains are pulled around a truck's outside rear tires and secured with two bungee cords, the second wrapped around the midpoint of the first at a (more or less) forty-five-degree angle.

The chain itself can't be so tight that it cuts into the treads, but it also can't have any slack lest it break and fly off the truck. Our instructors' warnings against this hazard are so graphic that the chains sound like malevolent entities yearning to leap from the wheels and garrote luckless passersby.

A plain collection truck is one kind of vehicle, but a collection truck wearing a plow and chains is an entirely different beast; its width, weight, turning radius, and general handling have changed. On warm autumn nights, dog walkers and other nocturnal New Yorkers startled to see plowed-up trucks and spreaders moving through quiet streets are seeing a new hire (or a new transfer) getting comfortable with the equipment and learning his plowing and salting routes while winter is still distant.

Even this isn't enough preparation for the real thing. Genuine snow training only comes by enduring the slings and icicles of night plow for many seasons. In the winter, the job becomes more difficult and more spirited.

Especially in the early hours of a big storm, energy runs high. Foremen talk to one another in tight voices while they scrutinize plow routes, the super shouts into the phone about orders from the snow office that take no account of what his district needs, and the garage clerk is on another phone pleading with someone at the borough for more manpower on a day when no garage can afford to be short. All troops are summoned; there is grousing about canceled vacations, leaves, and scheduled days off, but this is what we signed on for, and it's not without reward. Walking to our trucks, my fellow sanitation workers slap one another on the back. "It's not snowing white," they laugh, "it's snowing green!" They carry thermoses of coffee and remember to take transistor radios so they can listen to music (technically not allowed, but during a snowstorm such small rules are overlooked) during endless plowing.

Endless plowing. Sanitation work is dangerous, but the seemingly simple task of pushing snow off a road has its own special hazard. At night on a desolate highway or empty avenue, with the somnolent beat of the wipers, the scratching of the plow, and the erratic streaks of snow zigging and zagging out of the depthless dark straight at the windshield for hours and hours . . . and hours . . . workers often find themselves slipping into a kind of hypnosis as they slowly start falling asleep at the wheel—

—until out of nowhere a sound like a shotgun blast goes off right next to their heads and the truck leaps up and slams back down, and the sanitation worker is very suddenly very wide-awake. So startling and violent is the noise that san workers have been known to break a tooth or bite off a piece of their own tongue. If a new worker hasn't been warned to anticipate this, he might think the truck just detonated some part of itself, but it's nothing so dramatic. He just tripped the plow.

Because the plow moves over streets of uneven surfaces, it has to have some play, which it gets from the large spring at the center of the jack. If, while the truck is in motion, the bottom of the plow catches, say, the edge of a sewer cap sticking up even slightly from the street, the momentum of the vehicle pushes the top of the blade forward while the bottom of the blade jams. In the space of a few seconds, when the pressure on the top of the plow forces the bottom of the plow off whatever has caught it, it releases with a tremendous blast of noise while at the same time it shakes up the truck. The whole interaction happens fast enough that the driver rarely has time to anticipate it, especially if he's been hypnotized by the snow.

There are other ways to experience a near disaster in a plow. Workers with many years on the job but with little truck experience can find plowing an agonizing test, as one broom operator discovered when he was assigned to a spreader on hill blocks in a district far from his own. Because he was in a spreader, he carried a Department radio, but it did not serve him well.

"Help me . . . !" His first message, in a soft and whining voice,

was startling. "I'm a broom operator. I'm on a spreader . . ." He gave
his name and location, then took a deep, shuddering breath. ". . . I
shouldn't be expected to operate a spreader in a district I don't
know without any help! without any supervision! all alone! I can't
do it . . . !" He seemed to stifle a sob.

Radios provide an auditory backdrop to the work of Sanitation's
supervisory ranks all year, whether in the field or in the garage, but
during snow, radios are in continuous crackling chatter. Each communication starts and ends with a curt little beep; at the height of a
storm, it sounds as if R2-D2 is offering commentary while borough
chiefs, snow superintendents, district superintendents, supervisors,
and snow clerks call out road conditions and trouble spots, change
up routes, direct equipment from one part of a district to another,
and do their best to stay on top of the storm and ahead of the commissioner's quick eye and quicker tongue.

Especially during snow, he's on the radio all over the city. "Car
One to Queens West 1, you've got ice conditions at Astoria Boulevard and Twenty-First Street!" "Car One to Staten Island 3, you're
losing the Expressway!" "Car One to Bronx 10, why don't I see salt
on the Hutch?" John Doherty is known for his unstinting criticism,
which made it all the more surprising a few days after a particularly
heavy February storm to hear "Car One to Manhattan 1: You did a
beautiful job with Wall Street, Super. Go home and take a well-
deserved rest." The Department's entire Manhattan radio network
fell silent. I imagined officers throughout the borough struck dumb
with disbelief—until an anonymous falsetto filled the airwaves
with a sarcasm-laced "Attaboy, Supe!"

The despairing broom operator on the hill blocks was on a radio
frequency that broadcast to all Sanitation personnel working in
that borough and to headquarters in lower Manhattan. Hundreds
of people heard him. Like the commissioner's remark to the M1
super, the broom operator's plea inspired a moment of startled
silence. I wondered what he thought might be the reply. After a
pause, regular radio noise resumed as if the poor man had never

spoken. I hoped for his sake that he just needed his moment to vent and now he felt better, but half an hour later he was on the air again.

"Please . . ." His voice was weaker. "I'm slipping. My spreader. On the hills. I can't do this. Please, somebody help me . . ." Phone calls had been made immediately after his first message, and his supervisor had been dispatched to do something with him, but before the foreman arrived, the broomie sent one last, plaintive message. ". . . Can anybody hear me . . . ?" He seemed to be weeping. ". . . Is anybody there . . . ?"

He was not relieved of plowing duty, but he was definitely relieved of his radio.

I empathized with the poor san man, but not all plowing experiences are so tense. During a brief, sloppy December storm that sent the Department into battle mode, I was assigned to a team sent to tandem plow a section of the Bronx River Parkway. We climbed an entrance to the northbound side and spread out. The first truck tucked as close as possible to the far left guardrail, its plow—like all our plows—angled to the right. The second truck positioned its left front tire behind the first truck's right rear. The third plow was similarly lined up behind the second. I was fourth; behind me and hard up against the guardrail on the right was the last truck. The flow-and-dump, following us in the middle of the highway with its spindle set for maximum coverage, was sending a blanket of salt across all three lanes. Leading us was a young foreman I did not know, while the district super rode next to, ahead of, and behind us.

The world was painted grays, browns, and sooty whites. Our chains chirped steadily, like the beginning of a 1950s Christmas ditty, while my long windshield wipers opened wide and slapped together, as if praising and supplicating over and over.

Slush on the road ahead of us was thick. The first plow sent a rooster tail of it into the path of the second plow; the second plow's tail was a little bigger. The third plow created a curl taller than the truck, which I turned into a still bigger, more extravagant wave before the last plow sent it vaulting over the right lane guardrail. We were a mighty force, clearing all that stood before us. Maybe God used invisible tandem plows to part the Red Sea for Moses lo those many years ago.

We couldn't stop traffic—it was just before eight o'clock on a weekday morning, and this was a major commuting route—but we commanded the road. Cars driving behind or next to us were temporarily trapped. Sometimes a gap opened between two of the trucks and a motorist tried to slip by, but to pass the entire quintet, she had to run the momentarily blinding wall of mush rolling off the plow to her left. I was impressed with the moxie and foolishness of those who attempted it. Cars at off-ramps didn't anticipate us, though they couldn't have moved even if they did. The tsunami-like breaker rolling off the last plow resembled muffled machine-gun fire when it hit the sides of the cars, making them shiver one after the other like dogs shaking off water.

At our turnaround point, we followed the foreman off the exit, pulled over to a side street, climbed down to stretch, and listened to a pep talk of sorts. I suspected that it was his first storm in his new title.

"You gotta bust out this motherfucker!" He pounded his fist into his palm. "Get up tighter behind, don't let no space open up between yuz! We *got* this cocksucker highway! You gotta *get* this cunt of a storm, we have it, this motherfucker is *ours!*" He didn't notice that one of his workers was female. For my sisters on the job, I should have objected, but standing in the back of our little group, my hat pulled low, I considered the foreman's youth and suppressed a smile. Resuming our campaign on the southbound Bronx River Parkway, we did indeed bust out the motherfucker, just as we had the northbound.

Once the city's streets are cleared and the urgency of the snow response has lessened, the Department turns its attention back to its original job. No one has been on collection for a few days—or, in the case of a really big storm, a few weeks—but New Yorkers have been generating trash as steadily as ever, and the piles are immense. It's time to chase garbage. Large bag stops load out many trucks, but those are relatively easy. More difficult are the house-to-house routes. After even a short time without collection, accumulations from normally tidy lines of bags or cans will have been investigated and spread around by dogs, rats, and scavengers. Undone trash strewn from stoop to street adds to a sense of impending decay.

Phil Burton* and Percy Anderson, two senior men, set out in a cold drizzle early on a Sunday morning to begin clearing garbage. They were doing house-to-house. Burton, a muscular white guy, had an angular face and square shoulders. Anderson was a tall African American with an easy gait and a gentle voice. Both wore yellow slickers and rain pants, heavy rubber boots, thick orange gloves, and skullcaps. The rain would soak their caps soon enough, but neither their feet nor their hands would get wet.

Already-narrow streets were made tighter by banks of snow pushed up against the line of cars parked at both curbs. Heaps of snow between the cars and at the curbs had metamorphosed into kibbled ice full of uneven footing and unseen layers of trash. Burton and Anderson did their best to flatten the frozen lumps as they passed between cars when they were moving many bags. Otherwise, they tripped and stumbled, transforming an awkward chore into a humorless comedy. Trash bags and garbage cans were stacked high in rough layers; pulling just one the wrong way released a messy avalanche. Under the top layer were bags still frozen to one another or to the ground, and they had to be pulled, chipped, and kicked free. Rotted salad, old photographs, and bloodied tampons tumbled out. Every pile was shot through with small logs of dog shit, some neatly wrapped in little plastic bags but many sitting raw.

*Not his real name.

With each bag and can the men moved, ice water spilled across their pants, splashed their jackets.

There was little traffic, but the occasional car turned the corner and inevitably proceeded up the street. The truck made it impossible for any but the smallest vehicles to get by. Almost without exception, the blocked motorist cursed the men, but Anderson and Burton ignored them. Those who couldn't squeeze past gave up and drove backward to the corner.

On a regular day the street required less than twenty minutes to clear, but after working steadily for a long time, the men still had a long way to go. Wet and chilly, they took their fifteen-minute break at the counter of a nearby diner, where Anderson held his hands over his cup of hot coffee as if in blessing and let the steam warm his fingers.

18. Snowed Under

In the late nineteenth century, New York was hit with a storm that rewrote its future. On Saturday, March 10, 1888, temperatures in the city reached the fifties, and crocuses poking through the earth seemed to confirm that winter was finally over. Sunday afternoon brought rain, but it was even warmer than the day before. Anyone who thought to check the local forecasts, such as they were in that era, anticipated slightly cooler temperatures and clear skies on Monday.

While the city enjoyed the balmy weekend, a low-pressure system over the Great Lakes, part of a cold front extending from Canada to Texas, was barreling east. Another, wetter low-pressure area over the Gulf of Mexico was moving east as well, but then this southern system reached the Atlantic, turned left, and started up the coast. When the front coming across from the Midwest met the front coming up from the South, it was the meteorological equivalent of two military divisions merging forces. They combined warm air, cold air, cyclone-like winds, and a trough of low pressure.[1] This new, bigger storm marched north until an opposing high-pressure area over Canada's Maritime Provinces got in its way just when it reached the Bight, and the whole system stalled.

A bight is a curve or turn in a coastline. The New York Bight is the nearly perfect right-angle bend in the Eastern Seaboard that defines the entrance to New York Harbor. The vertical axis is the north–south line of the Jersey Shore, and the horizontal axis is the south side of Long Island, kicking east like the leg of a cancan dancer. When weather coming up the coast hits the New York Bight, it can do funny things. For instance, it can stop moving and intensify. Think of a stalled car revving at higher and higher RPMs.

New Yorkers had no idea what was about to hit. The weather was mild and rainy when they went to bed on Sunday night, but in the early hours of Monday temperatures dropped, the rain became heavy snow, a ferocious wind howled up the avenues, and the world transformed. Snow fell steadily into the morning and through the day. Trains in the city and all over the Northeast were literally stopped in their tracks; some were actually buried. Dozens of ships ran aground or sank. Workers who managed to get to their jobs on Monday couldn't get home later in the day; some died in the attempt. Telegraph, telephone, and electrical lines were completely disabled. Food supplies ran dangerously low. By the time the tempest abated on Wednesday night, more than three feet of snow had fallen, and winds as strong as eighty miles an hour had made drifts up to the second floor of many buildings. New York found itself paralyzed and isolated. At least two hundred and perhaps as many as four hundred people had been killed.[2]

The tragedy taught hard lessons. Communication and electrical wires strung in dense webs above city streets had been hazards for years, but their complete failure in the storm was a decisive factor in getting them moved underground.[3] After the elevated trains were rendered useless by snow and wind, a previously futile campaign to run the tracks below street level was finally given real attention. And in the weeks it took the city to dig itself out, the chronic inadequacies of the municipal system for clearing streets, whether of snow or of garbage, became even more painfully clear. It was partly the Department of Street Cleaning's failure in the storm's aftermath that let George Waring transform the DSC from the ground up six years later.

The Blizzard of 1888, so famous that it was marked with anniversary events as much as a century later, inspired lasting improvements to city infrastructure. A similarly positive outcome is harder to discern when weighing a storm's political impact. In that context, snow is either neutral or negative. When Sanitation's response matches public expectation, no matter if it's in answer to a short-lived squall or a historic blizzard, the thanks are brief and the event is largely forgotten. When it seems that Sanitation comes up short, however, the repercussions can be ruinous. New York's mayor John Lindsay lost his party's nomination for reelection in part because of how he dealt with the aftermath of a snowstorm in 1969.

There has never been a definitive account of everything that went wrong, but it started with the forecast. For Sunday, February 9, the National Weather Service predicted flurries turning to rain, but instead the flurries became snow and then more snow. Before it stopped, New York was under fifteen inches, the heaviest accumulation in eight years.

Sanitation had recently been made part of the Environmental Protection Administration, a new superagency that was meant to make municipal bureaucracy more efficient. The head of the agency was supposed to order the DSNY to respond, but he was out of town and couldn't be reached, and no one knew who could make that call in his place.[4] Even if the Department had leaped into action, 40 percent of its snow equipment was out of service. There were also allegations of labor irregularities. Lindsay had been unsympathetic to sanitation workers' demands in their strike the year before, and some people speculated that the storm was their chance for revenge.

The city was immobilized. Even the stock exchange closed. Six thousand passengers were stranded at Kennedy Airport for 2 days; 3 people were found dead in the airport parking lot. An initial toll of 14 fatalities and 68 injuries eventually rose to 42 deaths and 288 injured. The dig out, once it finally started, was slow and uncoordinated. Queens seemed particularly abandoned. When much of the city was restored to normal within a few days but snow in eastern Queens remained untouched, complaints grew loud and angry. It confirmed suspicions that the mayor cared little about the middle classes or about the people outside Manhattan.[5]

It took Lindsay a few days to realize that part of a borough had been neglected and that its residents were seething. To help make things better, he decided to take a goodwill tour of the neighborhoods that had been hardest hit, and he invited a full press corps to join him. When he reached the snowed-in sections, his limousine was stymied, so he switched to a four-wheel-drive vehicle. Then he was blocked by three DSNY plows stuck in drifts. He continued on foot. Reporters offered helpful observations about how the snow was ruining his expensive loafers, while the people of Queens jeered and booed. ("There were a good number of suggestions of what I might do with myself," Lindsay recalled years later, "and there was a good deal of fascinating speculation about my ancestry.")[6] As a finishing touch, every TV network broadcast the entire fiasco on that night's national news.

In the next election, the Republicans did not choose him as their candidate. He won a second term, but on the Liberal-Fusion ticket. The so-called Lindsay Storm taught mayors around the country the folly of not taking snow seriously, always. Four decades later, those lessons seemed to have been forgotten.

A common misunderstanding about snow is that one storm is much like the next, but each is its own contest. The equipment, supplies, and labor required to clear the streets remain more or less constant, but their deployment varies. Some storms are especially icy. Some carry more wet precipitation than the fluffy variety. After a stretch of extremely cold weather, snow fighting requires different methods than if the preceding days were warm.

In December 2010, the National Weather Service saw a storm system headed toward the Northeast that would arrive around Christmas, but its track was erratic and its strength uncertain. It sashayed up the coast, moving first inland, then out to the ocean, then back to shore. If it made landfall near New York, there would be snow, but maybe not much. If it didn't make landfall, forecasters predicted, it would spend its energy at sea. Then the meandering system reached the New York Bight and was blocked by a northern front. Like its ancestor storm in 1888, it settled in and gathered strength.

When snow started coming down straight and thick on Sunday, December 26, the Department stepped forward with its full force. Operations in every borough went smoothly for several hours, but late in the afternoon snow began falling as fast as two inches an hour, and soon it was joined by fifty-five-mile-an-hour winds. What had started as a garden-variety storm was metamorphosing into a combination blizzard-hurricane.

In a rare move, Sanitation asked the Departments of Transportation, Parks, Police, and Environmental Protection to join the fight. It made little difference. The mayor of Philadelphia had declared a snow emergency on Sunday afternoon. City commissioners in New York talked about doing the same thing, but Mike Bloomberg was the only one who could make that call, and he wasn't around. In fact, no one seemed to know where he was. The decision fell to Stephen Goldsmith, but he wasn't around, either; he was home in Washington for the holiday weekend. Besides, he didn't seem too concerned. While New York was getting pummeled, his single communication was the Twitter message "Good snow work."[7]

Monday, December 27, brought no relief. Even after the snow let up, plow operators cleared avenues that the wind buried again within minutes. Reports of plows dead in drifts and side streets started coming in from Brooklyn and Queens and Staten Island. By that evening, as many as 258 Sanitation vehicles all over the city were stuck. It wasn't a firm number, however, because the DSNY didn't have a system to track its equipment across boroughs or even across a single district. Drivers stayed with their disabled plows until help arrived, just as Sanitation regulations required, but there weren't enough wreckers to get to everyone, and some plow operators waited for twelve hours or more. Workers sent to rescue them in other plows also got stuck, as did the third worker sent after the first two. It was a slow-motion pileup.

Perhaps the people of New York assumed that Sanitation would save the day no matter how deep the snow or how strong the winds, and perhaps already limited public transportation choices in suburban neighborhoods meant that cars were the only way to get around, especially at the Christmas holiday, but whatever the reason, hundreds of people tried to drive even when their streets had yet to be cleared. Even when the news showed plows, fire engines, cop cars, ambulances, tractor trailers, and buses (more than six hundred, according to the MTA) trapped in the snow. Even when they saw that their neighbor, who'd had the same idea, had left his car abandoned in the middle of the street, blocking the plow when it eventually arrived.

No one could remember when Sanitation had so completely lost control of a storm or been so slow to recover. Entire neighborhoods were still not cleared by Tuesday, December 28. The mayor, back in town, held a press conference. When reporters started asking pointed questions, he became impatient. "The world has not come to an end," he snapped, adding that life in most of New York had already returned to normal and that people should stop complaining. He suggested that they take in a Broadway show.

It was hard to imagine a more callous response. Many people

already considered him a wealthy elitist who forgot that New York is more than Manhattan and who cared not at all about the city's middle class. He seemed unaware of how thoroughly his administration had botched the storm response, which was bad enough, but he also seemed unconcerned. To people who remembered the Lindsay Storm in 1969, it was eerily familiar.

A populace badly shaken by weather that had brought their town to its knees wanted their mayor to offer an explanation for what had gone wrong and to at least act as if he cared about their distress. They wanted to believe that despite evidence to the contrary, his administration was competent. When he dismissed them with a scolding instead, New Yorkers were not pleased.

Attention turned to Stephen Goldsmith. The storm had demanded a serious operational response—so why was the deputy mayor of operations not on hand? And, especially, why wasn't he on hand for operations while the mayor was AWOL? It seemed that he had bungled a snowstorm when he was mayor of Indianapolis.[8] Did anyone know that when he was put in charge of such matters in New York? On the Tuesday after the storm, while New York was still nowhere near being back to normal, he was tweeting about things like restaurant permits—just how clueless was he, anyway? ("Nero would have loved this guy," said Michael Daly in the *Daily News*.)[9] And what about those demotions he'd ordered in Sanitation a few months earlier? Had that made the problem worse?

All the while, stranded DSNY trucks were attracting attention from passersby with video cameras and cell phones who took pictures of workers napping, drinking coffee, and apparently just hanging out. It looked as if the san men were collectively giving New York the finger (and it might have made things worse to explain that the workers were following orders). People wanted someone to blame. Who better than plow operators sleeping in their vehicles and enjoying the crullers at Dunkin' Donuts while so many streets remained to be cleared?

Then Daniel Halloran, a councilman from Queens, provided

ammunition for just such an impulse. He told the *New York Post* that three Sanitation workers and two supervisors from the Department of Transportation had confessed to him that DSNY foremen had ordered them not to plow, or to plow slowly, or to skip entire routes. These sources supposedly told Halloran that the foremen were upset about the demotions and so wanted to stick it to the city. The claim made national headlines. Sanitation people across the city reported being cursed out, spat upon, threatened. The city council convened a hearing in early January, intent on learning exactly what had gone wrong. It lasted all day and into the night. Stephen Goldsmith and John Doherty were on the hot seat for a long time.

If Halloran's allegations were true, it meant that city employees had broken the law. The Department of Investigation launched a formal inquiry. Staffers spent six months talking with more than 150 witnesses, scrutinizing hours of footage from surveillance cameras all over the city, reading e-mails, studying photographs, and consulting various prosecutors. When investigators interviewed the DOT supervisors who allegedly told Halloran about DSNY misconduct, the men adamantly denied having said any such thing. The DOI also wanted to talk with the sanitation workers who the councilman said had spoken to him, but when pressed for their names, Halloran hedged, then said he couldn't reveal them because of attorney-client privilege. The DOI considered it a dubious claim.

The results of the inquiry were published in a twenty-five-page report in June 2011. It pointed to several problems within Sanitation that it urged the Department to correct. Communication procedures had been inadequate, as was equipment tracking. Wreckers had not been deployed as effectively as they should have been. The decision to suspend salting operations on December 26 hadn't considered the fact that the storm was hitting some parts of the city harder than others.

The report also included a detailed account of its research into Halloran's charges and concluded that they had no merit. The news made a few local media outlets, but it wasn't blared from the front pages the way his accusations had been.

Sanitation's snow-fighting protocols have been fine-tuned across decades, and the Department was successful in every storm to hit New York for many years, but the 2010 event revealed serious weaknesses. The DOI report pointed to several, but there's another that it didn't mention.

Orders about plowing up the trucks, putting on chains, spreading salt or suspending salt operations, turning plows to the left or right, all come from headquarters. But storms don't play out the same way in every part of the city. A district super on Staten Island might need to salt much longer than does his counterpart in the Bronx, for instance, but he must obey the stop-salt order no matter when it comes down. Such a command structure minimizes the risk of field officers making mistakes. It also prevents them from making and acting on good decisions. Sanitation workers and officers who have years of experience and who know the field well often have the best sense of what works and doesn't work in their own districts, but their street smarts and snow wisdom aren't always put to good use. It's a management approach common to many large bureaucracies and is partly in reaction to the litigiousness of contemporary America, but it weakens organizations as often as it protects them; it doesn't allow for flexibility when decisions made centrally don't fit the situation in the field—and it always bruises morale.

John Doherty still cringes when he talks about the Christmas Blizzard of 2010. It was the only time in his career, he said, when he was so discouraged he actually considered stepping down. He fervently hoped for a big snowstorm in the winter of 2011–2012 so his Department could redeem itself, but the weather stayed unseasonably warm. Vito Turso was disheartened to realize that all the goodwill for the DSNY that he had spent years fostering could dissipate so completely, so fast. Sanitation workers and officers who worked as long as forty-one days straight without a break because of that storm and its aftermath still become indignant when they remember how quickly the public assumed the worst of them. If a foreman ever gave an order not to plow during a snowstorm, several san workers told me, no one would listen. Sanitation pride wraps around many things, but snow fighting is one of the biggest. It makes no sense that anyone within the Department intentionally lay down when that storm hit. It makes just as little sense that the public believed they did.

The storm dented Sanitation's reputation, but it ruined Goldsmith's. He could no longer wear the mantle of management hero, and there was speculation that the mayor regretted appointing him. When Goldsmith was arrested on charges of domestic abuse after an altercation with his wife at the end of July, Bloomberg let him quietly resign.[10] Then the press found out why he left, and the quiet ended as they gave him a last drubbing on his way out the door. In early January 2012, the accusation against Goldsmith was found to have no merit.[11] Many sources reported the news, but—just as when Halloran's charges against the DSNY were determined to be baseless—it wasn't delivered with the same fanfare that had accompanied the original allegations.

19. Benevolence

They gather on the last Thursday of the month at a social hall in Maspeth, Queens, greeting one another with hearty embraces.[1] The loudest welcomes are given to the most recently retired, not yet so far from the daily life of the job; their smiles are wide and their cheeks flush as they endure huzzahs and backslaps. Almost all are men. Their sartorial choices run from T-shirts and jeans to sport coats and dress pants, though a few wear tailored suits. In the old days, a layer of smoke would hover at the ceiling, but now the smokers—fewer than there used to be—enjoy their habit outside, where they don't linger. A faint whiff of cigars drifts in after them.

The noise grows as more people arrive, the air thick with conversation. They trade rumors about who has what new assignment ("I heard he took that tissue in Queens East"), speculate on the most recent promotion list ("How'd she get such a low number?"); they shake their heads about transfers ("You know why he left the Bronx, right?"), inquire after one another's families ("Doesn't your daughter start college in the fall?"). Chiefs, officers, and sanitation workers mingle easily; when everyone is wearing civilian clothes, it's hard to discern rank, but forms of address give a clue. Familiar greetings of Frankie, Joey, or Ronnie are between equals, or from higher to lower status. From lower to higher, those same men are called Chief or Boss.

As the hour nears 7:00, people find their way to seats at the round tables that crowd the floor. Each table holds a jug of wine. Tantalizing smells of garlic and olive oil waft from a tiny kitchen in the back. The men in suits gather at the front of the room behind a pair of long tables set end to end, covered with white cloth, and anchored by a podium with a microphone. One of them taps the mic a few times, the room quiets, and the monthly meeting of the Department of Sanitation's Columbia Association is called to order.

The work of the DSNY is taken for granted by the larger public, but such disregard is not the measure that matters most to those who wear a Sanitation uniform. They are heroes or scoundrels to one another, some well respected or a few despised, but united by their shared understanding of what the job demands, what it gives back, what it denies, how profoundly it shapes their lives.

Everyone at a Columbia meeting knows exactly what it's like when the garbage seems too interminable, the rain too penetrating, the rules of the Department too punitive. There's no need for explanation when someone tells a story that mentions round-robins or bull pricks or saddlebags. If no one offers sympathy to the man who shakes his head about what it was like getting up in the middle of an eternally cold night for the umpteenth day to be at work well before dawn to steer a plow through snow-clogged streets at the start of another twelve-hour shift, the last day off nothing more than a distant memory, it's because everyone listening has been there, done that. At a benevolent society meeting, no one suffers the invisibility that marks their working hours. Quite the contrary. People come to the meetings because they know that here, at least, they are visible, known, and acknowledged.

In size and influence, the Columbia Association, the Emerald

Society, and the African American Benevolent Society are Sanitation's most powerful fraternals, but they are only three among many. The Hispanic Society, the Association de Latinos, Holy Name, Asian Jade, Steuben, Pulaski, and the Hebrew Spiritual have devoted members. Two newcomers are the United Women of Sanitation and Strongest Brotherhood, a benevolent society that is also a motorcycle club. Anyone who works for the Department is welcome to join any of the societies except the Hebrew Spiritual. Because it offers burial plots in a Jewish cemetery on Long Island, its membership is open only to fellow Jews.[2]

Sanitation's benevolent societies belong to a tradition that has been pivotal to American history almost since the country's start. Especially after the Revolutionary War, voluntary associations flourished, organizing themselves around religion, ethnicity, occupation, political sentiment. Many such groups first acted as burial societies to help pay for a casket and cemetery plot when a loved one died, but they also provided early forms of unemployment and medical insurance. Over time, organizations like the Odd Fellows, Elks, Masons, and Knights of Pythias were joined by the Ancient Order of United Workmen, Modern Woodmen of America, and other newcomers. These, in turn, were precursors to today's Rotary, Lions, and Kiwanis Clubs.[3] By the end of the nineteenth century, more than a third of the adult men in the United States—including American-born whites, African Americans, and immigrants—belonged to fraternal organizations.[4] These groups, though varied and many, shared goals of "sobriety, thrift, temperance, piety, industry, self-restraint, and moral obligation."[5]

In an institution as large and diverse as the DSNY, the societies provide smaller communities that are shaped around clearly defined and homogeneous measures. Fraternals inculcate their members in forms of social behavior that will help both the individual and the group by creating what the sociologist Cecilia Ridgeway calls "a shared definition of the situation." They also offer tangible forms of support in navigating the job by trying to foster in their members a combination of independence, compliance, and drive that defines what they consider a successful Sanitation employee.[6]

Independence implies patience with uncomfortable work rhythms, like bouncing all over the clock before seniority accumulates, and reluctance to complain about difficult job conditions. Compliance means following the Department's formal codes of conduct, but it also requires adherence to less formal social codes, like ignoring the job's stigma and not disrespecting higher-ranking colleagues. Drive is made evident through a willingness to take promotional exams and climb the Sanitation career ladder, which society leadership encourages all its members to do.

As with benevolents of old, members who prove themselves responsible and who are loyal participants in their association's dynamics create social capital within the group and for the organization within other contexts.[7] This, in turn, bolsters its power, which points to another, equally important purpose of the fraternals. Especially for the larger societies, inward cohesion is coupled with a political presence in Department life that has real consequence. Sanitation personnel who aren't much involved with the benevolents claim that promotions to higher ranks are based on requests from society leadership, which may or may not be true. At the same time, fraternals become guardians of at least nominal diversity within the upper ranks of DSNY hierarchy.

At the social hall in Maspeth, the man who tapped the microphone and quieted the room is the Columbia Association's recording secretary. He introduces himself and asks everyone to stand for the Pledge of Allegiance. After a mumbled rendition is finished and the sound of scraping chairs subsides, he introduces his elegantly dressed compatriots, the association's other officers, then turns the proceedings over to the president, Ron Cohen.

Cohen is tall, balding, and wears wire-rim glasses and a goatee. His mother is Italian, which fulfills the requirement that officers in the association have at least one Italian parent, and generations of his family have worked to better the image and standing of Italian Americans. He was raised in Italian neighborhoods with Italian friends and was an altar boy at Our Lady Help of Christians church in Midwood, Brooklyn, for years. He joined the Columbians when he first came on Sanitation in 1988 and quickly became one of the association's most active members. Fellow Columbians bragged that Cohen had more ethnic bona fides than many of them had themselves, but some people were unhappy when he was elected president.

Joe Siano, Cohen's predecessor, wasn't worried.[8]

Siano is a compact, slightly portly man with powerful arms and a mustache going to silver. He grew up in Brooklyn, joined the army in 1966, served in Vietnam, came out in 1969, took civil service exams for a variety of city jobs, married his sweetheart from Queens, and found work as a pipe fitter. He'd been in that job for sixteen years when the company went under. He was called for Sanitation at about the same time. He had no particular interest in or affinity with the DSNY, but he had a family to support.

He also had no particular interest in or affinity for the Columbia Association. When he was invited to a meeting, he and a couple of friends decided to see what it was about, but only out of mild curiosity. "We just sat there and listened the whole night," he recalled, "and we ate, and then we left." But he went back, and went back again, and after a while was asked to help with the annual journal, a book of tributes saluting the person within Sanitation whom the association has named Italian American of the Year. After that he was invited to join the board, where he took on the task of coordinating the group's annual family weekend at a local resort.

Then scandals involving its leadership rocked the organization. The president at the time was ousted, but not before months of acrimony left the association's reputation bruised and its membership rolls withered.

Siano agreed to serve as interim president, and when he was

elected to the office six months later, he made it his mission to re-build. "We started from the bottom," he said. He met with officers from the Department's other fraternals to begin repairing their trust in his society. And he deliberately changed the dynamic of the monthly meetings, standing at the door and personally greeting everyone who came.

"We do a lot of kissing," he explained. "First time it happened I was like, 'Oh my God, the hell is this? I got to get out of this organization!' But I learned. And I would meet you at the door and I'd hug you and give you a kiss on the cheek and I'd say, 'How is your family? What's going on?' And, I guess, the love got out there. People said, 'Hey, let's go to a meeting.' And actually our meetings are great."

So is their dinner dance, held every October at the El Caribe Country Club in Mill Basin, Brooklyn (association officers, the evening's proud and anxious hosts, look particularly debonair in black tuxedos with small red boutonnieres). Several of Sanitation's societies have dinner dances, but the Columbian's is acknowledged to be particularly well done. The cocktail hour is famously bountiful; the dinner itself is delicious. Speeches during dinner, when the Italian American of the Year Award is only the biggest of several honors doled out during the evening, can get a little long, though Siano tried to keep that in check even before he was president. (He was asked to emcee at many dances, he said, after organizers "realized I was able to read and speak and chew gum.") The evening regularly draws as many as eight hundred people, but there's another mark of its popularity. At similar Sanitation events, the brass tend to duck out as soon as possible after the formal presentations are finished; by the time dessert arrives, the hall is half empty. Not so at the Columbian dinner. The dance floor is crowded until late in the night, even though many of those attending must be at work by 6:00 the next morning.

In reviving the association, Siano took some inspiration from history. "You have to realize," he explained, "back in the day, the job was Italian. So, who had more members? We did. Who got more promotions? Italians. Our people were on the top for a long time, and the organization grew because of that."

When Cohen succeeded him, Siano knew that some among his membership didn't want a president with a Jewish name, but he saw the transition as a test. If the benevolent society he had helped revive was really as solid as he believed it to be, he knew it would not stumble on such pettiness. He said good riddance to those few who actually quit the group in protest.

Siano did well. Today the Columbia Association is thriving, and the difficult interludes are well past. This evening Cohen conducts the usual business of the meeting's start. He gives a special welcome to dignitaries in the crowd—chiefs of various ranks, presidents of some of the Department's other benevolents, Columbians from other city agencies.[9] He announces study groups for upcoming promotion exams and urges a good turnout for the annual golf outing, organized as a fund-raiser for the Cooley's Anemia Foundation. He reminds his listeners, though they know it already, that the disease especially affects children of Mediterranean heritage.

The audience listens politely, but when Cohen starts to introduce the evening's guest speaker, he's immediately drowned out by cheering and whistling. Harry Nespoli, president of the Uniformed Sanitationmen's Association, Local 831 of the International Brotherhood of Teamsters, is well-known to this crowd. He receives a standing ovation as he steps to the microphone.

Nespoli was elected president in 2003, only the fourth since the union was established in 1956.[10] He is powerfully built, with silver hair and a bearing that hints of his days playing semipro football. He grew up in Park Slope when that Brooklyn neighborhood was home to stevedores and others who worked on the waterfront. His accent and manner of speech sound more like Hollywood's idea of a blue-collar union man than the real thing, but he is one of the savviest labor leaders in recent city history. In 2008, his negotiating skills and tactical smarts helped him become head of the Municipal Labor Committee, a coalition that represents nearly half a million members of New York's municipal unions and that has considerable clout in local politics.

Sanitation bosses are respectful of Nespoli, but sanitation workers are adoring. In negotiations with the city, he has won solid contracts. He has made it a special cause to get the same death, heart, and lung benefits already available to the other municipal uniformed forces but long denied his workers, goals that eluded his predecessors. When the applause dies down, Nespoli gives quick reports on those efforts but soon moves to his real message.

Even if no one knew that Nespoli was tonight's guest, even if a different person were standing in front of them, everyone in the audience knows what they'll hear. It's one of the reasons they come to the meetings.

At all the benevolent societies, every guest speaker, every association or society officer, even the occasional member who's had a little too much to drink and takes an extemporaneous moment at the mic after the formal part of the meeting is over, sounds the same theme: Be proud. You *collect* garbage, that doesn't mean you *are* garbage. What you do is important. What you do *matters*. What you do is difficult and dangerous and absolutely fundamental to the well-being of this city. Never mind if the public ignores you or even scorns you. Look at what you've given your families; look at the children you're raising, the homes you can provide for them. Take pride in your job. Support your fraternal organizations. Support your union. Officers and chiefs, never forget where you came from. Remember that everyone in this room started on the street. Support one another. *Be proud.*

Benevolents offer respite not only from the imprecations of a surly public but also from another source of denigration as well: the job's harshest critics sometimes come from within the job itself.

Derision usually starts with accusations of ignorance, but those charges can be mere jumping-off points for a litany of slurs.

According to many san workers, foremen are lazy good-for-nothings, superintendents are heartless, assistant borough chiefs are merely garbagemen in jackets (within the DSNY there is a clear distinction between a "garbageman," which implies disapproval of an individual's ethics and character, and a sanitation worker), the borough chief never knew the street, three-star chiefs long ago forgot where they came from (and most never knew the job in the first place), while anyone with a higher rank than that either had to kiss a lot of ass to get there or only got promoted because of society hooks.

A similarly acerbic set of editorials can spew from employees across the chain of command, with changes in tone for those below or above them. The biggest criticism of sanitation workers by everyone higher up is that they are "crybabies," but foremen and superintendents are not immune from the same assessment by one-, two-, three-, and four-star chiefs. Even deputy commissioners will sometimes sling that insult about anyone of lower rank. The two most damning insults, however, are the purview of those at the bottom of the hierarchy.

The first is about claims to knowledge. If someone doesn't know the street, he doesn't know the job. "He's got no time" implies that the person in question hasn't been around long enough to learn anything worth knowing. I've heard it said of workers on the job a few months and on the job fifteen years (the speaker always has more time than the unfortunate soul he is skewering). Or if a san worker had an assignment that took him off the street, he can be on the job for many years and still be called ignorant by those who have little understanding of what his work actually entails.

The second insult points to affiliation and is reserved for people who have been promoted. If someone forgets where he comes from, he has proven himself disloyal. This is especially harsh to say of supervisors, who are only one step up from the street.

When I hear Sanitation folk cutting down other Sanitation folk, I yearn for a night with any of the benevolents. At least for one eve-ning, with friends, wine—and, at the Columbia meeting, some of the most delicious Italian food in New York—there is refuge from a cold, cruel world, even when that world is the DSNY itself.

Postlude: Someone Else

After Homer Simpson has an argument with Ray Patterson, Springfield's sanitation commissioner, he decides to run for the office himself, but his campaign isn't going well. Full of despair, he tells his troubles to his friend Moe, who suggests that he needs a good slogan. Nothing comes to mind. Moe encourages him to give it some real thought, but Homer isn't up to the task.

"Can't someone else do it?" he whines.

He has stumbled on the perfect message. At a rally, Homer reminds his audience how much they don't like dealing with their own garbage. Wouldn't it be so much better, he suggests, if they didn't have to? If it were someone else's responsibility? The crowd, quickly whipped into righteous indignation, sounds a loud and steady chant.

"Someone else! Someone else!"

Homer wins the election by a landslide.[1]

In the *Simpsons* episode called "Trash of the Titans," Homer is his usual self—absurd in a way that reveals to us our own absurdity. Of *course* we want someone else to deal with our mess, preferably someone like the san workers in Springfield: rough-looking men with stained uniforms, cigarettes dangling from their lips, and accents straight out of Brooklyn, circa 1954. It's the classic image of a "garbageman," but the few guys I met on the job who had any resemblance to it drew ridicule from coworkers. They were told to quit playacting. Though real sanitation workers don't recognize themselves in the cartoon, the stereotype still stands. It's part of the unseen-ness that attends labors of waste, mostly noticed only when something goes wrong.[2]

New York's sanitation workers walked out on strike for nine days in February 1968. It didn't take long before obscene quantities of garbage festooned every neighborhood, the stink spreading as heaps toppled and putrefying debris was strewn across sidewalks and thoroughfares. Various municipal employees in New York went on strike during that era, but Sanitation earned special venom. Maybe it was because of all the suddenly feral trash.[3] But maybe it was also because they demanded more than higher pay and a shorter workweek. They were no longer willing to endure equipment with broken switches, missing lights, sagging doors, and wiring so faulty that trucks sometimes burst into flames while drivers were in them, or filthy washrooms that crawled with rats, or falling-down facilities furnished with thirdhand amenities (lockers too old and battered for NYPD precincts were passed along to the DSNY).[4]

When they struck, the san men forced the city to actually see them. The previously anonymous Someone Elses were standing up and demanding to be recognized as honest-to-goodness, real live human beings. Sanitation workers in Memphis eloquently expressed the same sentiment in their strike later that year, carrying signs that read "I *AM* A MAN." They met even more resistance than their brethren in New York had faced.[5]

Mierle Laderman Ukeles remembers a story she heard during *Touch Sanitation*. As the ritual required, she faced a san man, shook hands with him, and thanked him for keeping New York City alive;

in return, he told her about a time he was on collection. "We were in Brooklyn. It was over 90 degrees, humid; we were very tired," he recalled. "We loaded a lady's garbage into the truck, and sat down on her porch steps for a minute. She opened up the door, and she said to us, 'Get away from here, you smelly garbagemen. I don't want you stinking up my porch.' For seventeen years that stuck in my throat, and today you wipe that out." Then he looked at Ukeles and asked, "Will you remember this?"[6]

His question inspired a 1984 performance work called *Cleansing the Bad Names*. Ukeles sent a message to Sanitation's entire workforce, asking them to tell her all the ugly names they'd been called over the years. Hundreds of responses came back. She painted them on seventy-five-foot-tall plate-glass windows in front of an art gallery in Manhattan, put up a two-story scaffolding so that all the names were within reach, and rebuilt the lady's porch at the gallery entrance.[7] Then she asked 190 people from various sectors of city life—government officials, politicians, artists, academics, bankers, athletes—to come wash off the bad names.

On the day of the event, the street was closed, chairs were set up, the participants were grouped into nine teams, and Ukeles invited them to begin. Some scrubbed from the upper levels of the scaffolding, some from the ground, and while an audience watched, Sanitation people among them, the bad names were slowly washed away.

It was a simple gesture that made a pointed statement. "Just as the DSNY washes away the dirt of the city for us—we who are dependent on the sanitation workers to do this work for us—it is up to us to wash away the bad names they are called on the street," Ukeles told me. "That is our work, not theirs."

While we are learning to do that work and teaching others to do that work, it's wise to remember how profoundly we depend on the slender vanguard of Sanitation that stands between our lives and the torrents of waste that would otherwise overwhelm us. A colleague put it succinctly one cold winter morning while we worked a heavy stop. "If you're lucky," he said as he tossed a couple of bags into the hopper, "you can go your whole life without ever having to call a cop." He pulled the handles; the hopper blade jerked into motion. "And you can also go your whole life without ever calling a fireman." The blade shoved under the trash, its machinery groaning. "But you need a sanitation worker every single day."

How to Speak Sanitation: A DSNY Glossary

57: The sign-in/sign-out sheet; used at the start and end of every shift.

350: The form that all sanitation workers receive, carry, fill out, and turn in at the end of their shifts. Different colors are for collection, recycling, sweeping, and other tasks. It is meant to account for mileage, fuel consumption, and route percentage completed, among other details.

air mail: Garbage thrown at the truck from windows above.

ASP: Alternate side parking regulations, also called street-cleaning regulations (see SCR).

bad time: Time spent on suspension, usually because of disciplinary action. Bad time doesn't count toward the years required for a full pension, so when you're ready to retire, you have to keep working the duration of that bad time until you make up the gap.

bale the truck: Squeeze the movable wall near the cab end of the truck body against the blade that pushes the garbage into the truck body. It compacts the trash as tightly as possible and can allow an extra ton or so of trash to fit in the truck.

banged: Disciplined. If you get banged, someone above you in the chain of command has filed a written complaint about you.

baskets: An assignment to empty public litter baskets along a defined route. It includes no truck money (see below). When you finish the route, you go back to the top and start over. It's one of the least popular assignments; junior workers are stuck on baskets.

beat: A word that defines seniority; when you say "I got you beat," it means "I have more time on the job than you do" and therefore have first choice of good assignments.

blade: The movable back wall of the truck body and/or the scooping mechanism of the hopper.

blood money: Overtime for working snow once the novelty has been replaced by the relentlessness of too many hours and no days off.

board: The assignments board, which changes from day to day. Sanitation workers scrutinize it at the start and end of their shifts; it tells them what they are doing and with whom they are doing it. It is ruled by seniority.

body bags: The big (120-gallon), long garbage bags that come from apartment buildings with compactors. They look as if they could hold a body. Also called sausage bags (see below).

bombed: An extremely heavy route.

bouncing: A highly erratic work schedule.

broom qualified: Someone who is trained to operate a mechanical broom.

bulk: Dead refrigerators, stoves, other large appliances, furniture, and so on. Describes what's collected and also describes the assignment ("I'm on bulk today").

bull prick: The large pin that holds the plow apparatus on to the front of a truck.

bumper cars: Mechanical brooms.

calling it out: Not finishing the route; same as giving back work (see below).

can man: How many workers are available to staff a particular need. Phrased as "What's your can man for today?"

carry: When one worker covers for another worker, usually in the context of collection. "That whole month Jimmy had back trouble, his partner carried him."

CDL: Commercial driver license; a Class B CDL is mandatory for getting the job as a sanitation worker.

chart or chart day: Day off. If you "get" your chart, it means you work it and will be paid time and a half. If you don't get your chart, it means you don't work on your scheduled day off. Chart days rotate from one week to the next. You are always off on Sunday (unless there's some special occasion or it snows), but because your chart day rotates, you rarely get two days off in a row.

chasing garbage: Returning to collection after having been diverted to snow. Depending on how big the storm, it can take weeks of chasing garbage to get caught up.

clean: What a route is or is not by the end of a shift.

clean garbage: Trash left out for collection in neatly organized piles.

collection: Picking up garbage.

coming on: Starting the job.

commingle: Lump metal, glass, and plastic recycling together for collection.

condition: A garbage-related problem; for example, the contents of many full and overturned litter baskets blowing around a street corner is a condition. So is a place used as a dump out (see below).

coned: A litter basket that's overloaded and overflowing.

cut-down: The DSNY dump truck.

cut the load: Fill the truck to less than its capacity.

deadheading: Driving a collection truck on a street that forbids commercial traffic. It's against DSNY regulations, but it can be a faster route than more crowded streets.

death march: A very long route.

detached: Working in a location for an indefinite period of time but not assigned there permanently. Example: A supervisor assigned to the Queens East 10 garage is detached to Safety and Training as an instructor. His home within the DSNY is still Queens East 10, but he works at Floyd Bennett Field.

disco rice: Maggots.

district: A field division within DSNY's operations. Sanitation divides the city into fifty-nine districts, coterminous with community boards. Each district has a garage and as many as eight sections (see below).

doesn't have a hair on his ass: A man who is not manly, not courageous, not macho.

doing a job: Collecting garbage that, by law, is not allowed in city Sanitation trucks.

dump out: A location used as an illegal dump site, often along railroad tracks, under overpasses, or in abandoned lots. Dump outs create conditions (see above).

even: Exactly the right number of workers for the day's assignments.

export: What happens to New York City's municipal waste now that there are no disposal options within the city's boundaries.

FEL: Front-end loader; used for, among other things, filling spreaders with salt.

flats: Collection from big bag stops, usually in high-density residential neighborhoods with large apartment buildings.

forced: Being ordered to work a particular shift or assignment.

foreman: Former title of a supervisor; it was officially changed in October 1983, but it's still commonly used.

fruit wagon: Collection truck.

gate district: A Sanitation district that has a lot of gate work (see next entry), like some neighborhoods in Brooklyn.

gate work: Lifting garbage cans and garbage bags over the gates that stand between a home and the street.

get it and go: An old practice of cleaning the route, dumping the truck, and then leaving for the day. A crew that ran it up (see below) and had a few heavy flat stops (see above) could be done in a few hours. Get it and go is no longer allowed.

getting hurt: To be on the receiving end of disciplinary action that costs pay.

getting it up: Getting the garbage up off the street. Someone who can really get it up is a good worker.

getting made: Being promoted.

getting over: Getting away with something, being sneaky, getting around a rule. Not unique to the DSNY, but heard with some frequency.

giving back work: Not finishing the task you're supposed to finish on your shift. If a route isn't cleaned by the time it's supposed to be, that collection crew gave back work.

go down: Get (down) out of the truck.

gold-chain garage: A garage with many workers of Italian heritage.

grounded: You can work, but you can't drive equipment.

GU: Garage utility person; a sanitation worker who is assigned to the garage to help the garage supervisor.

half: A truck that isn't filled when it finishes one section in a district so is moved to another section.

haul road: A road between a landfill's unloading area and the open face.

haulster: A small pickup truck; also called an LUV truck (see below).

Hi-Lo: Forklift.

hit the handle: Activate the hopper blade so it scoops garbage into the body of the truck (see below; same as "send it up").

hold the district: What a worker or officer with seniority can do when there are too many people for the jobs available. Workers or officers with less seniority can't hold the district, so they'll be sent to other work locations.

hook: Someone within the bureaucracy, usually of higher rank, who can do you a favor or help you out of a jam. A person with good hooks has a lot of juice (see below).

House of Pain: Nickname for the Bronx 7 garage, where the average weight on the day shift is sometimes as high as twenty tons (which means a crew must do a load and a piece; see below).

house-to-house: A route with many stops to pick up small quantities of garbage from individual homes or small apartment buildings.

hugging the side: Staying as close as possible to the curb or to parked cars when doing house-to-house.

ins and outs: Highway entrances and exits. Used in the context of snowplow routes.

in title: Refers to the uniformed jobs within the DSNY. A person just hired is in title as a sanitation worker. After his first promotion, he's in title as a supervisor.

juice: The power to make things happen; someone with good hooks (see above).

jumping the route: A broom operator who leaves his regular route for another one.

junior flip: New hire.

knocked down: When a complaint or summons is dismissed.

laying down: Not doing the job.

laying pipe: Working extremely slowly (slower than walking backwards; see below. Also has a sexual connotation).

left out: The status of garbage still uncollected on a route at the end of a shift.

lights: Empty barges.

list number: Based on hiring and promotional exams, this number indicates the likelihood of getting the job and later of moving up in rank. List number plus start date determines seniority.

load: A truck's worth of garbage.

load and a piece: A truck filled (also called "loaded out"; see next entry), dumped, and then partially loaded again.

loaded out: A full truck; the end of a truck's capacity. "I'm loaded out" means "My truck is full."

LODI: Line-of-duty injury. "He went LODI" means he is away from work because of an injury sustained on the job.

loop a load, loop a piece: To enter and leave a dump without emptying the truck (see also "swing a load," below).

LUV truck: Light utility vehicle; a small pickup truck, also called a haulster (see above).

make the truck: An assignment on collection (garbage) or recycling. Because it includes a pay differential, a worker usually requires some seniority to make the truck.

minute man: A worker who shows up as close to the exact start of the shift as possible.

MLP: Mechanized (or motorized) litter patrol; a fancy phrase for cleaning up messes in odd places, like under an overpass or along a side street. It can involve bulk pickup.

m'on back man: The person who guides a driver while the driver is backing up a truck (short for "Come on back").

mongo/mungo: (N.) objects plucked/rescued from the trash; (v.) to take objects from the trash.

MPG: Metal, plastics, and glass recycling.

mutual: Trading chart days. For example, Pete is chart on a Tuesday and I'm chart on a Friday but he needs Friday off, so we swap. I'd explain to our supervisor or to our superintendent, "Pete and I did a mutual."

nail-and-mail: A summons delivered by mail.

nanny goat route: An especially hilly route on collection or recycling.

night diff or night differential: A 10 percent add-on to the hourly pay of anyone who works a night shift.

night plow: The time between November and April when the DSNY is ready for snow. The day shift, which is 6:00 to 2:00 in the summer, becomes 7:00 to 3:00, and one section in each garage must work nights. The sections rotate from year to year.

on the arm: Unpaid labor. For instance: "Are you being paid for this work?" "Hell, yes! I'd never do it on the arm!"

O route: A broom operator's route on Wednesdays and Saturdays, when there is no alternate side parking. O stands for "ordinary" (though some sources say it stands for "other").

out of town: Having to work for the day at a garage (or location) that's not your home garage (or location). Depending on where you are assigned, you can pick up hours (see below).

over: Extra workers. When a garage is three over, it means three workers will be sent to work that day in garages that are under (see below).

Packman/Mrs. Packman: A male or female sanitation worker, respectively, assigned to an automated collection truck known as an E-Z Pack.

PAP: Stands for "policies and procedures" but refers to a drug and alcohol test. When the "PAP Wagon," a.k.a. the piss wagon, shows up at a garage, sanitation workers are randomly chosen to take a Breathalyzer test and to pee into a cup. In the event of a vehicular accident, sanitation workers are also PAPed.

papers, throwing (putting) them in: Retiring.

picking up: Where you work. Someone working in Greenwich Village around the university would say, "I pick up NYU." Someone working in Brooklyn 6 would say, "I pick up Park Slope."

picking up hours: Getting time in the books that you can take off with pay. This happens for a sanitation worker when he or she is sent outside the zone that includes her or his home garage. Officers at the rank of chief pick up hours instead of getting paid for overtime.

piss pots: An old-fashioned term for house-to-house routes (see above).

PM: Periodic maintenance.

Ponderosa: Old nickname for the Queens East 13 garage.

premium: A double-time day, like Sunday or a holiday.

put out: What happens to household garbage on the day or evening before a scheduled collection.

rabbi: A guide, mentor; someone who takes you under his or her wing, teaches you the ropes, helps you stay out of trouble (this is not unique to the DSNY, but I first learned it there).

red-bagged: Medical waste (it is not collected by the DSNY).

redlined: The line drawn under the last name on the 57; anyone who signs after the red line is drawn is counted as late.

relay: Driving a full truck to the dump, emptying it, driving it back to the garage. New hires often start with relays; they'll spend the shift just driving full trucks, dumping them, returning them, taking out another truck.

released: What happens to a worker when he or she takes on another responsibility for a short time. Someone is released from his or her usual duties to be trained on a new piece of equipment. Members of the DSNY Pipe and Drum Band are released from regular assignments when they play at Department functions.

resumed: What must happen before you can return to work after a medical leave. "Have you been resumed by the clinic? No? Then you can't work."

rib: A segment of the truck body.

rip: (1) Get garbage off the street fast. "Ripping both sides" means working both sides of a street at once. (2) A formal disciplinary complaint. A three-day rip, for instance, is a three-day suspension for some infraction of the rules.

RO: Rotating officer. A supervisor or superintendent who is not assigned to a permanent location but instead works all over the city, filling in when fellow officers have a day off or are out sick.

rocket: A written complaint (as in a foreman telling a sanitation worker, "If you don't clean your route today, I'll give you a rocket").

ro-ro: Roll-on/roll-off truck, used for some kinds of containers.

running or running it up: Working very fast.

running heavy: Your truck is loading out (see above) before your route is cleaned.

saddlebags: Tubs of liquid calcium chloride affixed to the sides of snow-fighting vehicles called spreaders and flow-and-dumps.

salad wagon: Collection truck (an old term, not used much anymore).

sausage bags: Big garbage bags (approximately 120 gallons) that come from large apartment complexes with compactors. Shaped like sausages. Also called body bags (see above).

scalping: Stealing garbage (see below).

schranked: Being paid truck differential (also called truck money; see below) even if you don't work the truck. This happens only when you are supposed to work collection or recycling but are involuntarily reassigned. The word evolved from the name of Robert Schrank, a labor mediator who helped negotiate the transition from three-man to two-man crews.

SCR: Street-cleaning regulations, a.k.a. alternate side parking rules (see "ASP").

sections: The way districts (see above) are divided.

segments: Bristles of the gutter brooms on a mechanical broom.

send it up: Activate the hopper blade to move garbage up into the body of the truck (see above; same as "hit the handle").

set the blade: Position a truck's compaction mechanisms so that it can be loaded to maximum capacity. A crew sets the blade at the start of a shift.

shop steward's route: It's lighter than all the others.

short dump: A temporary location where a truck is emptied instead of being taken to a transfer station.

sign nights: Volunteer to work a regular night shift.

sign the broom: When a supervisor meets a broom operator along the broom route and signs the operator's 350 to confirm how much and which portions of the route have been completed.

sitting bull: Back in the day when there were three men on a truck, the driver never got out and never helped load; he was called the sitting bull.

smokin' shoes route: An especially long route on collection or recycling.

sniping: Maneuvering the mechanical broom between and around obstacles, which are usually cars.

spillage: Garbage that falls to the street while workers are loading out the truck.

spitting: What the truck does when it's filled beyond capacity.

squatter's rights: Slight changes to seniority protocols, according to the house rules of a given garage or broom depot.

stealing a street: Driving down a one-way street the wrong way.

stealing garbage: What happens sometimes when a crew thinks they'll come up light on the truck's weight, so they take ("go into") garbage from another route, another section, or even another district. Also called scalping (see above).

stroke the book: What foremen (supervisors) did when they filled out time books. The stroke is a line drawn diagonally from corner to corner of a little box in the ledger; above the stroke is one set of information, below the stroke is another, all in codes that correspond to different payroll lines (overtime, snow, night shift, and so on). This has been replaced by electronic payroll systems.

Sunday and one day: The weekend when a sanitation worker's scheduled days off line up to include a Saturday or a Monday.

super's clerk: A sanitation worker who serves as the secretary and right-hand person for the garage superintendent. Often sets the board, troubleshoots on behalf of the super, fields phone calls, tracks paperwork, keeps the super administratively organized. A good super's clerk makes the difference between a disorganized garage and a well-run garage.

swing a load: Dumping only part of a load and returning to the garage with garbage still in the truck. Not done anymore, because trucks are weighed when they arrive at the dump and when they leave. In the old days, they were weighed only when they arrived. See also "loop a load," above.

Tiffany: A particularly neat and tidy job of collection. "He did a real Tiffany on that stop" or "That crew did a Tiffany on their last block."

time frames: When and how long breaks and lunch last. Schedules for such things are supposed to be tightly followed; if you are outside of or if you don't watch your time frames, you can get banged (see above).

tissue: A desk job, an easy job; often (but not always) assigned to a sanitation worker coming off medical leave who can work but isn't quite ready to be behind the truck again.

tit job: Same as a tissue (see above).

triple shift: Work the same piece of equipment on the day shift (6:00 a.m. to 2:00 p.m.), then on the evening shift (4:00 p.m. to 12:00 a.m.), and then on the night shift (12:00 a.m. to 8:00 a.m.). Not allowed, but it happens sometimes.

truck money: The extra pay a sanitation worker earns when assigned to collection or recycling. This was negotiated as part of the deal with the city when crews went from three-man to two-man in the mid-1980s.

under: Too few workers. A garage that is three under will need to get three more workers, probably from a garage that is over (see above).

urban white fish: Spent condoms floating in the water (this phrase isn't exclusive to the DSNY).

unusual: An unanticipated and/or uncommon incident during a shift that has an impact on the work.

walking backwards: Working very slowly.

white elephant: Collection truck.

white shirt: Superintendent-level officer or higher.

work out: How much work is left at the end of a shift. "There are three loads out in my section," a supervisor might tell his superintendent. This means there are three trucks' worth of garbage to be collected.

wrecker: Tow truck. A sanitation worker who is wrecker qualified must have a Class A CDL (commercial driver license).

zone, in or out of: Where you're sent when you go out of town (see above). If you're out of zone, you pick up hours (see above), but in zone you don't.

Notes

Prelude: Center of the Universe

1. This particular transfer station takes garbage out by rail; others use tractor trailers, and there are intentions to bring back barge transport. The *New York Times* editorial "A Fair Way to Handle Trash," May 28, 2012, gives an update on recent controversies around one facility.
2. In fact, each ton is meticulously accounted for, and the city is charged accordingly.
3. Ukeles calls this a process of "un-naming" ("Leftovers").
4. Garbage inside a rear-loading compactor truck is tightly compressed. When it's emptied, a wall near the cab pushes the trash toward the back, where it's slowly excreted. The force of compaction often melds the rubbish into one large clump, known in the world of garbage truck design as a turd. A successfully built, smoothly functioning compactor is measured by the uniformity of its turds and by the ease with which the turd is shat (Nagle, "Week-Long Journal"; Royte, *Garbage Land*, 39).
5. See Needham and Spence, "Refuse and the Formation of Middens," as well as Martin and Russell, "Trashing Rubbish," for a discussion of rubbish in archaeological context. Rathje and Murphy, *Rubbish!*, explain what classical archaeological analysis learns from modern-day garbage; White, "Fascinating World of Trash," reports on Rathje's work. Buchli and Lucas, *Archaeologies of the Contemporary Past*, sounded an early call for a thoughtful archaeology of the contemporary; Harrison and Schofield, "Archaeo-ethnography, Auto-archaeology," offer more recent overviews.
6. Mauss, *The Gift*, 11–12.

I. Garbage Faeries

1. Different-colored cards indicate what is to be collected: refuse is white, paper is green, and MPG (metals, plastics, and glass) is blue, while 350s for mechanical brooms and litter baskets are yellow.
2. When a route includes both sides of the street, the crew is to work one side at a time. Working both sides is a good way to get hit by passing cars and is against Department rules. Some workers do it anyway.
3. It works out to 890 New Yorkers per DSNY employee. Numbers are current as of July 2012.
4. Household waste accounts for about a third of the city's daily waste total. Commercial and business waste is another third, with C&D—construction and demolition debris—making up the last third.
5. Office of Management and Budget, "New York Executive Budget Fiscal Year 2013," 133.
6. All figures, courtesy of the DSNY Bureau of Cleaning and Collection, are current as of May 2012.
7. Manhattan 8, which is on the east side of Central Park roughly parallel to Manhattan 7, is the borough's busiest; it runs a weekly average of 120 trucks on collection and 61 on recycling. It's also the borough's heaviest district, followed by Manhattan 12, which serves the Washington Heights neighborhood, and then Manhattan 7.
8. Excerpt from Wilbur, "Transit."
9. There is a rich literature about the impact of uniforms on those who wear them and on those who interact with them. See, for instance, Craik, "Cultural Politics of the Uniform"; Fussell, *Uniforms*; Joseph and Alex, "Uniform"; Pratt, "Organizational Dress."
10. Sanitation workers are on the street every day, however, and often find themselves stepping into emergencies.
11. *Blue-Collar Journal*, an account of Coleman's experiences working as a ditch-digger, a short-order cook, and a "garbageman," was a prelude to the more politically charged *Nickel and Dimed*, Barbara Ehrenreich's 2001 book about living for a year while earning only minimum wage in various jobs.
12. Coleman, *Blue-Collar Journal*, 220–21.
13. To study something that does not already stand out, argues Brekhus, can be called "reverse marking" ("Sociology of the Unmarked," 45). He was building on work by Harold Garfinkel (*Studies in Ethnomethodology*) that argued for transforming the socially mundane into the analytically significant.
14. Some of Brekhus's examples include handedness (left-handedness is marked; right-handedness is not), intellectual ability (gifted and challenged are marked; average is not), and moral behavior (criminals and saints are marked; moral neutrality is not) ("Sociology of the Unmarked," 36–37).

15. MacBride, *Recycling Reconsidered*, and Wagner, *But Will the Planet Notice?*, make compelling arguments for this point.

16. William Rathje calls garbage and its attendant needs "the visible invisible." The writer China Miéville plays with the idea of purposeful not-seeing in many of his novels; he puts it to particularly wonderful effect in *The City and the City*.

17. Garbage collection and street sweeping have been mandates since the city's earliest days, but they weren't done consistently or effectively until 1896.

18. This is an example of what the sociologist Eviatar Zerubavel calls "temporal regularity," part of our time-based understanding of the world that he says "helps us attain some peace of mind regarding our environment" (*Hidden Rhythms*, 14).

19. There have been so many examples of extreme hoarding behavior—people unable to part with even the most trivial bits and scraps—that the word "disposophobia" has been invented to describe it and a reality show called *Hoarders* profiles heartbreaking cases. For a measured look at this phenomenon, see Kelly Anderson's documentary film *Never Enough: People's Relationship with Stuff* and also Frost and Steketee, *Stuff*.

20. See Strasser, *Waste and Want*, 161–201, for a look at how disposability, cleanliness, and convenience were bundled together to sell new products in the early years of the twentieth century, and how those products fostered a faster flow of goods and greater ease of disposability while helping encourage the quickened pace of modern life.

21. Goldstein, "Jan Kemp Dies at 59."

22. The precise figures, courtesy of the Sanitation Department's Office of Public Information: as of June 2012, the DSNY workforce is 55 percent white, 24 percent black, and 17.6 percent Hispanic. The remainder includes Asians and the category "Unknown."

2. In the Field

1. Rothschild, *New York City Neighborhoods*.

2. See Ballon and Jackson, *Robert Moses and the Modern City*, and Caro, *Power Broker*, for more on Moses, though neither mentions much about his waste management schemes.

3. Her statement "Manifesto for Maintenance Art 1969!" remains a seminal document in contemporary art. For the text, see www.moca.org/wack/?p=301.

4. Bourdon, "Apocalyptic Paperhanger Shows His Stripes."

5. Anthony Vaccarello was the DSNY commissioner who reached out to Ukeles.

6. For more about *Touch Sanitation*, see Dion and Rockman, "Interview with Mierle Laderman Ukeles," and Morgan, "*Touch Sanitation*." For a more complete overview of Ukeles's nearly forty-year legacy with the DSNY, see www .feldmangallery.com.

7. For different viewpoints on the discipline's history, see Asad, *Anthropology and the Colonial Encounter*; Marvin Harris, *Rise of Anthropological Theory*; and Hodgen, *Early Anthropology in the Sixteenth and Seventeenth Centuries*.

8. Michael Thompson, *Rubbish Theory*.

9. On time, see E. P. Thompson, "Time, Work-Discipline, and Industrial Capitalism"; on things, see Kopytoff, "Cultural Biography of Things."

10. Strasser, *Waste and Want*.

11. Certeau, "Unnamable."

12. William Miller, *Anatomy of Disgust*.

13. Douglas, *Purity and Danger*.

14. Melosi, *Garbage in the Cities*; Benjamin Miller, *Fat of the Land*; Rathje and Murphy, *Rubbish!*

15. "Kill" is common to place-names in parts of New York state (the Catskill Mountains, the towns of Fishkill, Peekskill, Kaaterskill Falls). It comes from the Renaissance Dutch word for creek, brook, or stream and is a vestige of the region's colonial history.

16. Fresh Kills sits on a major avian flyway, and when its wetlands were buried by heaps of edible debris, it became a mother lode of victuals for as many as forty-five species of migratory birds (Gertz, "Fresh Kills"). The laughing gull, with its black mask and distinctive cry, had been on the brink of extinction when the landfill opened. Now the species thrives all over northeastern North America.

17. Kruse and Ellsworth, *Geologic City*. For more on social meanings of Fresh Kills, see Nagle, "History and Future of Fresh Kills."

18. While the filmmaker Lucy Walker was a student at NYU, she joined us for one of our Fresh Kills tours. The landfill left a deep impression on her, and she vowed that someday she would make a documentary that focused on garbage. The result was her 2010 film *Waste Land*, about scavengers who work on a landfill in Rio de Janeiro. See blogs.wsj.com/speakeasy/2010/10/28/lucy-walkers -waste-land/.

19. See Reno, "Out of Place," for an excellent ethnographic study of workers at a landfill in the Midwest.

20. A more specific definition calls participant observation "a dynamic and flexible method of social inquiry that permits the researcher access to detailed information regarding a social reality that is not normally accessible for quantitative research methods" (Lauder, "Covert Participant Observation of a Deviant Community," 185).

21. Kelley, "Using Garbage as Text."

22. Doherty has been commissioner longer than any other since the Department was established in 1881.

23. See Rogers, *Gone Tomorrow*, 141–53, for a critique of the role of the beverage container industry in founding Keep America Beautiful.

24. It's now across the street, on the West Side Highway and West Fifty-Seventh Street.

3. On the Board

1. As of June 2012, there are 186 women in the uniformed ranks of the DSNY.
2. See E. P. Thompson, "Time, Work-Discipline, and Industrial Capitalism," and Zerubavel, "Standardization of Time," for some of the history that shaped industrialized and standardized measures of time.
3. Certainly there had been injuries caused by falling off the back step, though some observers within the Department weren't convinced that this was the union's real reason for eliminating the running boards.
4. Manhattan's municipal waste goes to two waste-to-energy facilities near Newark, New Jersey.

4. Body and Soul

1. My thanks to Jennifer Pliego of Manos Therapeutics for clarifying the mechanics of these motions.
2. American Public Works Association, *Refuse Collection Practice*, 141.
3. See Sullivan, *Rats*, for a fascinating look at facts, folklore, and phobias inspired by our oldest and nearest urban neighbor. Also see Corrigan, "'Ratopolis' of New York City."
4. Quoted in the *Daily News*, June 28, 2001, 6.
5. According to the story in *The Chief*, Bloomberg also took care to point out that he had contributed two million dollars to the Police and Fire Widows' and Children's Benefit Fund over the previous thirteen years (Van Auken, "Bloomberg Blooper Stirs Union Wrath"). www.nycpba.org/archive/ch/01/ch-010706-bloomberg.html.
6. Drudi, "Job Hazards in the Waste Industry."
7. Bureau of Labor Statistics, "National Census of Fatal Occupational Injuries in 2011 (Preliminary Results)."
8. In a 2008 analysis, 112 police officers died for 1,426 million hours worked, a fatality rate of 15.7 per 100,000 employed individuals; for firefighters, the 44 deaths for 806 million work hours is a fatality rate of 6.9. In contrast, there were 30 refuse collector fatalities for 169 million work hours, a fatality rate of 35.5 per 100,000 workers. This and a wealth of related information can be found on the BLS Web pages (www.bls.gov).
9. Incidents of needle sticks for DSNY workers between 1997 and 2002, as well as protocols and policies, are described in Lawitts, "Needle Sightings and On-the-Job Needle-Stick Injuries."
10. Hydrofluoric acid, one of the most corrosive substances known to humankind, is described as "exceedingly" hazardous. It "quickly penetrates the skin, destroys deep tissues and can result in acute-threatening liver, kidney and metabolism disorder . . . Serious effects can occur even if only small skin areas are exposed . . . Deep penetration through the upper layer of the skin results in

liquefaction and necrosis of deeper soft tissues" (Peters, "Symptoms and Treatment of Hydrogen Fluoride Injuries," 162). See also Horton et al., "Hydrofluoric Acid Releases in 17 States." Its normal concentration is 48 percent.

5. Mongo and Manipulation

1. These don't include New York City Housing Authority buildings. Those are serviced by the DSNY, but most often the garbage is containerized and collected by trucks called E-Z Packs that use an automated arm and only a single worker.
2. The origins of the word, sometimes spelled "mungo," are obscure. It has even eluded the investigations of Erin McKean and her savvy word sleuths when, as editor of *The New Oxford American Dictionary*, she put her team on the case. For more about mongo in New York and elsewhere, see Botha, *Mongo*.
3. In districts with short routes, writing on the back of the 350 is quick and easy. In districts with long routes, like in eastern Queens and on Staten Island, the routes run many printed pages and are stapled to the 350.
4. Over the last decade and a half, drug testing has cost several hundred sanitation workers their jobs. At the same time, although it is harder to measure, countless accidents and tragedies did not occur.

6. Being Uniform

1. In 2006, citing insurmountable structural problems, sky-high truancy rates, rock-bottom graduation numbers, and extraordinary overcrowding, the city closed Seward Park High School, but the building still serves its original purpose. It is home to several smaller "boutique" high schools.
2. Only about 10 percent of these forty-five hundred made it all the way from the test to the job, a ratio steady enough to be predictable. The DSNY uses it when deciding how deep to go on the list. At a talk I gave a while after this, I met a young man whose heart's desire was to become a sanitation worker. His list number was somewhere around 14,000. He didn't have a chance.
3. *Time*, March 11, 1940; *New York Times*, March 3, 1940, 12.
4. *New York Times*, February 19, 1940, 18.
5. The commissioner at the time was Robert Groh, former borough president of Queens ("Women 'White Wings' Planned," *New York Times*, April 18, 1974, 45).
6. Redd, *Newsday*, September 23, 1986. Steisel brought in the Center for Women in Government, now part of the Rockefeller College of Public Affairs and Policy at the State University of New York–Albany.
7. Johnson, "Ruling Paves the Way."

7. Tubbs of Nastiness

1. Martin Melosi started the conversation about the role of solid waste in the history of urban infrastructure (*Garbage in the Cities*). The definitive history of garbage in New York was written by Benjamin Miller (*Fat of the Land*). A shorter but essential work on the same subject is by Elizabeth Fee and Steven Corey (*Garbage!*).

2. The first colonists in New York were Walloons, the name given to Huguenots from a part of Belgium known then as Wallonia. The Dutch had a hard time convincing their compatriots to migrate to the New World because so many of them preferred to stay in Holland. In the late sixteenth and early seventeenth centuries, while much of Europe was torn apart by wars and bloody religious persecution, the Netherlands enjoyed political security, amicable pluralism, economic stability, and intellectual ferment. This atypical peace and prosperity contributed mightily to the well-being of the Dutch citizenry, and the official policy of explicit religious tolerance—an economic decision, not a moral one—drew refugees from all over Europe and beyond. See Shorto, *Island at the Center of the World*, for more detail.

3. Hansen and McGowan, *Breaking Ground, Breaking Silence*, 16; Leslie M. Harris, *In the Shadow of Slavery*, 14, 15, 30–31; Moore, "World of Possibilities," 37; Wagman, "Corporate Slavery in New Netherland."

4. Leslie M. Harris, *In the Shadow of Slavery*, 18.

5. They are mostly left out of the city's history, but it's hard to overemphasize the importance of enslaved laborers. Without them, notes the historian Christopher Moore, the colony would likely have foundered, for they "stood at the core of New Netherland's labor force" ("World of Possibilities," 38).

6. Burrows and Wallace, *Gotham*, 43.

7. Fernow, *Records of New Amsterdam*, 1:31; Stokes, *Iconography of Manhattan Island, 1498–1909*, 177.

8. For a comprehensive survey of New York's public health history during colonial and postcolonial eras, see Duffy, *History of Public Health in New York City*.

9. For details about colonial land making, see Geismar, "Landmaking in Lower Manhattan"; Rothschild, *New York City Neighborhoods*; Cantwell and Wall, *Unearthing Gotham*.

10. Burns and Sanders, *New York*, 13.

11. If he could have seen the future, Stuyvesant might have taken comfort in knowing that the problem of roaming livestock, especially pigs, would vex New Yorkers for the next two hundred years.

12. Butchers were among the most egregious illegal dumpers. Bridenbaugh singles them out as "especially obnoxious and lacking in public consideration" (*Cities in the Wilderness*, 85).

13. Fernow, *Records of New Amsterdam*, 1:33.

14. Fernow, *Records of New Amsterdam*, 5:45; see also Duffy, *History of Public Health in New York City*, 19.

15. Koeppel notes that the scarcity of water was one of the reasons Stuyvesant gave his bosses when he returned to Holland to explain why he gave up New Amsterdam. They found it hard to believe ("Rise to Croton," 29).

16. Bridenbaugh, *Cities in the Wilderness*, 18; see Deetz, "In Small Things Forgotten," for details about similar behavior in rural areas.

17. Bridenbaugh, *Cities in the Wilderness*, 62.

18. For details about filling in the canals, see ibid., 20. Today the courses of the Bevers and Heere Grachts can be traced by walking Beaver and Broad Streets in lower Manhattan.

19. Ibid., 85–86.

20. Ibid., 44; Hodges, "Cartmen of New York City," 26–27.

21. Bridenbaugh, *Cities in the Wilderness*, 18, 166.

22. Hodges, "Cartmen of New York City," 37.

23. Duffy, *History of Public Health in New York City*, 26–27.

24. According to Jackson's *Encyclopedia of New York City*, 4,937 people lived in the county of New York in 1698 (922). Duffy estimates the population between 4,500 and 5,000 in 1702, and thus calculates that the first yellow fever outbreak claimed between 10 and 12 percent of the city's population (*History of Public Health in New York City*, 35–36). Population counts for that era vary considerably, depending on the source.

25. Duffy, *History of Public Health in New York City*, 42–47; Koeppel, *Water for Gotham*, 25. Cadwallader Colden was something of a Renaissance man. He was a surveyor, a physician, and a passionate botanist who lived with his family on a three-thousand-acre Hudson Valley estate called Coldengham (Lewis, *Hudson*, 21–24).

26. Burrows and Wallace, *Gotham*, 185.

27. New-York City Common Council Minutes, May 14, 1788.

28. Koeppel, *Water for Gotham*, 57.

29. A "malignant fever" (likely yellow fever) took 750 New Yorkers in 1795, and a few dozen in 1796 and in 1797 (ibid., 62).

30. Quoted in Daley, *World Beneath the City*, 25.

31. Ibid., though one assumes that if frogs and reptiles were still enjoying the water, perhaps it wasn't yet *that* dirty.

32. Quoted in Koeppel, *Water for Gotham*, 65.

33. Jackson, *Encyclopedia of New York City*, 923.

34. New York City Common Council Minutes, May 7 and May 14, 1804. The fill didn't just trouble the people who lived near it; about 120 years later, it troubled people trying to dig through it to build the Holland Tunnel (Frazier, *Gone to New York*, 40–41).

35. Philadelphia was thought to be occupied by orderly, right-angled citizens, since that city's streets were orderly and right-angled. In contrast, New Yorkers, who

were continually being "tossed about over hills and dales, through lanes and alleys, crooked streets" had become "the most irregular, crazy-headed, quick-silver, eccentric, whim-whamsical [sic] set of mortals that ever were jumbled together on this uneven, villainous revolving globe." Quoted in Burrows and Wallace, *Gotham*, 420.

36. The original map is at the New York State Museum in Albany.
37. This was thought to be so far away that the city would surely not reach it for "centuries to come" (ibid., 422).
38. For more on the grid plan, see Ballon, *Greatest Grid*.
39. Gordon, "Real Estate."
40. Pete Hamill makes this observation in his beautiful novel *Forever*.

8. A Matter of Spoils

1. The Commission of Emigration, established by the city in 1847, was charged with aiding them—or rather, aiding immigrants who arrived from Europe; blacks were not in their purview. Between May and December of that year alone, the commission found medical care for eleven thousand new arrivals; by 1852, more than twenty thousand were spread among better than half a dozen infirmaries and hospitals across Manhattan and Brooklyn in what the public health historian John Duffy called "the largest hospital system in the country" (*History of Public Health in New York City*, 518).
2. Burrows and Wallace, *Gotham*, 588.
3. Between 1850 and 1854, the city averaged 40.7 deaths per thousand people, an alarming increase from the 22.9 deaths per thousand that had been the average between 1810 and 1814 (Duffy, *History of Public Health in New York City*, 575).
4. Brieger, "Sanitary Reform in New York City," 441.
5. Alfred T. White, city inspector in 1849, is one good example. After he demanded that bone-boiling establishments be removed from the city, he made himself a silent partner in a corporation that provided the rendering industry with land, facilities, and transportation. The plants that he helped open on Barren Island in Brooklyn's Jamaica Bay attracted similar enterprises, and eventually it was home to the world's largest concentration of offal industries (Benjamin Miller, *Fat of the Land*, 36-44). For conditions for the workers on Barren Island, see Johnson, "All the Dead Horses, Next Door"; Benjamin Miller, *Fat of the Land*, 87-88.
6. See, for instance, Bridenbaugh, *Cities in the Wilderness*, 166.
7. Child scavengers were so common a sight in this era that they drew the attention of various authorities, who treated them as thieves and pickpockets—which, in fact, they often were. For more on children as scavengers in nineteenth-century New York, see Stansell, *City of Women*, 50-51, 204-6.
8. Lot, "Autobiography of a Tramp"; Newman, "Home of the Street Urchin."
9. "Rag-Pickers of New York," *American Phrenological Journal*, October 1857, 84;

"Life Under the Dumps," *Harper's Weekly*, November 14, 1885, 747cd. For other detailed descriptions of scavengers and their work, see "Walks Among the New-York Poor: The Rag and Bone Pickers," *New York Daily Times*, January 22, 1853, 2; "For My Little Readers," *Independent*, January 4, 1854, 6; "The Street Scavengers," *Friends' Review*, February 15, 1862, 381. See also Gage, "Low Life in a Great City."

10. Strasser, *Waste and Want*, 115.

11. Thomas Edison filmed scow trimmers and rubbish carts at a New York dumping pier in 1903; the footage can be seen on YouTube, www.youtube.com/watch ?v=4Io9DM6WBzA&feature=relmfu.

12. "In the Dumps," *National Police Gazette*, March 9, 1889.

13. Burrows and Wallace, *Gotham*, 744; McShane and Tarr, *Horse in the City*, 38.

14. For the specific challenges of mastering teams of horses in urban settings, see McShane and Tarr, *Horse in the City*, 39-41.

15. Ibid., 39.

16. Ibid., 44.

17. Created in June 1861, the U.S. Sanitary Commission hoped to institute the health-care innovations first made famous by Florence Nightingale during the Crimean War. Frederick Law Olmsted, one of the principal designers of Central Park, was the commission's secretary and chief executive officer. Despite its efforts, three Union soldiers died of diseases like dysentery and pneumonia for every two killed in battle (Hoy, *Chasing Dirt*, 29-58).

18. Cadwallader Colden's assessment of sanitary conditions in 1740 was followed by many similar efforts. City Inspector John Griscom's survey of the early 1840s was especially thorough, and his recommendations based on it would have gone a long way toward improving life in New York, but he was more than a century ahead of his time. (See Griscom's *Sanitary Condition of the Laboring Population of New York*.)

19. Its centerfold was a detailed map of Manhattan, drawn by Egbert Viele, that showed the island's original waterways, marshes, streams, and inlets.

20. "Sanitary Condition of New York," *Medical and Surgical Reporter*, April 8, 1865.

21. Burrows and Wallace, *Gotham*, 919.

22. Duffy, *Sanitarians*, 119.

23. "Sanitary Condition of New York."

24. For more details on the history of the Metropolitan Health Bill and the Metropolitan Board of Health, see Burrows and Wallace, *Gotham*, 919-21; Duffy, *History of Public Health in New York City*, 540-71; Duffy, *Sanitarians*, 119-22; Hoy, *Chasing Dirt*, 59-64.

25. Named for a mythical Delaware Indian chief, Tamanend, the Tammany Society (complete with "braves," "sachems," and "wigwams") became the most significant force in New York City politics in the nineteenth century. For more details about Tammany, see Ackerman, *Boss Tweed*; Hershkowitz, *Tweed's New York*; Mandelbaum, *Boss Tweed's New York*; and Sloat, *Battle for the Soul of New York*.

26. Jackson, *Encyclopedia of New York City*, 1206.
27. Melosi, *Garbage in the Cities*, 15.
28. Tweed was gone, but his departure didn't mean the end of the Tammany organization.
29. The Bureau of Street Cleaning, said the state legislature, should own its stables, horses, carts, and tools so that it would be less vulnerable to corrupt contractors jacking up prices for such essentials. Street-cleaning equipment should be painted a distinctive color and employees at least wear a badge, if not an actual uniform. Likewise, each street-cleaning horse should carry a brand or mark. The legislature advocated dividing the city into districts, then assigning foremen, sweepers, and carters to specific streets within those districts, to "make every man responsible for the result of his own work." Ashes should be separated from garbage, and both should be removed from the streets no later than 9:00 in the morning. Affluent and heavily trafficked areas should have a full-time crew to pick up manure and other debris whenever it fell so that those particular thoroughfares (which included Fifth, Lexington, and Park Avenues) would always be pristine. Finally, the bureau's ledger should always be open for inspection. *New York Times*, April 11, 1874, 12.
30. *New York Times*, January 23, 1881.
31. *New York Times*, January 29, 1881, and March 24, 1881.
32. *Harper's Weekly*, June 18, 1881.
33. *New York Times*, December 20, 1889.
34. *New York Times*, December 6, 1890.
35. See Schultz and McShane, "To Engineer the Metropolis," for more on the history of municipal reform in this era.
36. Strasser, *Waste and Want*; Tomes, "Private Side of Public Health."
37. Sivulka, "From Domestic to Municipal Housekeeper."
38. "Women's Work for Health," *Independent*, July 9, 1896.
39. Melosi, *Garbage in the Cities*, 35–36.
40. "Women's Work for Health."
41. Melosi, *Garbage in the Cities*, 35–36.
42. The Republican state senator Clarence Lexow organized the inquiry. Among the many shocking revelations: policemen paid exorbitant fees to Tammany bosses in exchange for their jobs, then recouped the fees by extorting money from brothel owners, gamblers, abortionists, and saloon keepers. Counterfeiting, fight fixing, voter intimidation campaigns, strikebreaking, and confidence scams, among other offenses, rounded out the many charges. The Lexow Committee eventually gathered 10,576 pages of testimony from 678 witnesses (Burrows and Wallace, *Gotham*, 1192).
43. Strong asked a former U.S. Civil Service commissioner named Theodore Roosevelt to head the scandal-scathed police department.
44. *Brooklyn Daily Eagle*, January 28, 1896.

45. Hoy, *Chasing Dirt*, 78–79; Sivulka, "From Domestic to Municipal Housekeeper," 4; *New York Times*, February 11, 1914, 7.

9. Apostles of Cleanliness

1. Waring designed Central Park's drainage system (for more of his biography, see Cassedy, "Flamboyant Colonel Waring"; Melosi, *Garbage in the Cities*, 42–65). He's also credited with planting the elm trees that line the mall in the park's southeast quadrant. The elms there today are the fourth set, planted in 1920.

2. Waring designed the sewer systems of several American cities, but when he claimed the patent on parts that he changed only slightly and that had already been patented by the original inventors, he earned lifelong censure from the American Society of Civil Engineers; see Cassedy, "Flamboyant Colonel Waring," for more details.

3. *Brooklyn Daily Eagle*, January 28, 1896.

4. *New York Times*, March 30, 1895.

5. *Brooklyn Daily Eagle*, January 28, 1896.

6. *Brooklyn Daily Eagle*, December 13, 1895, 5.

7. *New York Times*, March 30, 1895, 2.

8. Ibid.

9. Benjamin Miller, *Fat of the Land*, 89.

10. *New York Times*, January 11, 1895.

11. *New York Times*, February 1, 1895. Waring's thoroughness with snow irked upper-class horsemen who lived near Central Park and who wanted to race their sleighs on the icy streets. After hearing their complaints, Waring—himself a lover of fine horses—left sections of the city around the park untouched in subsequent storms.

12. *Brooklyn Daily Eagle*, December 13, 1895; Melosi, *Garbage in the Cities*, 56.

13. Waring remained a staunch anticontagionist all his life. He scorned the daft "germ theory" gaining adherents in medical circles, believing instead that disease was caused by miasmas, or bad smells, rising from stagnant water and other odiferous sources.

14. Some of the DSC's workers protested that the bright white uniform was "a badge of servility" (*New-York Tribune*, May 23, 1896).

15. *Brooklyn Daily Eagle*, January 28, 1896.

16. *Brooklyn Daily Eagle*, August 16, 1896.

17. Burnstein, *Next to Godliness*, 96.

18. Rice, *Dignity and Respect*, 16–27, gives an alternative account of Waring's relationship with the DSC workforce.

19. *Harper's New Monthly Magazine*, August 1896, 480.

20. Consider only the problem of horse manure. A contemporary urban dweller might have trouble imagining the scale of the challenge. According to McShane

and Tarr, by 1900 there were approximately 130,000 horses on the streets of Manhattan, and every horse produced between 30 and 50 pounds of manure a day, or about 7 tons a year. No doubt some of this output was confined to stables, but even so, a significant portion of roughly 910,000 tons of horse manure was deposited on the streets of Manhattan every year (*Horse in the City*, 16, 26).

21. Part of the massive Croton Aqueduct system, the structure was built as a distributing reservoir between 1839 and 1842. It covered four acres, held twenty million gallons, and looked like the foundation of an Egyptian pyramid. The top was designed as a public promenade, and it quickly became a popular place for leisurely perambulations. The reservoir was torn down at the end of the nineteenth century. The same site today is home to Bryant Park and the main branch of the New York Public Library.

22. *New York Times*, May 27, 1896, 1.

23. Ibid.

24. Riis, *Battle with the Slum*, 271.

10. An Angry Sea

1. The Department of Street Cleaning had dumping piers at Old Slip and at Rutgers, Rivington, 17th, and 38th Streets on the East River. On the North River (called the Hudson today), dumping piers were at Canal, 19th, 35th, 47th, 79th, and 129th Streets. More than a dozen tugboats a day pulled garbage scows out to sea. For an account of tugboat history in New York, see Matteson, *Tugboats of New York*.

2. It specified the waters behind Bedloe's Island, the eventual home of the Statue of Liberty (now called Liberty Island).

3. Fee and Corey, *Garbage!*, 45–46.

4. *Harper's Weekly*, June 30, 1883, 403.

5. *Harper's Weekly*, July 23, 1892, 699.

6. "Mayor Gilroy's Message," *New York Times*, January 6, 1893, 9.

7. It took a U.S. Supreme Court order to stop the city from ocean dumping. The last garbage barge sailed in 1934, much to the relief of New Jersey, which had brought the lawsuit that finally forced New York to change its ways. For a more complete history of ocean-dumping legislation, see H. Miller, "Ocean Dumping—Prelude and Fugue."

8. Allen, "How New York Handles Her Garbage and Rubbish Problem," 21; Matteson, *Tugboats of New York*, 88.

9. "Freeboard" refers to the part of a boat above the waterline. A full scow sits lower in the water and is thus more stable than an empty scow.

10. *New-York Tribune*, January 27, 1892.

11. Several sailors said it was even worse than the Blizzard of 1888.

12. Details about these vessels were in the *Herald*, the *Evening Post*, the *Evening Sun* (on January 27, 1892), and the *Tribune* (January 30, 1892).

13. Equivalent amounts in 2012 would range from $250,000 to $650,000.
14. *New York World*, January 28, 1892, 1.
15. Ibid.
16. *New York Evening Sun*, January 28, 1892, 1.
17. *New York World*, January 27, 1892, 1.
18. Maybe it was 60 miles from Sandy Hook, or perhaps 112; the distance seemed to grow with the telling.
19. *New York World*, January 30, 1892, 1.
20. *New York World*, January 28, 1892, 1.
21. *New York World*, February 1, 1892, 1.
22. *New York Evening Sun*, February 3, 1892, 1.

11. You Are a San Man

1. Harry Nespoli, president of the Uniformed Sanitationmen's Association (International Brotherhood of Teamsters Local 831), told me the story of his first day on the job as a sanitation worker. It went kind of like this.
2. A version of this story happened to Frank O'Keefe.

12. Road Worthy

1. It was originally the headquarters of the New York Life Insurance Company.
2. Adams, *Hitchhiker's Guide to the Galaxy*, 48.
3. Floyd Bennett piloted the plane that flew Richard Byrd over the North Pole in May 1926. The pair was planning an expedition over the South Pole in 1928 when Bennett participated in a rescue of fellow aviators in Canada; he contracted pneumonia because of the exercise and died that April. He was thirty-seven years old.
    Air transportation had found a thriving hub in Newark, New Jersey, across the river from New York City. Local politicians, wanting a piece of that revenue, decided to build a municipal airport. The city took over a small private airfield on Barren Island in Brooklyn, expanded it, renamed it, and hosted a spectacular dedication ceremony in the spring of 1931. Floyd Bennett Field played a pivotal role in early aviation history—Charles Lindbergh, Amelia Earhart, Howard Hughes, and Douglas "Wrong Way" Corrigan were only a few of the notable aviators who flew from there—but it was never a commercial success.

14. Getting It Up

1. There is debate about whether or not the DSNY should pick up yard waste at all. One camp thinks it should be composted, but collecting for that purpose costs more money. Another camp thinks homeowners should be responsible for dealing with their yard waste and not burden the city with it.

2. This estimate assumes a load is thirteen tons or thereabouts. Another way to convey the same information is to call out forty tons.

16. We Eat Our Own

1. *Webster's* and other sources claim that "agita" comes from the Italian word *acido*, as in acid or heartburn, and means nervousness or anxiety—see www.merriam-webster.com/dictionary/agita—but as it's used in New York, "agita" sounds closer to a corruption of the Italian verb *agitare*: to fret, shake up, rattle, or annoy. "Don't give me no agita" means "Don't give me a hard time," "Don't give me trouble," "Don't give me pushback."
2. Van Gennep, *Rites of Passage*; Turner, *Ritual Process*.
3. For more about assumptions and implications of classifying systems, see Bowker and Star, *Sorting Things Out*.
4. If a worker is supposed to be on collection or recycling but then is given a different assignment through no fault of his own, he will still get the pay differential he would have received if he hadn't been pulled off the truck. Robert Schrank, a labor mediator who worked with Sanitation on the transition from three-man to two-man crews, figured out the details. Over time his name became the verb that stands for the policy.
5. Steinbeck, *Acts of King Arthur*, 406.
6. As of 2010, NYPD traffic agents also help with this chore. Handheld scanners allow the officers to upload a vehicle's registration information and then print a summons that is easy to read.
7. Saul and Barrett, "Bloomberg Taps Former Indianapolis Mayor."
8. Katz, "New Ed Skyler Is Older, More Experienced, and More Midwestern."
9. Lisberg, "Midwesterner Gets Deputy Post."
10. Lisberg and Colangelo, "New York City to Demote 100 Sanitation Supervisors to Help Cut Budget."
11. From November 2010.

17. Night Plow

1. Chris Glorioso, "Surprising Salaries at the Department of Sanitation," WNBC Television News, January 31, 2011. Ironically, Mr. Glorioso did not confirm or deny the rumor that his father was a sanitation worker out of Queens East.
2. The city acquires its supply from International Salt, a Pennsylvania-based subsidiary of the Chilean company SPL (for Sociedad Punta de Lobos), itself an affiliate of the German firm K + S, which says it is the world's largest salt producer. The salt originates in Chile's Tarapacá Salt Flat, is transported on cargo ships, and is off-loaded in Red Hook, Brooklyn.

18. Snowed Under

1. Ludlum, "Blizzard of '88 in Historical Perspective," 11–12.
2. See Caplovich, *Blizzard!*; High and Filippucci, *City of Snow*; and Ludlum, "Blizzard of '88 in Historical Perspective," for more detail. Photographs and personal stories give a vivid sense of the storm's impact. A good collection of both is found through Virtual New York, an online history archive created by the City University of New York; see www.vny.cuny.edu/blizzard/stories/stories_set.html.
3. Starting in 1884, various ordinances mandated that the lines be moved belowground, but corporate interests refused to comply and instead challenged the laws in court. See www.virtualny.cuny.edu/blizzard/building/building_fr_set.html.
4. For details about Lindsay's reorganization of city government, see Mantel, "Reorganization of the New York City Government," and McFadden, "John V. Lindsay, Mayor and Maverick, Dies at 79." For more on the Lindsay Storm, see Cannato, *Ungovernable City*, 395–97.
5. Siegel, "Those Fun City Years Recalled by Insiders," 38.
6. McFadden, "John V. Lindsay, Mayor and Maverick, Dies at 79," A1.
7. Einhorn, "Stephen Goldsmith, Deputy Mayor of New York, Tweeted 'Good Snow Work' During Blizzard"; Ortiz, "City Leaders Face Hearing on Poor Snowstorm Response."
8. Chen, "Goldsmith's Other Bad Snow Day."
9. Daly, "Clueless Deputy Mayor Goldsmith."
10. Barbaro, "Deputy Mayor Was Arrested Before He Resigned."
11. Newman, "Stephen Goldsmith, Ex-Deputy Mayor, Absolved of Domestic Violence."

19. Benevolence

1. Frank Kowalinski Post 4 of the Polish Legion of American Veterans.
2. When I describe Sanitation's benevolent societies to friends and colleagues outside the Department, many of them assume that the fraternals are like quaint "clubs," throwbacks to an era when religious affiliation or ethnic heritage was considered fundamental to one's sense of self. The societies, they tell me, sound like charming anachronisms; in today's world, few people cling to such old-fashioned markers of identity. This reaction surprised me. I know that there's a cultural divide between many different elements of American life, but I hadn't realized just how big the gap is. Religion and ethnicity are exactly the markers of identity and inclusion around which most Americans still understand themselves.
3. Gamm and Putnam, "Growth of Voluntary Associations in America," 521. So prevalent were mutual aid associations in the young United States that they

drew comment from the French chronicler Alexis de Tocqueville, who wrote in the 1830s that Americans "are forever forming associations" (*Democracy in America*, 514).

4. Trotter, "African American Fraternal Associations in American History," 355–56.
5. Quoted in Dumenil, *Freemasonry and American Culture*, xii.
6. Ridgeway, "Linking Social Structure and Interpersonal Behavior," 6.
7. Kaufman and Weintraub, "Social-Capital Formation and American Fraternal Association." I use the phrase rather lightly, but Kaufman and Weintraub point out that its definitions sometimes conflict.
8. Joe Siano's stories are part of the DSNY Oral History Archive. The interview from which these quotations are drawn was conducted by Hilary Crowe on March 25, 2011. The full transcript and audio are available at www.dsnyoral historyarchive.org/?s=Siano.
9. The DSNY Columbia Association belongs to the National Council of Columbia Associations in Civil Service.
10. See Rice, *Dignity and Respect*, for a history of the union.

Postlude: Someone Else

1. From *The Simpsons*, episode 200 (#5F09, Season 9; airdate April 26, 1998). The show has provided cogent social commentary on American life for more than two decades; in 2008, it tied *Gunsmoke* as the longest-running prime-time series in the country's history.
2. See Star, "Ethnography of Infrastructure," and Graham and Thrift, "Out of Order," for more about the ethnographies of maintenance and of infrastructure.
3. This is China Miéville's marvelous term, from his novel *Un Lun Dun*.
4. For analysis of the strike, see Cannato, *Ungovernable City*; Maier, *City Unions*; Rice, *Dignity and Respect*. For a detailed account of the strike from the union's perspective, see *Nine Days That Shook New York City*.
5. For more on the sanitation-worker strike in New York, see Arvid Anderson, "Strikes and Impasse Resolution in Public Employment." For more on the strike in Memphis, see Beifuss, *At the River I Stand*; Collins, "Analysis of the Memphis Garbage Strike of 1968"; Estes, " 'I *Am* a Man!' "; Green, "Race, Gender, and Labor in 1960s Memphis"; Lentz, "Sixty-Five Days in Memphis"; McKnight, "1968 Memphis Sanitation Strike and the FBI."
6. Quoted in Finkelpearl, "Interview."
7. The Ronald Feldman Gallery on Mercer Street in SoHo.

Sources

Historical Newspapers and Magazines

American Phrenological Journal
Brooklyn Daily Eagle
Friends' Review
Harper's Weekly and *Harper's New Monthly Magazine*
Independent
New York Daily Times
New York Evening Sun
New York Evening Telegram
New York Herald
New York Times
New-York Tribune
New York World

Books and Articles

Ackerman, Kenneth D. *Boss Tweed: The Rise and Fall of the Corrupt Pol Who Conceived the Soul of Modern New York*. New York: Carroll & Graf, 2005.

Adams, Douglas. *The Hitchhiker's Guide to the Galaxy*. New York: Ballantine, 1997.

Allen, Kenneth. "How New York Handles Her Garbage and Rubbish Problem." *Municipal Sanitation*, January 1930, 16–21.

American Public Works Association. *Refuse Collection Practice*. Chicago: American Public Works Association, 1941.

Anderson, Arvid. "Strikes and Impasse Resolution in Public Employment." *Michigan Law Review* 67, no. 5 (1969): 943–70.

Anderson, Kelly. *Never Enough: People's Relationship with Stuff.* AndersonGold Films, 2010.

Asad, Talal, ed. *Anthropology and the Colonial Encounter.* Amherst, N.Y.: Humanity Books, 1973.

Ballon, Hilary, ed. *The Greatest Grid: The Master Plan of Manhattan, 1811–2011.* New York: Columbia University Press, 2012.

Ballon, Hilary, and Kenneth Jackson. *Robert Moses and the Modern City: The Transformation of New York.* New York: W. W. Norton, 2007.

Barbaro, Michael. "Deputy Mayor Was Arrested Before He Resigned." City Room blog, *New York Times*, September 1, 2011.

Beifuss, Joan Turner. *At the River I Stand: Memphis, the 1968 Strike, and Martin Luther King, Jr.* Memphis: B&W Books, 1985.

Botha, Ted. *Mongo: Adventures in Trash.* New York: Bloomsbury, 2004.

Bourdon, David. "An Apocalyptic Paperhanger Shows His Stripes." *Village Voice*, October 4, 1976, 105.

Bowker, Geoffrey C., and Susan Leigh Star. *Sorting Things Out: Classification and Its Consequences.* Cambridge, Mass.: MIT Press, 2000.

Brekhus, Wayne. "A Sociology of the Unmarked: Redirecting Our Focus." *Sociological Theory* 16, no. 1 (1998): 34–51.

Bridenbaugh, Carl. *Cities in the Wilderness: The First Century of Urban Life in America, 1625–1742.* New York: Ronald Press, 1938.

Brieger, Gert H. "Sanitary Reform in New York City: Stephen Smith and the Passage of the Metropolitan Health Bill." In *Sickness and Health in America: Readings in the History of Medicine and Public Health*, edited by Judith Leavitt and Ronald Numbers. 3rd ed. Madison: University of Wisconsin Press, 1997.

Buchli, Victor, and Gavin Lucas. *Archaeologies of the Contemporary Past.* London: Routledge, 2001.

Bureau of Labor Statistics. "National Census of Fatal Occupational Injuries in 2011 (Preliminary Results)." September 20, 2012.

Burns, Ric, and James Sanders, eds. *New York: An Illustrated History.* New York: Knopf, 1999.

Burnstein, Daniel. *Next to Godliness: Confronting Dirt and Despair in Progressive Era New York City.* Urbana: University of Illinois Press, 2006.

Burrows, Edwin G., and Mike Wallace. *Gotham: A History of New York City to 1898.* New York: Oxford University Press, 1999.

Cannato, Vincent J. *The Ungovernable City: John Lindsay and His Struggle to Save New York.* New York: Basic Books, 2001.

Cantwell, Anne-Marie, and Diana diZerega Wall. *Unearthing Gotham: The Archaeology of New York City.* New Haven, Conn.: Yale University Press, 2001.

Caplovich, Judd. *Blizzard! The Great Storm of '88.* Vernon, Conn.: VeRo, 1987.

Caro, Robert. *The Power Broker: Robert Moses and the Fall of New York*. New York: Knopf, 1974.

Cassedy, James H. "The Flamboyant Colonel Waring: An Anticontagionist Holds the American Stage in the Age of Pasteur and Koch." In *Sickness and Health in America: Readings in the History of Medicine and Public Health*, edited by Judith Leavitt and Ronald Numbers. Madison: University of Wisconsin Press, 1978.

Certeau, Michel de. "The Unnamable." In *The Practice of Everyday Life*. Berkeley: University of California Press, 1988.

Chen, David W. "Goldsmith's Other Bad Snow Day." City Room blog, *New York Times*, January 10, 2011.

Citizens' Association of New York. *Report of the Council of Hygiene and Public Health of the Citizens' Association of New York upon the Sanitary Condition of the City*. 1866. Reprint, New York: Arno Press, 1970.

Coleman, John. *Blue-Collar Journal*. Philadelphia: J. B. Lippincott, 1974.

Collins, Thomas W. "An Analysis of the Memphis Garbage Strike of 1968." In *Anthropology for the Nineties: Introductory Readings*, edited by Johnnetta B. Cole. New York: Free Press, 1988.

Corrigan, Robert. "The 'Ratopolis' of New York City." *PCT Magazine*, April 2007, 115.

Craik, Jennifer. "The Cultural Politics of the Uniform." *Fashion Theory* 7, no. 2 (2003): 127–47.

Daley, Robert. *The World Beneath the City*. New York: J. B. Lippincott, 1959.

Daly, Michael. "Clueless Deputy Mayor Goldsmith Deserves Blame for Fiasco Following Blizzard." *Daily News*, January 2, 2011.

Deetz, James. *In Small Things Forgotten: An Archaeology of Early American Life*. New York: Anchor Books, 1996.

Dion, Mark, and Alexis Rockman. "Interview with Mierle Laderman Ukeles, Artist for the New York Sanitation Department." In *Concrete Jungle*. New York: Juno Books, 1996.

Douglas, Mary. *Purity and Danger: An Analysis of the Concepts of Pollution and Taboo*. London: Ark Paperbacks, 1985.

Drudi, Dino. "Job Hazards in the Waste Industry." *Compensation and Working Conditions* 4, no. 2 (Summer 1999): 19–23.

Duffy, John. *A History of Public Health in New York City, 1625–1866*. New York: Russell Sage Foundation, 1968.

———. *The Sanitarians: A History of American Public Health*. Urbana: University of Illinois Press, 1990.

Dumenil, Lynn. *Freemasonry and American Culture, 1880–1930*. Princeton, N.J.: Princeton University Press, 1984.

Ehrenreich, Barbara. *Nickel and Dimed: On (Not) Getting By in America*. New York: Metropolitan, 2001.

Einhorn, Erin. "Stephen Goldsmith, Deputy Mayor of New York, Tweeted 'Good Snow Work' During Blizzard." *Daily News*, December 30, 2010.

Estes, Steve. "'I *Am* a Man!': Race, Masculinity, and the 1968 Memphis Sanitation Strike." *Labor History* 41, no. 2 (2000): 153–70.

Fee, Elizabeth, and Steven H. Corey. *Garbage! The History and Politics of Trash in New York City.* New York: New York Public Library, 1994.

Fernow, Berthold, ed. *Records of New Amsterdam, 1653–1674.* Vol. 1. Baltimore: Genealogical Publishing Co., 1976.

———. *Records of New Amsterdam, 1653–1674.* Vol. 5. Baltimore: Genealogical Publishing Co., 1976.

Finkelpearl, Tom. "Interview: Mierle Laderman Ukeles on Maintenance and Sanitation Art." In *Dialogues in Public Art.* Cambridge, Mass.: MIT Press, 2001.

Frazier, Ian. *Gone to New York: Adventures in the City.* New York: Picador, 2005.

Frost, Randy O., and Gail Steketee. *Stuff: Compulsive Hoarding and the Meaning of Things.* New York: Houghton Mifflin Harcourt, 2010.

Fussell, Paul. *Uniforms: Why We Are What We Wear.* New York: Houghton Mifflin, 2002.

Gage, Frances D. "Low Life in a Great City: What Comes from the Ash Barrels." *Ohio Farmer*, January 25, 1868, 58.

Gamm, Gerald, and Robert Putnam. "The Growth of Voluntary Associations in America, 1840–1940." *Journal of Interdisciplinary History* 29, no. 4 (1999): 511–57.

Garfinkel, Harold. *Studies in Ethnomethodology.* Englewood Cliffs, N.J.: Prentice-Hall, 1967.

Geismar, Joan. "Landmaking in Lower Manhattan." *Seaport* 14, no. 3 (1980): 16–19.

Gertz, Emily. "Fresh Kills: An Unnatural Context." *WorldChanging*, April 2, 2004. www.worldchanging.com/archives/000525.html.

Goldstein, Richard. "Jan Kemp Dies at 59; Exposed Fraud in Grades of Players." *New York Times*, December 11, 2008.

Gordon, John Steele. "Real Estate: When and Where." *American Heritage*, November 1990.

Graham, Stephen, and Nigel Thrift. "Out of Order: Understanding Repair and Maintenance." *Theory, Culture & Society* 24, no. 3 (2007): 1–25.

Green, Laurie B. "Race, Gender, and Labor in 1960s Memphis: 'I *Am* a Man' and the Meaning of Freedom." *Journal of Urban History* 30, no. 3 (2004): 465–89.

Griscom, John. *The Sanitary Condition of the Laboring Population of New York.* 1844. Facsimile ed., New York: Arno Press, 1970.

Hamill, Pete. *Forever.* New York: Little, Brown, 2003.

Hansen, Joyce, and Gary McGowan. *Breaking Ground, Breaking Silence: The Story of New York's African Burial Ground.* New York: Henry Holt, 1998.

Harris, Leslie M. *In the Shadow of Slavery: African Americans in New York City, 1626–1863.* Chicago: University of Chicago Press, 2003.

Harris, Marvin. *The Rise of Anthropological Theory: A History of Theories of Culture.* Walnut Creek, Calif.: AltaMira Press, 2001.

Harrison, Rodney, and John Schofield. "Archaeo-ethnography, Auto-archaeology: Introducing Archaeologies of the Contemporary Past." *Archaeologies* 5, no. 2 (2009): 185–209.

Hershkowitz, Leo. *Tweed's New York: Another Look.* Garden City, N.Y.: Anchor Press/Doubleday, 1977.

High, Linda Oatman, and Laura Francesca Filippucci. *City of Snow: The Great Blizzard of 1888.* New York: Walker, 2004.

Hodgen, Margaret T. *Early Anthropology in the Sixteenth and Seventeenth Centuries.* Philadelphia: University of Pennsylvania Press, 1971.

Hodges, Graham. "The Cartmen of New York City, 1667–1801." Ph.D. diss., New York University, 1982.

Horton, D. Kevin, et al. "Hydrofluoric Acid Releases in 17 States and the Acute Health Effects Associated, 1993–2001." *Journal of Occupational Environmental Medicine* 46, no. 5 (2004): 501–8.

Hoy, Suellen. *Chasing Dirt: The American Pursuit of Cleanliness.* New York: Oxford University Press, 1995.

Independent. "Women's Work for Health." July 9, 1896, 7.

Jackson, Kenneth, ed. *The Encyclopedia of New York City.* New York: Yale University Press, 1995.

Johnson, Kirk. "All the Dead Horses, Next Door: Bittersweet Memories of the City's Island of Garbage." *New York Times*, November 7, 2000.

———. "Ruling Paves the Way for Hiring City's First Female Trash Haulers." *New York Times*, July 29, 1986, B5.

Joseph, Nathan, and Nicholas Alex. "The Uniform: A Sociological Perspective." *American Journal of Sociology* 77, no. 4 (1972): 719–30.

Katz, Celeste. "The New Ed Skyler Is Older, More Experienced, and More Midwestern." *Daily News*, April 30, 2010.

Kaufman, Jason, and David Weintraub. "Social-Capital Formation and American Fraternal Association: New Empirical Evidence." *Journal of Interdisciplinary History* 35, no. 1 (2004): 1–36.

Kelley, Tina. "Using Garbage as Text: Class at NYU Looks for Deeper Meaning at Fresh Kills." *New York Times*, March 23, 2000, B1.

Koeppel, Gerard. "The Rise to Croton." In *Water-Works: The Architecture and Engineering of the New York City Water Supply*, edited by Kevin Bone. New York: Monacelli Press, 2006.

———. *Water for Gotham: A History.* Princeton, N.J.: Princeton University Press, 2000.

Kopytoff, Igor. "The Cultural Biography of Things: Commoditization as Process." In *The Social Life of Things: Commodities in Cultural Perspective*, edited by A. Appadurai. Cambridge, U.K.: Cambridge University Press, 1986.

Kruse, Jamie, and Elizabeth Ellsworth. *Geologic City: A Field Guide to the Geoarchitecture of New York.* New York: Smudge Studio, 2011.

Lauder, Matthew. "Covert Participant Observation of a Deviant Community:

Justifying the Use of Deception." *Journal of Contemporary Religion* 18, no. 2 (2003): 185–96.

Lawitts, Steven. "Needle Sightings and On-the-Job Needle-Stick Injuries Among New York City Department of Sanitation Workers." *Journal of the American Pharmaceutical Association* 42, no. 6 (2002), supplement 2.

Lentz, Richard. "Sixty-Five Days in Memphis: A Study of Culture, Symbols, and the Press." *Journalism Monographs* 98 (1986): 10–11.

Lewis, Tom. *The Hudson: A History*. New Haven, Conn.: Yale University Press, 2005.

Lisberg, Adam. "Midwesterner Gets Deputy Post." *Daily News*, May 3, 2010.

Lisberg, Adam, and Lisa L. Colangelo. "New York City to Demote 100 Sanitation Supervisors to Help Cut Budget." *Daily News*, October 22, 2010.

Lot, Arthur. "Autobiography of a Tramp." *Puck*, March 3, 1880, 844.

Ludlum, David. "The Blizzard of '88 in Historical Perspective." In *Blizzard of 1888 Centennial*, edited by Mark Kramer. Unpublished collection of essays, 1988.

MacBride, Samantha. *Recycling Reconsidered: The Present Failure and Future Promise of Environmental Action in the United States*. Cambridge, Mass.: MIT Press, 2011.

Maier, Mark. *City Unions: Managing Discontent in New York City*. New Brunswick, N.J.: Rutgers University Press, 1987.

Mandelbaum, Seymour J. *Boss Tweed's New York*. New York: John Wiley & Sons, 1965.

Mantel, Howard. "Reorganization of the New York City Government." *Public Administration* 48, no. 20 (1970): 191–212.

Martin, L., and N. Russell. "Trashing Rubbish." In *Towards Reflexive Method in Archaeology: The Example at Çatalhöyük*, edited by Ian Hodder, 57–69. Cambridge, U.K.: McDonald Institute Monographs, 2000.

Matteson, George. *Tugboats of New York: An Illustrated History*. New York: New York University Press, 2005.

Mauss, Marcel. *The Gift: Forms and Functions of Exchange in Archaic Societies*. New York: W. W. Norton, 1967.

McFadden, Robert D. "John V. Lindsay, Mayor and Maverick, Dies at 79." *New York Times*, December 21, 2000, A1.

McKnight, Gerald. "The 1968 Memphis Sanitation Strike and the FBI: A Case Study in Urban Surveillance." *South Atlantic Quarterly* 83, no. 2 (1984): 138–56.

McLaughlin, Terence. *Dirt: A Social History as Seen Through the Uses and Abuses of Dirt*. New York: Stein & Day, 1971.

McShane, Clay, and Joel A. Tarr. *The Horse in the City: Living Machines in the Nineteenth Century*. Baltimore: The Johns Hopkins University Press, 2007.

Medical and Surgical Reporter. "Sanitary Condition of New York." April 8, 1865, 418.

Melosi, Martin. *Garbage in the Cities: Refuse, Reform, and the Environment*. Rev. ed. Pittsburgh: University of Pittsburgh Press, 2005.

Miéville, China. *The City and the City*. New York: Random House, 2009.

————. *Un Lun Dun*. New York: Random House, 2007.

Miller, Benjamin. *Fat of the Land: The History of Garbage in New York the Last Two Hundred Years*. New York: Four Walls Eight Windows, 2000.

Miller, H. Crane. "Ocean Dumping—Prelude and Fugue." *Journal of Maritime Law and Commerce* 5, no. 4 (1973): 51–76.

Miller, William. *The Anatomy of Disgust*. Cambridge, Mass.: Harvard University Press, 1997.

Moore, Christopher. "A World of Possibilities: Slavery and Freedom in Dutch New Amsterdam." In *Slavery in New York*, edited by Ira Berlin and Leslie M. Harris. New York: New Press, 2005.

Morgan, Robert C. "*Touch Sanitation*: Mierle Laderman Ukeles." In *The Citizen Artist: 20 Years of Art in the Public Arena*, edited by Linda Burnham and Steve Durland. Vol. 1. Gardiner, N.Y.: Critical Press, 1998.

Nagle, Robin. "The History and Future of Fresh Kills." In *Dirt: The Filthy Reality of Everyday Life*, edited by Nadine Monem. London: Profile Books, 2011.

————. "A Week-Long Journal of a Sanitation Worker in Training." *Slate*, October 4–8, 2004.

National Police Gazette. "In the Dumps." March 9, 1889, 3.

Needham, Stuart, and Tony Spence. "Refuse and the Formation of Middens." *Antiquity* 71 (1997): 77–90.

Newman, Andy. "Stephen Goldsmith, Ex-Deputy Mayor, Absolved of Domestic Violence." City Room blog, *New York Times*, February 17, 2012.

Newman, Bernard J. "The Home of the Street Urchin." *National Municipal Review*, October 1915: 587–93.

New York City Common Council Minutes. Various dates.

New York Times. "Editorial: A Fair Way to Handle Trash." May 28, 2012.

Nine Days That Shook New York City. New York: Uniformed Sanitationmen's Association Record, n.d.

Office of Management and Budget, City of New York. "New York Executive Budget Fiscal Year 2013." 2012.

Ortiz, Erico. "City Leaders Face Hearing on Poor Snowstorm Response." *amNew York*, January 9, 2011.

Peters, D. "Symptoms and Treatment of Hydrogen Fluoride Injuries." *Journal of Fluorine Chemistry* 79 (1996): 161–65.

Pratt, Michael. "Organizational Dress as a Symbol of Multilayered Social Identities." *Academy of Management Journal* 40, no. 4 (1997): 862–98.

Rathje, William, and Cullen Murphy. *Rubbish! The Archaeology of Garbage*. Tucson: University of Arizona Press, 1992.

Redd, Lisa. *Newsday*, September 23, 1986, 32.

Reno, Josh. "Out of Place: Possibility and Pollution at a Transnational Landfill." Ph.D. diss., University of Michigan, 2008.

Rice, Kevin. *Dignity and Respect: The History of Local 831*. New York: United Sanitationmen's Association, Local 831, IBT, 2009.

Ridgeway, Cecilia L. "Linking Social Structure and Interpersonal Behavior: A Theoretical Perspective on Cultural Schemas and Social Relations." *Social Psychology Quarterly* 69, no. 1 (2006): 5–16.

Riis, Jacob. *The Battle with the Slum*. 1902. Mineola, N.Y.: Dover, 1998.

Rogers, Heather. *Gone Tomorrow: The Hidden Life of Trash*. New York: New Press, 2005.

Rothschild, Nan. *New York City Neighborhoods: The 18th Century*. New York: Academic Press, 1990.

Royte, Elizabeth. *Garbage Land: On the Secret Trail of Trash*. New York: Little, Brown, 2005.

Saul, Michael Howard, and Joe Barrett. "Bloomberg Taps Former Indianapolis Mayor." *Wall Street Journal*, May 1, 2010.

Schultz, Stanley K., and Clay McShane. "To Engineer the Metropolis: Sewers, Sanitation, and City Planning in Late-Nineteenth-Century America." *Journal of American History* 65, no. 2 (1978): 389–411.

Shorto, Russell. *Island at the Center of the World: The Epic Story of Dutch Manhattan and the Forgotten Colony That Shaped America*. New York: Vintage Books, 2005.

Siano, Joseph. Oral history interview with Hilary Crowe, March 25, 2011. DSNY Oral History Archive. www.dsnyoralhistoryarchive.org/?s=Siano.

Siegel, Joel. "Those Fun City Years Recalled by Insiders." *Daily News*, December 21, 2000, 38.

Silva, Mariana. *Waste and Recycling News*, August 2, 2010. www.wasterecyclingnews.com/article/20100802/NEWS99/308029990/aug-2-2010.

Sivulka, Juliann. "From Domestic to Municipal Housekeeper: The Influence of the Sanitary Reform Movement on Changing Women's Roles in America, 1860–1920." *Journal of American Culture* 22, no. 4 (1999): 1–7.

Sloat, Warren. *A Battle for the Soul of New York: Tammany Hall, Police Corruption, Vice, and Reverend Charles Parkhurst's Crusade Against Them, 1892–1895*. New York: Cooper Square Press, 2002.

Stansell, Christine. *City of Women: Sex and Class in New York, 1789–1860*. Urbana: University of Illinois Press, 1987.

Star, Susan Leigh. "The Ethnography of Infrastructure." *American Behavioral Scientist* 43, no. 3 (1999): 377–91.

Steinbeck, John. *The Acts of King Arthur and His Noble Knights*. New York: Penguin, 1976.

Stokes, I. N. Phelps. *The Iconography of Manhattan Island, 1498–1909*. Union, N.J.: Lawbook Exchange, 1998.

Strasser, Susan. *Waste and Want: A Social History of Trash*. New York: Metropolitan, 1999.

Sullivan, Robert. *Rats: Observations on the History and Habitat of the City's Most Unwanted Inhabitants*. New York: Bloomsbury, 2005.

Thompson, E. P. "Time, Work-Discipline, and Industrial Capitalism." *Past and Present* 38 (1967): 56–97.

Thompson, Michael. *Rubbish Theory: The Creation and Destruction of Value*. New York: Oxford University Press, 1979.

Tocqueville, Alexis de. *Democracy in America*. Edited by J. P. Mayer. Translated by George Lawrence. Garden City, N.Y.: Doubleday, 1969.

Tomes, Nancy. "The Private Side of Public Health: Sanitary Science, Domestic Hygiene, and the Germ Theory, 1870–1900." In *Sickness and Health in America: Readings in the History of Medicine and Public Health*, edited by Judith Leavitt and Ronald Numbers. 3rd ed. Madison: University of Wisconsin Press, 1997.

Trotter, Joe. "African American Fraternal Associations in American History: An Introduction." *Social Science History* 28, no. 3 (2004): 355–66.

Turner, Victor. *The Ritual Process: Structure and Anti-structure*. Ithaca, N.Y.: Cornell University Press, 1969.

Ukeles, Mierle Laderman. "Leftovers/It's About Time for Freshkills." *Cabinet* 6 (2002).

Van Auken, William. "Bloomberg Blooper Stirs Union Wrath." *The Chief*, July 6, 2001.

van Gennep, Arnold. *The Rites of Passage*. London: Routledge and Kegan Paul, 1960.

Wagman, Morton. "Corporate Slavery in New Netherland." *Journal of Negro History* 65, no. 1 (1980): 34–42.

Wagner, Gernot. *But Will the Planet Notice? How Smart Economics Can Save the World*. New York: Hill and Wang, 2011.

White, Peter T. "The Fascinating World of Trash." *National Geographic*, April 1983.

Wilbur, Richard. "Transit." In *Collected Poems, 1943–2004*. New York: Harcourt, 2005.

Zerubavel, Eviatar. *Hidden Rhythms: Schedules and Calendars in Social Life*. Berkeley: University of California Press, 1981.

———. "The Standardization of Time: A Sociohistorical Perspective." *American Journal of Sociology* 88, no. 1 (1982): 1–23.

Acknowledgments

This book reflects the generosity of many people and the sharing of many forms of wisdom.

I bow in deep gratitude and respect to the men and women of New York City's Department of Sanitation. Their intelligence, fortitude, and dedication really do keep the city alive. They are also deeply generous. In every borough, in every garage and office and repair shop and classroom and section station, behind the trucks and in the brooms and on the street, in snow and heat, on the day line and the night shift, at union halls and society meetings and dinner dances and barbecues, whether retired or newly hired, civilian or uniformed, they welcomed me with patience and good humor, then taught me about their labors and their lives. It is my hope that this book will inspire a larger world to better understand and more fully appreciate the work they do, why it's so important, and what it takes to do it well.

For his welcome, his encouragement, and his many stories, Commissioner John Doherty forever has my thanks. So does Vito Turso, deputy commissioner of public information and community affairs, who opened the DSNY to me and who provided steadfast support from our first conversation.

Robert Dimit, Larissa Kyzer, and Georgia Jelatis-Hoke Lowe at New York University held down the fort no matter what; this book would never have come into being without them. Thanks also to Bruce Altshuler, John Beckman, Tom Bender, Laurie Benton, Tom Carew, James Devitt, Dick Foley, Phil Furmanski, Haidy Geismar, Faye Ginsburg, Joe Juliano, David Ludden, Samantha MacBride, Gwynneth Malin, Emily Martin, the Material Culture Study Group, Noah McClain, Harvey Molotch, Fred Myers, Joel Oppenheim, Ann Pellegrini, David Potash, Sandra Rozental, Todd Selby, Mal Semple, Kate Stimpson, and Kathy Talvacchia.

Friends, students, teachers, and colleagues near and far offered encouragement: Chris Alley, Ted Bestor, Norman Brouwer, James Burnett, Catherine Burns, Alex Carp, Claire Cesario, Mary Marshall Clark, Robert Corrigan, Leila Darabi, Kevin Doughton, Lisa Dowda, Mitch Duneier, Jenine Durland, Doug Elliott, Brian Ferguson, Eric Friedman, Zsuzsa Gille, Carrie Grassi, Kathy Gunderson, Ari Handel, Sarah Hill, Eloise Hirsh, Mark Hurst, Maggie Hutton, Tina Kelley, Bill Kornblum, Raj Kottamasu, Venetia Lannon, Max Liboiron, Carey Lovelace, Setha Low, James Luongo, Liza McAlister, Kate McCaffrey, Liz McEnaney, Erin McKean, Martin Melosi, Ben Miller, Michael Miscione, Rick Muller, Alexandra Murphy, Richard Ogust, Patty O'Toole, Su Yon Pak, Karen Peterson, Jennifer Pliego, Jason Price, Samar Qandil, Louise Quayle, Josh Reno, Elana Resnick, Kevin Rice, Anne Savarese, Amy Smiley, Laine Snowman, Sparky, Amy Starecheski, Laura Starecheski, Glenn Stone, Elizabeth Streb, Harriet Taub, Bill Tucker, Ben Turner, Mierle Laderman Ukeles, Jennifer Vinopal, Lucy Walker, Terry Walton, Howard Warren, and Tom de Zengotita. The Writers Room provided an oasis for productive quiet, and the writer-friends I've found through the Academic Ladder helped me stay focused and sometimes even fearless.

Remarkable research assistants made this much stronger than it otherwise would have been; heartfelt thanks to Mario Cancel-Bigay, Claire Dougherty, Ryan Gavaghan, Chandani Patel, Rachel Riederer, Mariel Rose, Shalini Shankar, Amy Shaw, Julia Shaw, and Tod Van Gunten. Casey Lynn was exceptionally insightful with her meticulous reads of many chapter drafts. Thank you, also, to the librarians and archivists at New York University, Columbia University, the Municipal Library and Municipal Archives, the Museum of the City of New York, the New-York Historical Society, the New York Public Library, and the South Street Seaport Museum.

The work of many journalists informed this writing. Special thanks to Lars Åberg, Molly Bentley, Alex Carp, Bob Edwards, Amanda Fortini, Ira Glass, Clyde Haberman, Ben McGrath, Heather Rogers, Edward Rothstein, Elizabeth Royte, Emily Rueb, and Nicholette Zeliadt.

Michelle Tessler, my agent, embraced this before a word of it was written. At FSG, many people were involved in its creation. Paul Elie helped shape it, Karen Maine gave it a thorough polishing, and Alex Star brought it into the light of day. First Mark Krotov and then Christopher Richards provided patient guidance on countless details. Sam Bayard asked thoughtful questions in tending to legalities. Lenni Wolff was a patient production editor and Ingrid Sterner an eagle-eyed copy editor. Jennifer Carrow designed the brilliant cover, using Jason Fulford's images from our autumnal photo shoot. Debra Helfand managed all aspects of production with skill and aplomb. Jeff Seroy, Amanda Schoonmaker, Sarita Varma, Lottchen Shivers, and Nicholas Courage make a formidable marketing team.

Zachary DeLano-Nagle has never known a time when his mother wasn't immersed in Sanitation. He has endured it with patience and goodwill. He has also learned his own rock-solid respect for the DSNY, which he shares with friends and teachers at every opportunity. For both, he has my immeasurable gratitude. David DeLano stepped into the gap more times than I can count. George and Margo Nagle, Susan Nagle Olsen, Eric Olsen, Garth Olsen, and Evan Olsen have had unflagging faith even when the project puzzled them. James Kinsella, the best brother a girl could wish for, kept me moving forward with his smarts and his customary high-octane enthusiasm.

There are four people whose influence infuses this book but who will not read it (at least, not on this side of the divide). Annette Weiner, my boss, mentor, and friend, nudged me to start, but didn't live to see me finish. Neither did Bob Schrank, a labor mediator, activist, and scholar whom I met for the first time several years ago and whose work even unto his dying breath was an inspiration for me and for so many others. Steve Rubenstein, the most intellectually generous anthropologist I ever knew, was another source of early encouragement; his untimely death leaves a permanent tear in many lives. And Bill Rathje, archaeologist, garbologist, and general all-around wise man, whose visionary stubbornness started it all with the Garbage Project in Arizona decades ago and whose advice to me was always savvy, is too soon gone and will be long missed. Wherever he is, may his garbage smell sweet or not at all.

Index

A NOTE ABOUT THE AUTHOR

Robin Nagle has been anthropologist-in-residence at New York City's Department of Sanitation since 2006. She is a clinical associate professor of anthropology and urban studies at New York University, where she also directs the John W. Draper Interdisciplinary Master's Program in Humanities and Social Thought.